Through the Flames

American Society of Missiology Monograph Series

Chair of Series Editorial Committee, James R. Krabill

The ASM Monograph Series provides a forum for publishing quality dissertations and studies in the field of missiology. Collaborating with Pickwick Publications—a division of Wipf and Stock Publishers of Eugene, Oregon—the American Society of Missiology selects high quality dissertations and other monographic studies that offer research materials in mission studies for scholars, mission and church leaders, and the academic community at large. The ASM seeks scholarly work for publication in the series that throws light on issues confronting Christian world mission in its cultural, social, historical, biblical, and theological dimensions.

Missiology is an academic field that brings together scholars whose professional training ranges from doctoral-level preparation in areas such as Scripture, history and sociology of religions, anthropology, theology, international relations, interreligious interchange, mission history, inculturation, and church law. The American Society of Missiology, which sponsors this series, is an ecumenical body drawing members from Independent and Ecumenical Protestant, Catholic, Orthodox, and other traditions. Members of the ASM are united by their commitment to reflect on and do scholarly work relating to both mission history and the present-day mission of the church. The ASM Monograph Series aims to publish works of exceptional merit on specialized topics, with particular attention given to work by younger scholars, the dissemination and publication of which is difficult under the economic pressures of standard publishing models.

Persons seeking information about the ASM or the guidelines for having their dissertations considered for publication in the ASM Monograph Series should consult the Society's website—www.asmweb.org.

Members of the ASM Monograph Committee who approved this book are:

Susan Maros, Affiliate Assistant Professor of Christian Leadership
Fuller Theological Seminary

Sue Russell, Professor of Mission and Contextual Studies
Asbury Theological Seminary

RECENTLY PUBLISHED IN THE ASM MONOGRAPH SERIES

George Shakwelele, *Explaining the Practice of Elevating an Ancestor for Veneration*
Peter T. Lee, *Hybridizing Mission: Intercultural Social Dynamics among Christian Workers on Multicultural Teams in North Africa*

Through the Flames

Early Christian Responses to Persecution and Implications for Christians in Northern Nigeria

Yakubu T. Jakada

◈PICKWICK *Publications* · Eugene, Oregon

THROUGH THE FLAMES
Early Christian Responses to Persecution and Implications for Christians in Northern Nigeria

American Society of Missiology Monograph Series 68

Copyright © 2024 Yakubu T. Jakada. All rights reserved. Except for brief quotations in critical publications or reviews, no part of this book may be reproduced in any manner without prior written permission from the publisher. Write: Permissions, Wipf and Stock Publishers, 199 W. 8th Ave., Suite 3, Eugene, OR 97401.

Pickwick Publications
An Imprint of Wipf and Stock Publishers
199 W. 8th Ave., Suite 3
Eugene, OR 97401

www.wipfandstock.com

PAPERBACK ISBN: 978-1-6667-8219-6
HARDCOVER ISBN: 978-1-6667-8220-2
EBOOK ISBN: 978-1-6667-8221-9

Cataloguing-in-Publication data:

Names: Jakada, Yakubu T. [author].

Title: Through the flames : early Christian responses to persecution and implications for Christians in northern Nigeria / by Yakubu T. Jakada.

Description: Eugene, OR: Pickwick Publications, 2024 | American Society of Missiology Monograph Series 68 | Includes bibliographical references.

Identifiers: ISBN 978-1-6667-8219-6 (paperback) | ISBN 978-1-6667-8220-2 (hardcover) | ISBN 978-1-6667-8221-9 (ebook)

Subjects: LCSH: Persecution—Nigeria—Religious aspects. | Christianity—Nigeria. | Christians—Violence against—Nigeria. | Violence—Nigeria—Religious aspects. | Persecution—History—Early church, ca. 30–600. | Boko Haram. | Religious tolerance—Nigeria. | Christianity and other religions—Islam.

Classification: BR1608 J35 2024 (paperback) | BR1608 (ebook)

VERSION NUMBER 01/12/24

Scripture quotations are from the Holy Bible, New International Version®, NIV®, copyright ©1973, 1978, 1984, 2011 by Biblica, Inc.® Used by permission. All rights reserved worldwide.

Contents

Acknowledgments | vii
Dedication | ix
Abbreviations | xi

1. The Challenge | 1
2. Background of Conflicts in Northern Nigeria | 18
3. Responses to Persecution: Northern Nigerian Experience | 55
4. Biblical and Historical Responses to Persecution | 99
5. Towards a Proper Response to Persecution | 150

Appendix A: Methodology | 167
Appendix B: Questionnaires | 179
Appendix C: Interviews and Questionnaire Responses | 181
Appendix D: Analysis of Questionnaires: Kaduna State | 183
Appendix E: Analysis of Questionnaires: Borno State | 190
Appendix F: Interview Protocol | 197
Appendix G: Informed Consent Letter | 199
Appendix H: Research Permission Letter | 201
Appendix I: Research Permission Letter | 203
Appendix J: Research Assistant Confidential Agreement | 205
Appendix K: IRB Approval | 206
Appendix L: Debate about the Myth of Persecution | 207
Bibliography | 211

Acknowledgments

I WOULD LIKE TO first recognize God with gratitude for making it possible to study for a PhD. He gave me sound health, strength, wisdom, and intellectual abilities for this accomplishment. He made all physical and spiritual provisions and stood by me in my trying times. If not for his help, the completion of this study would not have been possible. All glory to him.

I would like to recognize the efforts of my mentor, Dr. Sue Russell, a great woman of substance who walked me through to the end of my studies. Your quality advice, encouragement, scholarly insights, and motherly corrections have stepped up my scholarship. The time and commitment you gave to this work is highly appreciated. Thank you for the resources you made available to me. I am forever grateful to you. I want to also recognize Dr. W. Jay Moon for the time spent as my reader to go through the manuscripts; thank you for the insights you brought into this work. I want to recognize Dr. Lalsangkima Pachuau for agreeing to be my alternate reader. The three of you have been a great team that helped produce this successful work. I want to also recognize Dr. Stephen Ybarrola for being my examiner. The observations you raised added much to improve this work. I want to recognize all the professors who taught me and made themselves available for advice and prayer. I recognize Dr. Timothy Tennent, president of Asbury Theological Seminary, who taught me and greatly encouraged me.

I would like to recognize Dr. Reuben Chuga, under whose able leadership I was permitted by the Baptist Theological Seminary Kaduna (BTSK) to further my studies. Thank you for all your support. I want to thank the board of governors of BTSK for their continuous support during my studies. I want to recognize the current president of BTSK, Dr. Moses

Audi, for his support in ensuring that this work is completed. Thank you, entire BTSK family, for your support.

I acknowledge the efforts of my wife Yagana, and my children, Gamaliel, Comfort, Irene, and Karen, who have struggled with me. I know there were times when you needed my attention, and I was not there because I had to meet deadlines. The financial burden of the studies has caused you some suffering, but you endured. I appreciate your prayers and encouragements.

I am thankful to Bill Johnson and family for the Johnson Scholarship awarded for this study. It was a great help for the entire period of the study.

I also recognize Pastor Nathan Elliott, the deacons, and all members of Mount Freedom Baptist Church, Wilmore, Kentucky, for financial and moral support. You stood by us during our trying times. God will not forget your labor of love.

There are numerous families and friends who did much in supporting this effort and are truly part of this success story, including Mr. Benjamin Quigg and wife Sarah; Mrs. Janine Damran; Pastor Shedrack Para; Mr. Alan Peed and wife Karen; Wasiu Jakada; Sarah Jakada and the entire Jakada Family; my mother-in-law Comfort Kashim; Ken Dean and his family; Pastor Kenric Prescott, former pastor of Union Baptist Church, Hartford, Connecticut; Mr. Bulus Drambi; Rev. Titus Pona for help with research; Rev. Joshua Enock; Bishop Mohammed Naga; Rev. Sunday Ibrahim; Joshua Jacob; Dr. Medine Keener; and so many others who supported. God will abundantly reward you.

I would like to recognize Katrina Sally and Pilar Mackinnon for their help editing this work. It is not possible to remember and mention all who contributed to my studies and the dissertation this book is based upon, but the Lord who rewards saw your contribution and will bless you abundantly in return.

Dedication

I DEDICATE THIS RESEARCH work to God who saw me through this program, as the twenty-four elders in the book of Revelation have cast their golden crowns before him. This work and the PhD are hereby laid at his feet. I also dedicate this work to my family, my wife Yagana, and children, Gamaliel, Comfort, Irene, and Karen, who prayed and persevered with me until the completion of this work. Finally, I dedicate this work to the following individuals: Leah Sharibu, who has been held captive in the den of Boko Haram for over two years, at this writing, for refusing to deny her faith in Christ; Rev. Lawan Andimi, who was beheaded for his faith in January 2020; the eleven Christians beheaded for their faith by Boko Haram in Nigeria on Christmas Day 2019; and all Christians who are suffering for the faith all over the world.

Abbreviations

CAN	Christian Association of Nigeria
CMS	Church Missionary Society
COCIN	Church of Christ in Nigeria (now Church of Christ in Nations)
ECWA	Evangelical Church of West Africa (now Evangelical Church Winning All)
EYN	Ekklesiyar Yanuwa a Nigeria
FCS	Fellowship of Christian Students
ISWAP	Islamic State West Africa Province
NCEF	National Christian Elders Forum
NIREC	Nigeria Inter-Religious Council
SIM	Sudan Interior Mission
SUM	Sudan United Mission

1

The Challenge

INTRODUCTION

EXPERIENCING PERSECUTION IS NOT new to the church. It has always been with the church to varying degrees. The persecution of Christians attracts much attention when it involves a massive loss of lives and property. This research focuses on how proper response to persecution from Christians impacts evangelism and discipleship within the context of persecution.

Luke, in the Acts of the Apostles, recorded several experiences of persecution of the apostles and early disciples of Christ. Persecution for the Christian faith in the first three hundred years of the church was mostly sporadic and sometimes sponsored by the state. Roman persecution of the early church is traditionally accepted to have taken place under ten emperors.[1] The persecutions resulted in the martyrdom of thousands of Christians. Constantine ended the persecutions by making Christianity the legal state religion.

In northern Nigeria, there has not been official, state-sponsored persecution of Christians, but Muslim traditional rulers and government officials have directly or indirectly supported the efforts of fundamentalist Muslims to persecute Christians. Muslims have used the political power at their disposal to maltreat, marginalize, and oppress Christian minorities in northern Nigeria.[2] There have been attacks on Christians and their

---

1. The emperors who are known to have persecuted Christians include Nero, Domitian, Trajan, Marcus Aurelius, Septimus Severus, Decius, Valerian, and Maximus the Thracian, and climaxed with Diocletian and Galerius.

2. Bitrus, "Persecution of the Church," 380–81. Stefanos Foundation, *Religious Intolerance*, 55–214, documents examples of such maltreatment and marginalization by Muslims of Christian minorities in northern Nigeria with the involvement of traditional rulers and government officials.

properties, claiming the lives of thousands of Christians in the region.³ The introduction of the Shari'a legal system in twelve of the nineteen states of the northern part of Nigeria, the emergence of Boko Haram, and the deadly Fulani herdsmen who are ravaging and destroying Christian villages all introduce a new dimension to the persecution of Christians in northern Nigeria. Bishop Joseph Bagobiri has stated correctly that this new dimension is a systematic attempt by some groups of Muslims to wipe out Christianity in northern Nigeria.⁴

The persecution of Christians is a growing phenomenon throughout the world.⁵ The need to prepare the church for proper responses to this development cannot be overemphasized. If Christians properly respond to persecution, as this study considers, then evangelism, discipleship, and growth of the church will thrive in the context of persecution.

STATEMENT OF THE PROBLEM

Nigeria in West Africa has a population of about 180 million people, covering a land area of 923,768 km². While English is the official language used in the country, there are about 520 spoken languages in Nigeria. Hausa is widely spoken in the north, Igbo in the east, and Yoruba in the west. The northern part of Nigeria is predominantly Muslim, and the southern part consists mainly of two groups: Christians and followers of the African traditional religion. Christians are 52.61 percent of the total population of Nigeria according to *Operation World*.⁶ In northern Nigeria, Christians have been oppressed by Muslim traditional institutions and Muslim government officials.⁷ Muslims have inflicted harsh treatments such as denial of land for places of worship, denial of certificates of occupancy for church buildings, ridicule as infidels, confiscation of land and property, denial of promotions, forceful marriage of Christian girls to Muslims, persecution of Muslim converts to Christianity, and destruction of church buildings.⁸

The rise of Islamic fundamentalism and fanaticism from the 1970s substantially increased persecution of Christians in northern Nigeria,⁹ while assuming a new dimension in the 1980s with the Kafanchan religious

---

3. Ukanah, *In God's Name*, xii.
4. Bagobiri, "Asso Village Massacre," para. 2.
5. Marshall, "Persecution of Christians," para. 4.
6. Johnstone and Mandryk, *Operation World*, 488. The current population of Nigeria is over two hundred million people and still growing.
7. Ishaku, *Boko Haram*, 175–80.
8. M. Gaiya, "History of Christian-Muslim Relationship," 299–300.
9. Gwamna, "Turning Tides," 271.

crisis in 1987, the Reinhard Bonnke riot in Kano in 1991, and the Zangon Kataf crisis in 1992, followed by many other crises in various parts of the north. An uncountable number of church buildings, Christian homes, and businesses worth billions of Naira (Nigerian currency) have also been destroyed and several thousands of lives lost.[10]

As noted, the introduction of the Islamic legal system, Shari'a, in twelve out of nineteen states of northern Nigeria in the year 2000 added another dimension to the persecution of Christians in the affected areas: being subjected to living under Islamic rules. This development provided the ideal environment for the emergence of the Boko Haram insurgency, which is now fighting for an Islamic state in Nigeria. Massive killings of Christians commenced with other crimes, including bombing and destruction of church buildings.[11] Massive, alarming killings by Fulani herdsmen who target predominantly Christian villages have recently happened.[12] These experiences of persecution in northern Nigeria are affecting social relationships between Christians and Muslims and the theology of many Christians, as well as making missionary activities more difficult.

Research for this study observed a trend in the responses to persecution by Christians in northern Nigeria. In the 1980s, Christians were pacifists and left vengeance to God. When violence increased in the 1990s, Christians saw the need to defend their lives and property. Self-defense, therefore, became another option of their response to persecution. In the 2000s, occasional vengeance from Christians became a response to persecution in some areas. These developments have created a concern for the future of Christianity in northern Nigeria.

Christians in northern Nigeria want to know whether it is appropriate for them to respond with vengeance after an attack, since the attackers view the nonresistant pacifism of the Christians as weakness. These Christians ask about self-defense, since the government is not adequately protecting the Christians in northern Nigeria, and whether there is any biblical and/or theological justification for self-defense. The church in northern Nigeria, however, needs to address the more fundamental question of how to respond to persecution in a way that positively impacts evangelism and discipleship. This book considers how different Christian responses to persecution in postcolonial northern Nigeria impacted evangelism and discipleship, and

10. Gwamna, "Turning Tides," 278.
11. P. Gaiya, *Religion and Justice*, 77–78.
12. Ukanah, *In God's Name*, 296–300. The Fulani herdsmen killers have targeted Christian villages in the part of northern Nigeria referred to as the Middle Belt where Christianity is stronger. The states most affected include Plateau, Kaduna, Benue, Taraba, Adamawa, Southern Bauchi, and Nasarawa.

how these varying Christian responses in northern Nigeria compare to the historical accounts of the early Christian responses to persecution.

RESEARCH QUESTIONS

This study attempted to answer whether the different Christian responses to persecution in postcolonial northern Nigeria impacted evangelism and discipleship and how these responses compare to the historical accounts of responses to persecution in the early Christian church. The types, nature, and reasons for persecuting Christians were investigated, as well as Christian responses to persecution. The objective was to identify how these responses affect evangelism and discipleship to develop a framework for Christian response to persecution in northern Nigeria. Following are the specific research questions that guided this study.

1. What are the root causes of conflicts in northern Nigeria?

   I attempted to examine factors such as legacies of colonialism, Shari'a, religion and politics, Islamic fundamentalism and radicalism, and other ethnic, sociocultural, and economic factors that trigger the conflicts experienced; and how these oppressive factors connect with Christian persecution in the region.

2. What were early Christian responses to persecution and what impact did the responses have on evangelism and discipleship?

   Addressing this question, the persecution of early Christians was investigated, including ways Christians were persecuted and reasons for the persecution, as well as early Christian responses to persecution and how these responses effected evangelism and discipleship.

3. What has been the Nigerian Christian response to persecution since postcolonial era and how has it impacted evangelism and discipleship?

   The history of persecution of Christians in northern Nigeria was traced, including reasons for persecution, types of persecutions, extent of persecution, responses to persecution by Christians in northern Nigeria, and effects of these responses on evangelism and discipleship.

4. What are the biblical/historical bases for Christian responses to persecutions?

Researched was whether Scripture provides one specific response or multiple types of responses to persecution, whether there are biblical and historical grounds for self-defense or vengeance, and the consequences of conflicts between contextual and biblical responses to persecution.

SIGNIFICANCE OF THE STUDY

Persecution has been a part of the experience of many Christians in postcolonial northern Nigeria. As evidenced by the early church, believers experiencing persecution can still live out their lives as light and salt in the world. Learning from the responses of the early church may bring encouragement to Christians in northern Nigeria to remain steadfast and faithful in the faith despite difficult times.

The need for promotion of peaceful coexistence between Christians and people of other faiths in Nigeria cannot be overemphasized. Bitter experiences of religious violence in cities like Kaduna and Jos have segregated communities by two faiths, Islam, and Christianity. Such balkanization is not healthy for evangelism and discipleship. This research may benefit those who seek to mediate peace and reconciliation. Proper responses to persecution may help build bridges and improve interfaith relationships.

As extreme persecution of Christians was the experience of early Christians, it is reality in many Christian communities today. Persecution of Christians is growing globally and there is a need to prepare the church on how to respond. Jesus prepared his disciples for persecution (Mark 13:9–13), and the contemporary church should be prepared. This work hopes to contribute to Christian preparation in responding to persecution with positive attitudes.

Although the goal of persecution is to weaken the church, the church often flourishes because of the persecution. Learning from the early church and contemporary experiences on how the church grew in the context of persecution will be of great benefit to Christians in northern Nigeria. Early Christians were not perfect in their responses, and this research seeks to uncover the pitfalls of early Christian responses to persecution to help the contemporary church avoid them.

This research work is of significance to my teaching ministry in northern Nigeria. Deeper insights may be realized concerning persecution and how to respond, preparing those in the teaching ministry for future challenges of persecution. The findings of this book may serve as a tool to prepare Christian leaders and train pastors in theological schools, specifically the Baptist Theological Seminary, Kaduna, Nigeria. These leaders will in turn prepare other Christians in different communities in northern Nigeria. This work will be an additional resource about Christian persecution, unique in its focus on responses to persecution and their effects on Christian life and ministry.

SCOPE AND DELIMITATION

To study persecution in the early church is an enormous task. Therefore, the scope of the study has been narrowed to the responses of early Christians to persecution, in order that the lessons learned may be applied in the context of persecution of Christians in northern Nigeria.

Nigeria covers a land area of 923,768 km² with a population about 180 million.[13] As such, it is difficult within the scope of this book and available human, material, and financial resources to perform a thorough research on the whole of Nigeria. This study is limited to northern Nigeria with samples from Kaduna State and Borno State, which are major areas of persecution of Christians in Nigeria. Another limitation is security. Some regions to be researched could not be accessed due to security issues caused by Boko Haram, Fulani herdsmen, and kidnappers. I narrowly escaped a major crisis in Kaduna that led to a citywide imposition of a twenty-four-hour curfew on October 21, 2018. Returning from Maiduguri, I was delayed for three days in Kano until a safe travel report to Kaduna was issued. The first trip scheduled for Gwantu in Southern Kaduna was cancelled because of a report of an impending attack on some communities by Fulani herdsmen, which did occur that weekend. The dangerous research trip to Chibok in Borno State was like going into the lions' den and emerging alive amid frequent Boko Haram attacks in the area.

An additional limiting factor was the level of education of some leaders, as evidenced by the responses on some questionnaires lacking sufficient information. The research assistants were instructed to explain the questions or administer the Hausa[14] version to those who did not understand English very well. Fear of attacks or victimization in places of work prevented a few from responding, even with codes used in place of their names to conceal their identities. Other research-hindering factors included bad roads, erratic power supply, poor internet service, health issues, and lack of cooperation from some respondents, such as failure to complete or return questionnaires.

---

13. Fleck, *Bringing Christianity to Nigeria*, 27–28.
14. A language widely spoken in northern Nigeria and some parts of West Africa.

DEFINITION OF KEY TERMS

The following key terms are defined for this research.

Discipleship: The process of maturing new believers who agree to follow Jesus on his terms, which is to grow into his image and reflect his glory. W. Jay Moon defines intercultural discipleship as "a transforming process whereby people center their lives on the Kingdom of God (Matt 6:33), such that they obey Christ's commands in the cultures in which they live (Matt 28:19–20)."[15] The emphasis on obedience to the commands of Jesus in cultures where the disciples live is unique to this definition. For Christianity to truly take root in cultures, it must be the type that emphasizes discipleship within that culture wherein the new believer grows and matures in faith and commitment to Christ and his causes. Following Christ in the context of persecution may include suffering, shame, reproach, pain, and even death. Many have failed to become disciples because they wish to follow Jesus on their own terms. In discipleship, there is a willing submission to Christ with the goal of becoming like him (2 Cor 3:18).

Early Christians: Followers of the Christian religion in the first four decades of the existence of Christianity. Sometimes the term "early church" may be used to denote early Christians in this research.

Evangelism: Scott Jones defines evangelism as "that set of loving, intentional activities governed by the goal of initiating persons into Christian discipleship in response to the reign of God."[16] In this definition, Jones makes a strong connection between evangelism, discipleship, and the kingdom. Evangelism is defined in this research as the practical expression of the love of God for the dying world, in that God uses believers as instruments for the completion of his divine purpose of saving and bringing people into the kingdom. In the context of persecution, this love is expressed through loyalty to Christ despite the suffering and pain endured, as well as through acts and words of love from the persecuted to the persecutor.

Fundamentalism: R. M. Burrell defines fundamentalism as "an assured and unwavering conviction that a certain body of beliefs, usually derived from 'sacred' writings and often associated with the life and teaching of a particular personality, unquestionably represents the truth, and that it is the duty of all the faithful to live their lives and direct their activities in accordance with

---

15. Moon, *Intercultural Discipleship*, 50.
16. Jones, *Evangelistic Love of God*, loc. 1849–50.

those beliefs."[17] This definition is important in this book in that it addresses the key elements of fundamentalism: the believer, body of beliefs, unwavering conviction, sense of duty, and commitment to persuade other believers to share their convictions. Fundamentalism is not limited to religion. There are political, economic, and ethnic/racial fundamentalists. Fundamentalism taken to its extremes is radicalism. This study focuses on religious fundamentalism and radicalism within a geographical area—northern Nigeria.

Northern Nigeria: Nigeria in West Africa is the largest black nation in the world with a population of about 180 million people. The 1914 amalgamation of Nigeria into a British protectorate gave Nigeria the three distinct regions of north, west, and east. The northern part is hereby called northern Nigeria. Northern Nigeria is predominantly Muslim, and Hausa is the widely spoken vernacular.

Persecution: A form of inconvenience, suffering, or pain inflicted intentionally upon a person due to their opinion, beliefs, or affiliation. Charles Tieszen defines Christian persecution as an "unjust action of varying levels of hostility perpetrated primarily on the basis of religion and directed at Christians, resulting in varying levels of harm as it is considered from the victim's perspective."[18] Tieszen's definition addresses the experiences of both extreme persecution and those who endure mild hostility. This definition is clear that persecution directed at Christians distinguishes political and ethnic persecution, which Christians who belong to either group may suffer. Sometimes, Christian persecution in Nigeria may occur from a combination of religious, political, and ethnic reasons. In this research, Tieszen's approach is used to define Christian persecution.

Responses to Persecution: Actions, reactions, or inaction by the person being persecuted and caused by internal influences, external influences, or both.

LITERATURE REVIEW ON RESPONSES TO PERSECUTION

The purpose of this research project was to examine the Christian responses to persecution and their impact on evangelism and discipleship. Literature that examines responses to Christian persecution was reviewed. In his book *In the Shadow of the Cross: A Biblical Theology of Persecution and*

17. Burrell, *Islamic Fundamentalism*, 5.
18. Tieszen, *Re-Examining Religious Persecution*, 48.

Discipleship, Glenn Penner examines the theology of persecution in both the New Testament and Old Testament. Penner outlines the three kinds of responses permitted in Scripture, which he calls fight, flight, and fortitude.[19] Each of these types of responses—vengeance (fight), pacifism (flight), and defense (fortitude)—has been part of the conversation on how Christians in northern Nigeria should manage persecution. This framework of persecution responses provides the structure for analysis of the data.

Fight

The first type of response to persecution, as outlined by Glenn Penner, is fight. This response has found support in the just war theory of St. Augustine. The theory sets the background for Christian involvement in war when doing so has proper justification. Philip Wynn contends that Augustine did not originate the idea of "just war." He insists that there were other voices, such as Origen and Ambrose.[20] Wynn maintains that Augustine was the major voice but not the only voice. Although Augustine was not a pacifist, he saw "war at times as a harsh necessity."[21]

The *Summa Theologica* of Thomas Aquinas, part 2, elaborates on the just war theory. Aquinas approves of Christian involvement in military service as soldiers are needed to defend divine worship, ensure public safety, and protect the poor and the oppressed.[22] In Aquinas's opinion, Christians can only get involved in war on the authority of the sovereign or the church.[23] In *The Nature and Destiny of Man*, Reinhold Niebuhr agrees with the idea of just war but cautions that "not all wars are equally just and not all contestants are equally right."[24]

Jay Beaman argues that early Pentecostals were pacifists. Pacifism was closely related to their eschatological worldview. He states that "change in status since the world wars affected Pentecostal thinking about pacifism."[25] The movement from poverty to religious and social mainstream changed their values and ethics. Beaman gives this vivid example: "In 1953, the Assemblies of God statement on military service was altered without comment. Reference to the Decalogue (Ex. 20:13) as a reason for not

---

19. Penner, *In the Shadow*, 132–33.
20. Wynn, *Augustine on War*, 134.
21. Wynn, *Augustine on War*, 135.
22. Aquinas, *Summa Theologica*, 268.
23. Aquinas, *Summa Theologica*, 269.
24. Niebuhr, *Nature and Destiny*, 283.
25. Beaman, *Pentecostal Pacifism*, 107.

participating in bloodshed during time of war was removed."[26] In *The Weight of Glory*, C. S. Lewis argues that the audience of the Sermon on the Mount did not take "turning the other cheek" literally. He insists that those listening "were private people in a disarmed nation; it seems unlikely that they would ever suppose our Lord to be referring to war. They would not have been thinking of war. The friction of daily life among villagers was more likely to be in their minds."[27]

Just war theory is about the justification of Christian involvement in war declared by the state or the church, which has a different context than religious persecution in Nigeria. Though it is hard to find Christian literature that encourages vengeance, there is evidence of vengeance by Christians in Africa and in northern Nigeria in particular. Daniel Philpott and Timothy Shah report how Christians in Central African Republic, who suffered violence at the hands of Muslims, in turn massacred their persecutors.[28]

In Nigeria also there have also been instances where Christians murdered Muslims in retaliation for Christians killed. A vivid example is that of Christians in Yelwa Shendam in Plateau State, Nigeria, who killed hundreds of their Muslim persecutors in 2004.[29] Sunday Bobai Agang reports about a Christian militia poised for vengeance in northern Nigeria: "A northern Christian militia named *Akhwat Akwop* emerged in September 2011 vowing to match 'blood for more blood, violence for more violence, and life for more lives.'"[30] Writing from the perspective of a pacifist, he laments the advice given to him by some retired pastors who said to him, "Sunday, make sure when Muslims burn two churches, you burn four mosques."[31] Agang does not discuss the reason for this attitude toward violence.

Although there are works written by Christians discouraging vengeance, this approach is used as a response to persecution. The reason why Christians being persecuted resort to vengeance needs to be examined, an important perspective of this study.

Flight

The second response to persecution is flight, or pacifism. This has been an age-old response to persecution based on an understanding of the pacifist teachings of Christ in the Sermon on the Mount and some of Paul's pacifist

26. Beaman, *Pentecostal Pacifism*, 114.
27. Lewis, *Weight of Glory*, 86–87.
28. Philpott and Shah, "In Response to Persecution," 8.
29. John et al., "Gun Violence in Nigeria," 425.
30. Agang, *No More Cheeks*, 47.
31. Agang, *No More Cheeks*, 46.

teachings on the treatment of the enemy. Sampling church traditions that are pacifist, the literature of writers who are Mennonites were examined. Daniel A. Dombrowski argues that early Christians were universally pacifists, as he notes, "The first Christians who were known to be soldiers are not found until A.D. 177."[32] In reaction to just war theory, Dombrowski concludes that "the 'just war theory' is practically dead."[33] Pacifism, in the context Dombrowski discusses, is whether Christians can serve in the military or not, which is different than the context of mob violence against Christians with little or no protection by the Nigerian government.

Howard Yoder in his book *Reinhold Niebuhr and Christian Pacifism* looks at Niebuhr's concepts of impossibility, necessity, and responsibility, which he uses to argue in support of America's involvement in World War II.[34] Yoder argues for pacifism and the law of love as he examines the teachings of Christ on treatment of the enemy. He sees in Niebuhr's position a contradiction of the love ethics of the New Testament. Yoder further sees the pacifism of Jesus as an intensification of the nonviolence that the prophets of Israel proclaimed. Interestingly here, Yoder is trying to strike a balance by saying, "Just war theory and pacifism should not be seen as enemies but as complementary." He further argues that the two "battle side by side against the usual war ethic, which is either crusade or justification of whatever wars the state decides to wage."[35]

Another discussion on pacifism as the proper Christian response to persecution is Jonathan Dymond's article "An Inquiry into the Accordancy of War with the Principles of Christianity," which provides the official position of Quakers on pacifism. The basic argument is that they cannot reconcile the life and teachings of Jesus and Christian principles with war.[36] To buttress the claim of the Quakers' position, Margaret E. Hirst says that the Society of Friends (Quakers) have stood for their conviction on pacifism not only in the time of peace, but also in time of war when they were left to stand alone. Hirst wrote this about the Quakers: "Our conviction of the unlawfulness of war to the Christian, which prevents us from giving to our country the military service willingly rendered by many, should specially call us to voluntary service in other ways, even at the cost of much personal sacrifice."[37]

---

32. Dombrowski, *Christian Pacifism*, 13.
33. Dombrowski, *Christian Pacifism*, 21.
34. Yoder, *Reinhold Niebuhr*, 18.
35. Yoder, *War of the Lamb*, 20.
36. Dymond, *Quakers against War*, 174.
37. Hirst, *Quakers in War*, 487.

There are examples of outstanding Christian leaders and theologians who follow the Christian pacifism as described above. These leaders include Martin Luther King Jr., who writes about nonviolent action. "Nonviolence is a powerful and just weapon. It is a weapon unique in history, which cuts without wounding and ennobles the man who wields it. It is a sword that heals."[38] He argues for the effectiveness of nonviolent resistance and cites as evidence "the nonviolent actions of early Christians . . . and the nonviolent actions of Mahatma Gandhi and his followers in India."[39]

King also does not support self-defense as a response to persecution, because it often includes violence. If it includes violence, he writes, "It is extremely dangerous to organize a movement around self-defense. The line between defensive violence and aggressive or retaliatory violence is a fine line indeed."[40] He further stresses, "When violence is tolerated even as a means of self-defense there is grave danger that in the fervor of emotion the main fight will be lost over the question of self-defense."[41] King has a valid argument for nonviolent resistance. The context of violence that Martin Luther King Jr. and the African Americans had to contend with is comparably like that which northern Nigerian Christians are experiencing. In northern Nigeria, the Shari'a law is used as an instrument of persecution of Christians and other religious minorities compared to the Jim Crow law in the Southern part of the United States that was used to marginalize, segregate, and persecute blacks and people of color.[42] Other similarities include the denial of justice to their victims, the use of mob violence for wanton destruction, and the use of terrorist groups to achieve their aims.[43] In the south of the United States, the Ku Klux Klan used terrorism, as Boko Haram and Fulani Herdsmen do in northern Nigeria. There is a difference—the persecution in northern Nigeria is primarily religious with a sometimes ethnic undertone, while in the southern states of America, it was primarily racist, which in turn affected religion. This unique difference is addressed in this research.

Dietrich Bonhoeffer was also a pacifist. In his teaching on discipleship, he advocates pacifism as the only right way to adhere to the teachings of Jesus on how to react to evil. He writes, "The only way to overcome evil is to let it run itself to a standstill because it does not find resistance it is looking for." He adds, "Resistance merely creates further evil and adds fuel

---

38. King, *Why We Can't Wait*, 26.
39. King, *Why We Can't Wait*, 37.
40. King, *Testament of Hope*, 57.
41. King, *Testament of Hope*, 57.
42. Teach Democracy, "Jim Crow," paras. 9–13.
43. Urofsky, "Jim Crow Law," para. 2.

to the flames."⁴⁴ The pacifist Bonhoeffer later changed and became a champion of violent resistance to the extent of becoming involved in the attempt to assassinate Adolf Hitler. Eberhard Bethge, who was a close disciple of Bonhoeffer, claims that "Bonhoeffer introduced us in 1935 to the problem of what we today call political resistance."⁴⁵ Bonhoeffer's concern about the escalation of the persecution of the Jews in Germany turned him from pacifism to resistance. The ideas of Bonhoeffer will be used as a case study in the discussion of persecution in the context of northern Nigeria.

Ibrahim Bitrus also argues that the appropriate response to persecution in the context of northern Nigeria is nonviolent resistance. He states that "neither armed struggle nor reverting to traditional worship of the ancestral gods is a valid response to such persecution."⁴⁶ He discusses the theology of the cross as a basis for understanding the theology of suffering and suggests for the Christians in northern Nigeria "an unwavering faith rooted in the liberating presence of the crucified God in the midst of God's suffering people."⁴⁷ He claims that this response will bring victory to the Christians in northern Nigeria more than armed resistance. In accordance with Bitrus's views, Musa Adziba Mambula observes that the Ekklesiyar Yanuwa a Nigeria (EYN) practices pacifism. With roots from the Church of the Brethren, the EYN is one of the dominant Christian denominations in the northeast of Nigeria, which probably accounts for the Christians in the region tending toward pacifism. Mambula argues that the pacifism of the EYN church will bring a lasting solution to the problem of persecution in northern Nigeria.⁴⁸ Similarly, Agang also from the Middle Belt of Nigeria writes in support of pacifism and advocates the continual turning of the cheek in his book *No More Cheeks to Turn?* He contends, "In teaching about turning the other cheek, Jesus was essentially stating the obvious to help them understand a not so obvious principle of life in a violent context."⁴⁹ Agang further explains that turning the other cheek "does not mean that we simply accept any injustice done to us. It does mean that we respond with dignity and are free to appeal to the law and to injustice."⁵⁰

---

44. Bonhoeffer, *Cost of Discipleship*, 141.
45. Bethge, *Friendship and Resistance*, 24.
46. Bitrus, "Persecution of the Church," 381.
47. Bitrus, "Persecution of the Church," 385.
48. Mambula, *Ethno-Religious and Socio-Political Violence*, 123.
49. Agang, *No More Cheeks*, 57–58.
50. Agang, *No More Cheeks*, 58.

Agang believes that Christians can and should practice nonviolent self-defense as a more biblical response to persecution.[51]

Joseph Bagobiri adds to the "turning the other cheek" discussion by considering various contexts. He argues, "There are instances that call us to turn the other cheek. But there are others that doing so or taking to flight instead of fight will amount to a betrayal of the gospel of Christ."[52] Bagobiri insists that both the use of force to repel the persecutor and exhibition of the pacifistic character are valid options for Christians in their response to persecution. However, he argues that Christians need to be prayerful and discern which approach the Lord is leading them to employ.[53] While Bagobiri accepts Tertullian's maxim that the "blood of the martyrs is the seed of the church," he also argues that "in many other places discrimination, violence and martyrdom have been reason for the death of the church and Christian communities."[54] The church in the Middle East and in North Africa (Tunisia and Libya) give evidence to Bagobiri's claim.

In conclusion, many of those who write in support of pacifism often do so as a reaction to the just war theory, which seeks to justify the prohibition of Christians participating in military service. This is different from the context of persecution in northern Nigeria involving mob violence and genocide. This study is not aware of any Christian tradition in Nigeria that is opposed to military service. Nigerian Christians serve in the military. The following important questions need to be considered if we think of pacifism to be the only option for Christians in Nigeria. If all Christians in Nigeria flee from Muslim persecution and flight is the only option, where will seventy-plus million people go? Will the multitudes of people that move out of Nigeria result in a major humanitarian disaster on the African continent? Will nonviolent resistance work with Muslim persecution, which has a pattern of displacing religious groups and cultures? Will pacifism work where persecution has developed to the level of terrorism? Is nonviolent resistance reconcilable with genocide as in the case of Fulani herdsmen killings in Christian villages in northern Nigeria? Will nonviolent resistance work in the context of injustice like that in Nigeria where demonstrations and cries from the oppressed masses seem to be falling on deaf ears? These questions guided this research in examining further whether the age-old tradition of pacifism should be the only option in responding to persecution. Consequently, there

---

51. Agang, *No More Cheeks*, 31.
52. Bagobiri, *Seed of Another Humanity*, 118.
53. Bagobiri, *Seed of Another Humanity*, 119.
54. Bagobiri, *Seed of Another Humanity*, 8.

are gaps in response to persecution literature that need to be addressed as to how Christians should respond to persecution.

Fortitude

Fight and flight have been discussed thus far as responses to persecution. Are fight and flight the only options for Christians responding to persecution? What about self-defense? There has been less discussion on whether it is a valid option for Christians to defend themselves when attacked, as in the case of mob violence and genocide in northern Nigeria and elsewhere. In his *Christianity Today* article, "No Cheeks Left to Turn," Sunday Oguntola reports on a meeting where Christian leaders argued for and against self-defense. The former national president of the Christian Association of Nigeria (CAN), Pastor Ayo Oritsejafor, stated that he has the "responsibility to defend himself and his family." Bishop John Praise of Dominion Chapel called on churches to "raise young people to defend the church." Praise further commented, "People say, 'when they slap your cheek, you turn the other.' We have turned both, and they have slapped us. There is nothing else to turn."[55]

In contrast, Bishop Wale Oke, the vice president of Pentecostal Fellowship of Nigeria, Southwest, argues that Christians should not yield to such temptation. He stresses, "To fight back is contrary to the position of our Lord Jesus Christ."[56] He emphasizes the continual turning of the cheek to conquer the battle, as Christ did the same and conquered the world.

Ephraim Kadala, on the other hand, includes self-defense as a viable response to the persecution of Christians in northern Nigeria. In his opinion, pacifist Christians take "turning the other cheek" to the extreme. He advocates that Christians should be prepared to defend their lives and the lives of their loved ones against evildoers.[57] However, he cautions that self-defense should not degenerate to vengeance. In *Religious Intolerance: A Threat to Nigeria's Unity*, the Stefanos Foundation also suggests that victims of religious violence can undertake self-defense if well-coordinated.[58]

Another writer, Gary Corwin, counsels Christians in Nigeria on using self-defense as a response to persecution. He writes, "I cannot help wondering if the answer does not lie in encouraging the development of local but well-disciplined Christian self-defense forces in each vulnerable

---

55. Oguntola, "No Cheeks Left to Turn," 14.
56. Oguntola, "No Cheeks Left to Turn," 14.
57. Kadala, *Turn the Other Cheek*, 176.
58. Stefanos Foundation, *Religious Intolerance*, 234.

community."⁵⁹ He cautions that they should be defensive only and not attack innocent civilians. He concludes his article with a question: "While turning the cheek is an appropriate and godly personal response to unjust behavior toward oneself, is it the only appropriate community response to genocide?"⁶⁰ This question is important in the conversation on self-defense.

Bagobiri is in full support of self-defense as well. He says, "Self-defense is an act of love toward oneself, and in defense of God's gift of life." To support this viewpoint, he cites 1 Tim 5:8, "Anyone who does not look after his own relations, especially if they are living with him, has rejected the faith and is worse than an unbeliever," to argue that the protection and defense of one's family against harm is a religious duty.⁶¹

Dialogue with the aggressor is seen in this book as self-defense because of its preventive and/or curative potentials. It takes boldness to confront and engage an opponent in dialogue. Since the source of persecution of Christians in northern Nigeria is largely from Muslims, interreligious dialogue may be a valid form of response in Nigeria. John Onaiyekan believes that in order to achieve peace in Africa, religions must dialogue and live up to their founding principles. He reiterates that "the purpose of dialogue is to be able to understand one another, dissolve suspicion and prejudices, and so pave the way for collaboration and mutual respect."⁶² If Nigerian Christians and Muslims are able to work together toward understanding and mutual respect for each other, there will probably be less violence.

An example of this type of working together is seen in Badru D. Kateregga and David W. Shenk's book, *A Muslim and a Christian in Dialogue*. In the book, a Christian and Muslim each present views of their religion on certain theological issues, and responses are made in a respectful manner on each issue. They note that there are areas of agreement in the beliefs of both Christians and Muslims, and there are areas where Christianity and Islam disagree.⁶³ They have worked together to present a model of dialogue which promotes openness and respect for the other's religious beliefs.

Marinus Iwuchukwu advocates a similar view to that of Kateregga and Shenk on "respect for religious freedom and appreciation for each other's cultural and religious differences."⁶⁴ He believes that mutual respect and understanding is a way out of the Nigerian predicament. Iwuchukwu

---

59. Corwin, "Question of Self-Defense," 11.
60. Corwin, "Question of Self-Defense," 11.
61. Bagobiri, *Seed of Another Humanity*, 73.
62. Onaiyekan, *Seeking Common Grounds*, 17.
63. Kateregga and Shenk, *Muslim and Christian*, 206.
64. Iwuchukwu, *Christian-Muslim Dialogue*, 176.

adds an important observation, "It is both imperative and possible that Muslims and Christians collaborate to not only talk the talk of faith but also walk the walk of the faith traditions."[65] Adherence to faith traditions is essential for progress in the context of dialogue in Nigeria.

Bagobiri looks at dialogue in a new perspective as he introduces the evangelistic dimension in the discussion on dialogue. He writes, "Dialogue with other religions, especially Islam and African traditional religion, is an integral part of the proclamation of the gospel and the church's pastoral activity on behalf of reconciliation and peace."[66] Many advocates of dialogue—even Christians—often miss or downplay the importance of the gospel in bringing lasting peace among peoples, groups, and/or nations.

The Bad Urach Statement, a document produced as a result of a consultation held in Bad Urach, Germany to address the problems of Christian suffering and persecution, also recommends that the option of self-defense "be examined and compared critically with the alternative of pacifistic resistance." The document observes that self-defense has been "insufficiently studied and researched."[67] This study will make significant contributions in examining the option of self-defense more deeply as a Christian response to persecution.

CONCLUSION

The literature reviewed has focused on response to persecution using the framework of fight, flight, and fortitude. The themes included pacifism, nonviolence resistance, self-defense, and vengeance, each helpful in understanding the ongoing conversation concerning how Christians in Nigeria should respond to persecution. This research will advance the discussion of when self-defense is a viable response to persecution. It will also examine the effects of responses to persecution on evangelism and discipleship both in the early church and contemporary churches in northern Nigeria.

---

65. Iwuchukwu, *Christian-Muslim Dialogue*, 178.
66. Bagobiri, *Seed of Another Humanity*, 91.
67. Sauer and Howell, *Suffering, Persecution and Martyrdom*, 102.

2

Background of Conflicts in Northern Nigeria

INTRODUCTION

RELIGIOUS CONFLICT HAS BECOME a great concern to Nigerians across ethnic and religious communities because they have resulted in the deaths of thousands of people, destruction of property worth multibillion Naira, and relationships destroyed between Muslims and Christians. The conflicts in northern Nigeria are often between Christians and Muslims. Christianity and Islam are the two largest religious bodies in Nigeria. Concern about continual conflicts and their negative effects have prompted some citizens of Nigeria to reach across faith barriers and seek ways to bring peaceful coexistence. This research is concerned with responses to the persecution of Christians who suffer the most violent attacks in northern Nigeria, and how to maintain a vibrant Christian witness and discipleship in the context of persecution.

This chapter on the background and development of conflict in northern Nigeria discusses the role that legacies of colonialism have in the current crises in the region. The structures created by the Islamic and British colonial systems are considered by some scholars to be a major source of conflict between the Muslim Hausa-Fulani and the non-Muslim minority tribes of northern Nigeria. This chapter first assesses the contribution of colonialism to the current conflicts in northern Nigeria. It then examines the background and spread of the two major religions in Nigeria, Islam and Christianity, and their influence on politics. Finally, how Islamic fundamentalism and radicalism contribute to the conflicts in the region is studied. This research analysis identifies how the underlying ideology of an Islamic state governed by Shari'a law, actualized by the instrumentality of jihad, is a source of conflict in the region.

Though economic, social, and ethnic problems are contributing factors to the generation of conflicts in the region, they are strongly tied to religion. In the contemporary setting of Nigeria, the incompatible ideologies of Shari'a and democracy are one of the main sources of conflicts in northern Nigeria. The desire of Muslims to incorporate Shari'a into the Nigerian constitution is antithetical to a secular state. Understanding the background of current conflict in northern Nigeria helps readers understand how to best respond to conflict.

THE LEGACIES OF COLONIALISM AND NEOCOLONIALISM

Nigeria, the most populous black country in the world, was colonized by the British who controlled the area until independence in 1960. The name Nigeria came from combining two words, "Niger" and "area," to form Nigeria. When the British colonialists came to northern Nigeria, they found an existing Islamic colonization system imposed on non-Muslim minority tribes and built a governing system upon it. This attitude of the colonial masters empowered the Hausa-Fulani Muslims and gave them dominance over the non-Muslim tribal groups that later accepted Christianity. This section discusses the role of the British colonial government, with its indirect rule policy in northern Nigeria, in the expansion of Islam and the adverse effect of indirect rule on relationships between Muslims and Christians. This friction resulted in several ethno-religious riots in northern Nigeria. The legacy of colonialism in this context helps readers understand how the domination of non-Muslims with an Islamization agenda were strengthened by British colonialism and are now being resisted by Christians in northern Nigeria. The tension between the oppressor, Hausa-Fulani Muslims of northern Nigeria, and the non-Muslim oppressed is a source of conflict.

Legacy of British Rule

There existed before the arrival of the British colonialists, in what was later to be known as Nigeria, several independent states and/or empires such as the Hausa states, the Oyo Empire, and Benin Kingdom. The Berlin Conference of 1884 partitioned Africa, and Nigeria fell under the British. After the Berlin Conference, Frederick Lugard "paid his first visit to Nigeria to organize troops for subjugation on behalf of Royal Niger Company."[1] Lugard

---

1. Chinweizu, "Caliphate Colonialism," 185.

proclaimed the protectorate of northern Nigeria on January 1, 1897. The first emirates to be conquered in northern Nigeria were Kabba, Kontagora, and Ilorin. Kano fell in February 1903, and Sokoto, the capital of the caliphate, was captured on March 13, 1903.[2]

Some argue that Lugard was able to conquer the caliphate because he had superior weapons and gun powder. Matthew Kukah and Toyin Falola concur with this argument, but add the dimension that "the collapse of the emirates was possible because of the decadence and the incapacity of the system to sustain itself for things having fallen apart, a weak center could no longer hold."[3] This argument is supported by Abdullahi, the brother of Usman Dan Fodio, who soon after the reformation expressed his disappointment that the decadence of the Hausa rulers was practiced by the succeeding Fulani rulers.[4]

The British created Northern Nigeria in 1900 and Southern Nigeria in 1906. Northern Nigeria gained independence on March 15, 1953, with Sir Ahmadu Bello as its first and only premier. Northern and Southern Nigeria were amalgamated in 1914. Chinweizu claimed that in the amalgamation, the British colonial government made "Northern Nigeria 'the husband,'" who "would financially live off the dowry/revenue/resources of Southern Nigeria, 'the wife.'"[5] The British colonial government handed over power to the Fulani caliphate as successor.[6] Lugard was compelled by limited resources and manpower to adopt indirect rule for northern Nigeria, which later developed into a sophisticated political theory.[7] Arguably, indirect rule became a tool for the expansion of Islam among the non-Muslims of northern Nigeria.

The policy of indirect rule was a child of necessity that helped the British colonizers cope with the administration of a vast, conquered territory, which they did not have the funds and manpower to run. Ricardo Laremont gives a clear picture of the necessity of the policy of indirect rule and how it was helpful to the colonial administrators in this statement:

> This system in Northern Nigeria was remarkable because in 1906 it enabled seventy-five British administrative officers, supported by a small but efficient army, to control a territory of nearly 300,000 square miles inhabited by approximately seven

2. Falola, *Colonialism and Violence*, 13–16.
3. Kukah and Falola, *Religious Militancy and Self-Assertion*, 101.
4. Azumah, *Legacy of Arab-Islam*, 105.
5. Chinweizu, "Caliphate Colonialism," 178.
6. Chinweizu, "Caliphate Colonialism," 178.
7. Falola, *Colonialism and Violence*, 31.

million people, a great convenience for the British who were constrained by limited funds and personnel.⁸

When the British came to northern Nigeria, they met an effective system of administration through which they could easily control the region and collect taxes. The order of authority was as follows: sultan, the emirs, the district heads, the *dakatai* (village heads), and the *maiunguwas* (ward heads). Since this system was already working for the caliphate, the colonial masters saw no reason to abolish it. E. P. T. Crampton further commented on indirect rule, "Lugard and even more so his successor, raised 'Indirect Rule' from being 'just an expedient in times of financial hardship and lack of staff to a complete philosophy of government to Britain's colonial peoples.'"⁹

The system was favorable to the Muslim rulers in northern Nigeria, but it was an instrument of oppression for the non-Muslims. Kukah and Falola wrote, "The non-Muslims did not fare better. According to the colonial ladder of priorities, it was the emir first, the Muslim communities were next, and the bottom of the ladder was occupied by non-Muslims."¹⁰ The British used indirect rule to meet their needs at the expense of the rights of the non-Muslim minorities in northern Nigeria. To this, Laremont adds that "the British policy of Indirect Rule actually buttressed the Islamization of the society in ways that were not replicated in adjacent areas . . . to the former Hausa states that were under French rule just across the border in Niger."¹¹

From this discussion, it can be argued that the British colonial administration helped the expansion of Islam among the non-Muslim tribes and communities of northern Nigeria and hence further strengthened the Islamization agenda of Muslims in the region. However, Muslim writers viewed the colonialists in northern Nigeria as collaborators with Christian missionaries towards the proselytism of Muslims to the Christian faith.

Muslim Views on Colonization

Muslims view the British conquest as primarily truncating the Islamic agenda. Azumah writes, "Europe is blamed for interrupting and preventing Islam from accomplishing noble tasks."¹² This sentiment about the effect of colonialism on Islam is shared by Muslims in northern Nigeria as Abdulkareem Mohammed writes in *The Paradox of Boko Haram*,

8. Laremont, *Islamic Law and Politics*, 94.
9. Crampton, *Christianity in Northern Nigeria*, 52.
10. Kukah and Falola, *Religious Militancy and Self-Assertion*, 103.
11. Laremont, *Islamic Law and Politics*, 115.
12. Azumah, *Legacy of Arab-Islam*, 8.

> The colonial masters have been known to tamper with the conceptual and operational levels of both Islamic faith and religion in the conquered territories of the Muslim World. They were known to reduce the religion to secondary position or in some incidences to one of total irrelevance. This is why the post political independence era of the Muslim territories is marked by ideological efforts to rediscover its battered personality. The efforts are geared towards drawing upon Islamic spiritual and historical sources so as to develop new attitudes which symbolizes the revivalist movement of Islam.[13]

The Islamic state being run by the Dan Fodio caliphate was interrupted by British colonial rule, though certain elements were retained for indirect rule. Mohammed's comment makes a connection between the effect of colonialism on Islam and its culture that produces the ripple effects of violence in the name of Islamic revivalism. Christians, other non-Muslims, and even innocent Muslims in northern Nigeria are at the receiving end of what is termed Islamic revivalism.

Mohammed further seeks to justify the Islamic rule under the caliphate over the British colonial government as he asserts, "Although Pre-British rule period was characterized by inter-tribal and inter-state wars, it is noteworthy that people of different socio-cultural identities lived more in peace before the advent of colonial rule."[14] I argue that it was the Pax Britannica, the Christian message, and the introduction of Western education that reduced intertribal wars and interstate wars to the barest minimum. Under pre-British rule, non-Muslims were considered the "house of war" by the caliphate and a slave-raiding field.[15]

Expressing similar sentiments as Mohammed, Abdur Rahman Doi alleges, "Although Christianity came late, it came, as we have seen with the blessings of Imperial Power of Western Europe. Whenever, Christianity came, they were provided with all facilities by the former colonial masters, from anti-malarial drugs to dangerous weapons, educational facilities to material means to bribe the natives, health services to highest government positions."[16] I sympathize with Doi's feelings because Christianity had a phenomenal growth in Nigeria that, within a short time, conquered territories that Islam would have taken several centuries before Christianity came but could not. The coming of Christianity to Africa and colonialism from

---

13. Mohammed and Haruna, *Paradox of Boko Haram*, 2.
14. Mohammed and Haruna, *Paradox of Boko Haram*, 9.
15. Turaki, *Tainted Legacy*, 153.
16. Doi, *Islam in Nigeria*, 83.

Europe at almost the same time makes it easy for critics to criticize Christianity as collaborators with colonialism, which Doi does as a Muslim apologist. However, in his book *Islam in Nigeria*, he is not able to substantiate his portrayal of Christian missionaries as corrupt and dangerous criminals who took advantage of the poor local people.[17]

Contrary to Doi's depiction, Christians did not depend on government funding to carry out mission activities. Funds were raised by Christian individuals, families, and local church congregations to further the cause of the gospel. It should be noted that most of the colonial masters were not Christians, and many were rather anti-Christian. To accuse missionaries of possession of dangerous weapons is the highest form of negative criticism. Conversely, it is well documented that many missionaries were killed for the sake of the gospel.[18]

Christian missionaries in northern Nigeria excelled in social services, especially in education and health. Christians, Muslims, and pagans were educated without being forced to accept Christianity. Christian missionaries helped the poor without discrimination. The health services of missionaries in northern Nigeria saved the region from numerous deaths caused by leprosy and many other dangerous diseases. Many initial converts to Christianity were beneficiaries of these kindnesses. The same Muslim elites educated in missionary schools and benefitting from missionary health services schemed with the Nigerian government in the 1970s to seize these institutions and destroy them. Many of those schools and hospitals that were seized from the Christian missions by the Nigerian government in the pretext of better and effective management and services are today either in ruins or malfunctioning.

Contrary to Doi's claim that Christian missions came with the blessing of the imperial power, Christian missionaries were not allowed to operate in the Muslim northern Nigerian region. Crampton writes, "Lugard felt that he would be interfering with the Muslim religion if he allowed missions to operate where they are not welcomed by the rulers before the British conquest."[19] Colonial masters, who sought to pacify the northern rulers, required some missionaries to leave. With the support of the colonial administrators, the Muslim rulers were also able to send missionaries away from their domains. For example, the emir of Kano sent away Bishop Herbert Tugwell, a Church

---

17. Sanneh, *Translating the Message*, 210. Sanneh also notes that missionaries were often portrayed as the oppressors in ethnographic literature. For him this was a misrepresentation because it did not consider what he calls "reciprocity" between missionaries and the community.

18. Benge and Benge, *Rowland Bingham*, 110.

19. Crampton, *Christianity in Northern Nigeria*, 46.

Missionary Society missionary, telling him, "We do not want you: you can go. I give you three days to prepare: a hundred donkeys to carry loads back to Zaria, and we never wish to see you here again."[20] Akintude Akinade summarizes the experience of missionaries in northern Nigeria under the colonial authorities: "The politically protected status of Islam, coupled with the sense of right, muffled early Christian activities and intimidated Christian missionaries who were mainly from the mission churches."[21]

Another aspect of colonial rule that advanced the cause of Islam is the subjugation of the pagan societies under the Muslim rulers and the suppression of them with the support of the colonial powers. Crampton opines that "it can hardly be doubted that the practice of placing large numbers of 'pagans' under *Fulani* District Heads and supporting the authority of these by the powers of government when and where necessary led to an extension of Islam."[22] Pagan societies that were autonomous and self-governed before the British came were forcefully placed under Muslim rulers. To gain any political or economic advantage, one had to become a Muslim, which compelled many pagans to become Muslims. The Akurmi people, for example, were placed under the emir of Zaria. The emir determined who became a chief of a community, and the condition was conversion to Islam. When a chief became a Muslim, it was common for his subjects to be converted to Islam.

The native authority under the emirs became a tool for conversion to Islam. Crampton writes, "There was a general belief that employment in the emirate Native Administration was open only to those who were Muslims."[23] Most of the positions occupied by Christians were those that the Muslims were not capable to handle since Christians, through their missionaries, embraced Western education earlier than the Muslims. Ibrahim James argued that in the native authority "there was nothing 'native' in the system as far as the Southern Zaria Communities are concerned."[24] In James's view, if the native authority was truly native, then pagan communities such as those of southern Zaria should have been administered by native southern Zarians and not by Hausa-Fulani who were foreigners. The domination of pagan communities by Muslims resulted in many people converting to Islam and hence expanded the frontiers of Islam in northern Nigeria. Yusufu Turaki is blunter: "The British Colonial structure helped Islam to expand its influence and dominance over those non-Muslim

---

20. Crampton, *Christianity in Northern Nigeria*, 39.
21. Akinade, *Fractured Spectrum*, 46.
22. Crampton, *Christianity in Northern Nigeria*, 53.
23. Crampton, *Christianity in Northern Nigeria*, 68.
24. James, *Studies in the History*, 125–26.

groups of the Middle Belt that previously resisted it."[25] The struggle to free themselves from this dominance is a major contributor for the Zangon Kataf violence of 1992, which started because of the relocation of a market. The Kataf, indigenous people who are Christians, wanted the market to be relocated. On the other hand, the Hausa-Fulani Muslims wanted it to continue where it was to maintain their controlling influence on the market, so that the economic control of the town remained theirs.[26]

The domination of the non-Muslims in northern Nigeria empowered by the decision of the colonial masters to favor Muslims affected not only the economy of the non-Muslims but also the expansion of Christianity. Christianity in Nigeria came through the coastal areas of the southern part of the country. As missionaries worked in the south, southerners had the advantage of Western education and became the chief suppliers of manpower in the north. Most of the workers and traders from the south were Christians who were restricted from propagating their faith. As Crampton writes, "In the early years Nigerians from the south were restricted to the *sabon garis* and were almost as inhibited in propagating their faith as the expatriate officials and traders."[27] Indigenous Christians were not allowed to propagate their Christian faith because the British colonial administrators did not want to offend the Muslim rulers by going against the policy of the indirect rule.

Laremont clearly states this argument about the British colonial government's support for Islam and its propagation by comparing the policy of the indirect rule in northern Nigeria to the Francophone area of the caliphate in Niger Republic and other Francophone countries as he writes, "The British policy of indirect rule actually buttressed the Islamization of the society in ways that were not replicable in adjacent areas . . . to the former Hausa states that were under French rule just across the border in Niger."[28] While the French colonial policies restrained the Islamization of the society, they did not Christianize the society. This comparison is a strong support for the claim that in northern Nigeria, the colonial administration aided the expansion of Islam through the indirect rule policy.

Continued Effects of Colonial Policies

The non-Hausa Fulani have been dominated since the caliphate regime and later in the colonial period, which still affects non-Hausa Fulani today.

25. Turaki, *Tainted Legacy*, 33.
26. Gwamna, *Religion and Politics*, 79–80.
27. Crampton, *Christianity in Northern Nigeria*, 47.
28. Laremont, *Islamic Law and Politics*, 115.

When the government was turned over to the Nigerians by the British. The premier of northern Nigeria, Bello, boasts:

> The new nation called Nigeria should be an estate of our great grandfather, Uthman dan Fodio. We must ruthlessly prevent change of power. We use the minorities of the North as willing tools and the south as conquered territory and never allow them to rule over us, and never allow them to have control over their future.[29]

The indirect rule and manner of the colonialist British transition of power in Nigeria to the Hausa-Fulani Muslims implied that Nigeria was to be ruled by the Hausa-Fulani Muslims. This claim to ownership of Nigeria is one of the major sources of ethno-religious conflicts in the country. Reflecting on this domination and its effect, Kukah and Falola write, "The Hausa-Fulani whom they regard as 'strangers' and 'settlers' were not indigenous to the area; they alone have continued to control the traditional political power which was bequeathed to them by the colonial administration to the total exclusion of all other ethnic communities believed to be indigenous to the area."[30] This domination is what has manifested in the ethno-religious conflicts in Kafanchan, Tafawa Balewa, Zangon Kataf, and many more towns and cities in the Middle Belt of Nigeria. To buttress this point, Jan Boer states:

> A major colonial policy with long term repercussions was the practice of subjecting previously independent nations to the rule of Muslim emirs. These nations, most of them in Nigeria's Middle Belt, adhered to the Traditional Religion. Majority of the citizens of many of them later became Christians. That was the situation that obtained in much of Southern Zaria as well as in Tafawa Balewa, Bauchi state. The colonial policy became a major cause of some riots, if not the major cause.[31]

Many people blame ethno-religious conflict in Nigeria on economic deprivation, but the problem is deeper than that. Many tribal groups have been marginalized in the past and are still being marginalized by the dominant Hausa-Fulani Muslim group. In my opinion, the Hausa-Fulani Muslims wish to maintain their oppressive and dominant position as seen in the statement of Bello above, while the non-Muslim Middle Belt tribes are struggling to liberate themselves from this yoke of bondage that their

---

29. Chinweizu, "Caliphate Colonialism," 175.
30. Kukah and Falola, *Religious Militancy and Self-Assertion*, 157.
31. Boer, *Why this Muslim Violence*, 86–87.

ancestors suffered by the hands of the Hausa-Fulani. This struggle has caused the destruction of lives and property in northern Nigeria as well as religious bigotry and intolerance. Some religious intolerance is a manifestation of anger from the domination and marginalization of the past.

BACKGROUND OF RELIGION AND POLITICS IN NORTHERN NIGERIA

Nigeria is a multireligious country. Three religions are predominantly practiced by Nigerians: Christianity, Islam, and African traditional religion. Of the religions, Christianity and Islam are the largest. Islam predates Christianity in Nigeria, coming to the region in the eleventh century through Kanem-Borno Empire, while Christianity was introduced in the eighteenth century from the coastal areas of the south.

Religion plays a crucial role in Nigerian politics. Christianity and Islam, being the dominant religions, have great influence. Muslims and Christians each have a preferred party and candidates in the elections. Politicians appeal to religion for votes and to win elections. This we-versus-they political ideology of Christians and Muslims is a source of conflict in Nigeria. The postelection violence in northern Nigeria in 2011 attests to this fact. Violence erupted when a Christian won the presidential election. Several Christians were killed, churches burned, and businesses belonging to Christians looted and destroyed because of the outcome of an election.[32] It is important to understand the dynamics between religion and politics, their significance, and how they trigger violent crises. This is the focus of this section. A brief history of the spread of Islam and Christianity in Nigeria is important in understanding the background of the conflict in northern Nigeria.

Spread of Islam

Islam came into Nigeria from the north and has been moving southward, and Christianity came in from the coastal areas in the south and has been spreading northward. The meeting point and battleground for these two religions is the Middle Belt. I am of the opinion that the southward push by Islam, the northward push by Christianity, and the contest for the soul of the Middle Belt are contributing factors to the conflicts experienced in the Middle Belt states like Kaduna, Plateau, Bauchi, Nasarawa, Taraba, and Benue.

With a population of about 180 million, Nigeria is the most populous black country on earth. It has 520 ethnic groups and three major tribes:

32. Turaki, *Historical Roots*, 32.

Hausa, Igbo, and Yoruba.[33] Nigeria is situated between latitude four and fourteen degrees north of the equator. Three distinct vegetation zones run across the country from the south to the north—the tropical rain forest in the south, the Savannah grassland in the Middle Belt, and the semidesert in the extreme north. The two great rivers, Niger, and Benue, join at Lokoja and flow to the Atlantic Ocean, giving Nigeria its natural division of north, east, and west.

The story of one united country called Nigeria began in 1914 with the amalgamation of the north and south of Nigeria into one British protectorate with three distinct political regions of north, east, and west. The north is the largest with almost half of the population of the country.[34] The southern part of Nigeria is mostly Christian and followers of the African traditional religion, while the north is predominantly Muslim. Hausa is the major trade language spoken in northern Nigeria.

Islam came into what is now Nigeria through the Kanem-Bornu Empire in the eleventh century. The state of Borno was created in the northeast of Nigeria. Doi quotes Al-Bakri as saying, "The presence in *Kanem* in 1068 of people who descended from the Umayyad adherents who had fled south to escape persecution at the hands of Abbasid Caliphs when they came to power in 750."[35] This migration of persecuted Muslims was the genesis of the penetration of Islam in what was later called Nigeria. The introduction of Islam to *Kanem* through the Trans-Sahara trade routes established a relationship with the Arab world in the Middle East and the Maghrib.[36] Today the Kanuri of Borno State in Nigeria are proud to be the first recipients of Islam in Nigeria.

The introduction of Islam in the Hausa states is linked with Kano. According to the *Kano Chronicle*, "Islam came to Kano for the first time in the reign of *Yaji* (1319–1385 A. D.) when *Wangarawa* or *Mandingo* traders introduced it from Mali."[37] Doi said that Kano and the environs were fully Islamized under the patronage of Muhammad Rumfa (1463–99). The first mosque in Kano replaced the sacred tree of *Madabo*, which was cut down.[38] In Katsina, the first chief to accept Islam was Muhammad Korau, who ruled from 1380 to 1420.[39] It is surprising that the Fulani, who championed

---

33. Falola and Heaton, *History of Nigeria*, 4–6.
34. Falola and Heaton, *History of Nigeria*, 117.
35. Doi, *Islam in Nigeria*, 57.
36. Doi, *Islam in Nigeria*, 57.
37. Doi, *Islam in Nigeria*, 19.
38. Doi, *Islam in Nigeria*, 21.
39. Doi, *Islam in Nigeria*, 20.

the jihad in northern Nigeria with the claim to purify the religion, accepted Islam at the close of the seventeenth century and were mostly converted in the eighteenth and nineteenth century from paganism. Doi admits that some records show an earlier date of the conversion of the Fulani to Islam.[40] The Fulani, as roving shepherds, were ambassadors of Islam throughout the northern region, and remain so today.

Apart from the Hausa, Kanuri, and Fulani, the two tribes most influenced by Islam in northern Nigeria are the Nupes and the Ebirras. The first *Etsu* (Nupe chief) to accept Islam was Jibril, who reigned towards the end of the eighteenth century.[41] The present central mosque in Bida was built in 1870. The Nupes are said to be 97 percent Muslim. The spread of Islam among the Ebirras was the work of the Ulamas and credited to "the pupils of Uthman Dan Fodio."[42] Some Ebirras encountered Islam when they travelled out to Ilorin, Kano, Ibadan, and Zaria and were converted. Doi further comments that it was "during the reign of Ibrahim Atta Islam spread far and wide and it is estimated that about 90% of the Ebirras are Muslims."[43]

Having discussed the spread of Islam in Nigeria, focus will now shift to the role of politics and religion in fueling conflict in northern Nigeria. It is important to understand that in Islam, religion and politics are not separate. The belief that "Islam is superior to every other culture, faith, government and society and that it is ordained by Allah to conquer and dominate them" provides the justification in Islam for a strong emphasis on politics.[44] The foundation of Islamic society and Muslim politics in northern Nigeria is traceable to the reformation and jihad of Dan Fodio, where the caliphate was governed by Islamic laws. Al-Kanemi, the Borno chief who delivered Borno from the jihadists, refers to the jihad of Dan Fodio as efforts of "ambitious Fulani Mallams and politicians" who used the jihad "as a cover to achieve power and prominence."[45] Muhammad *al-Amin al-Kanemi* rightly views the Fulani jihad of Dan Fodio as a political maneuver instead of religious reformation. In the same way, Christians in northern Nigeria suspect that the Fulani herdsmen attacks on Christian communities in northern Nigeria were a revival of Dan Fodio's jihad and caliphate and must be resisted.

---

40. Doi, *Islam in Nigeria*, 28.
41. Doi, *Islam in Nigeria*, 61–62.
42. Doi, *Islam in Nigeria*, 65.
43. Doi, *Islam in Nigeria*, 66.
44. Asemota, "Project Nigeria 2018," para. 50.
45. Kukah and Falola, *Religious Militancy and Self-Assertion*, 31.

Kukah and Falola say that it is not difficult to understand the political nature of Islam because the religion was founded on politics.[46] The political nature of Islam manifested during the formative years of Nigeria as a nation and was especially prominent in the northern part of the country. There were three important Muslim political leaders who emerged between 1950 and 1966: Ahmadu Bello, Aminu Kano, and Abubakar Gumi, each articulating different versions of Islam in politics.[47] Bello wanted to unite the north under the umbrella of Islam against western and eastern Nigeria. Kano mixed Islamic and socialist ideology in his effort to liberate the *talakawas* (masses). Gumi, a Wahhabi legalist, sought to purify Islam. Kukah and Falola write, "The feeling that if Islam transformed the politics in Iran, Algeria, Egypt, or Pakistan, it should do the same in Nigeria is partly responsible for the radicalization of Islam and bigotry."[48] This idea has given birth to movements like the Muslim Students Society of Nigeria, the Muslim Brotherhood led by *Al-Zakzaky* and a strong Wahhabi influence of the *Izala*.

The military also used religion as a tool for creating a political constituency in Nigeria. Out of the eight military leaders in the history of Nigeria, five were Muslims. As a result of the influence of the military, "Islam serves as a political tool for an ambitious Northern elite."[49] Islam does not practice the separation of church (mosque) and state—all is the same. Bello, the premier of northern Nigeria, is quoted by Kukah and Falola: "The government of which I am leader will not do anything outside of Muslim law. You know that I myself have no strength except the strength of our religion."[50] During Bello's leadership, he used public funds to build mosques and promote Islamic activities.[51] Following Bello's example, Muslim government officials and politicians in northern Nigeria build mosques and Qur'anic schools for their communities with public funds to fulfill their duty as public office holders. Kukah and Falola reiterate that "in an Islamic state, [there is] no distinction between the religious sphere and that of politics."[52] Kukah and Falola's claim is evident in northern Nigeria, where the dominant religion is Islam, and any effort to separate Islam from politics is to misunderstand Islam.

---

46. Kukah and Falola, *Religious Militancy and Self-Assertion*, 13.
47. Laremont, *Islamic Law and Politics*, 126.
48. Kukah and Falola, *Religious Militancy and Self-Assertion*, 112.
49. Kukah and Falola, *Religious Militancy and Self-Assertion*, 2.
50. Kukah and Falola, *Religious Militancy and Self-Assertion*, 42.
51. Kukah and Falola, *Religious Militancy and Self-Assertion*, 43.
52. Kukah and Falola, *Religious Militancy and Self-Assertion*, 13–14.

Spread of Christianity

The history of Christianity in sub-Saharan Africa began in the fifteenth century when Portuguese missionaries came to the area.[53] After the Portuguese, Roman Catholics started working in the Congo in 1491 without success. In West Africa where Nigeria is located, Protestant missionary work began with the resettled freed slaves in Sierra Leone. Some of the slaves had become Christians when they were in England or America. They had their own pastors and built their own churches.[54]

In 1840, the liberated slaves from Nigeria returned home to Abeokuta and saw the need to evangelize their people. They sent a message requesting missionaries to come to Freetown. The Wesleyan Missionary Society and the Church Missionary Society (CMS) responded to this plea in 1842. The first missionary to arrive in Nigeria was Henry Townsend of the CMS. He was joined by another party of missionaries in 1844. Samuel Ajayi Crowther was a member of this party.[55] In 1843, the Wesleyan Methodists sent Thomas Freeman and William de Graft from the Gold coast to Badagry to pioneer their work.[56] In 1850, Thomas Jefferson Bowen, from the Southern Baptist USA, arrived in Badagry and went inland to Abeokuta to establish Baptist work.[57] The Scottish Presbyterian Mission worked in the eastern part of Nigeria.[58] After the failure of the Portuguese attempt in the fifteenth-century, the next attempt of the Catholic missions was through the Society of African Mission that arrived Nigeria in 1861. The prefectures apostolic were later formed to cover the Upper Niger in 1884, and the Lower Niger in 1889. In 1911, the prefecture of Eastern Nigeria was created. The Holy Ghost Fathers shared in the labor with the Society of African Missions in advancing the Catholic missions in Nigeria.[59]

There were waves of missionary movements in Nigeria that connected the Western missionary efforts and those of the indigenous missionaries. The first was the denominational missionary societies who pioneered the work of missions in the coastal areas.[60] The second wave was the Inland Missions, pioneered by nondenominational and faith missions. The most notable persons and mission organizations who pioneered the work in

---

53. Pobee, *AD 2000 and After*, 14.
54. Hildebrandt, *History of the Church*, 62.
55. Thiessen, *Survey of World Missions*, 195.
56. Hildebrandt, *History of the Church*, 105.
57. Falk, *Growth of the Church*, 340.
58. Hildebrandt, *History of the Church*, 105.
59. Falk, *Growth of the Church*, 343.
60. Johnstone, *Operation World*, 422.

northern Nigeria are Samuel Ajayi Crowther who worked along the Niger River;[61] the Sudan Interior Mission (SIM) pioneered by Thomas Kent, Walter Gowan, and Rowland Bingham; and the Sudan United Mission (SUM) led by Karl Kumm. The efforts of CMS missionaries Dr. Walter Miller and Bishop Herbert Tugwell as pioneer missionaries to the Hausa land are commendable.[62]

The third wave was the indigenous church movement, which started with some breakaways from the Western mission churches. Examples include Mojola Agbebi, who broke away to form in Lagos the first indigenous Baptist church, and the African church, which broke away from the CMS over leadership succession. Mission work was also turned over to indigenous leadership, such as the SIM work that became the Evangelical Church of West Africa (ECWA) and the work of SUM that produced churches such as Church of Christ in Nigeria (COCIN). Also, Anglican, Baptist, Methodist, and other denominational mission work was given to indigenous people.[63]

The third wave saw the development and explosion of indigenous-initiated churches. The most prominent indigenous-initiated churches in Nigeria are the Celestial Church of Christ, Cherubim and Seraphim Movement, the Church of the Lord (Aladura), and Christ Apostolic Church. Examples of the recent explosion of Pentecostal churches launched by Nigerian pastors include the prominent Deeper Life Bible Church, Redeemed Christian Church of God, and Winners Chapel. Most of these churches have significant work in northern Nigeria. For example, ECWA, COCIN, and other churches that are a product of SIM/SUM mission work in Nigeria are northern Nigerian-based churches. Much effort is being made to expand their territories beyond northern Nigeria, with branches in the southern part of Nigeria and neighboring countries, such as Niger Republic, Chad, and Cameroon.[64]

The 1960s and 70s began the era of establishing indigenous missionary societies and evangelistic ministries. Prominent ministries include the Evangelical Missionary Society of ECWA,[65] Calvary Ministries, Global Missions Board of the Nigerian Baptist Convention, and others who fellowship together in ministry under the Nigeria Evangelical Missionary Societies. Examples of evangelistic ministries include The New Life for

61. The work of Samuel Ajayi Crowther and other CMS missionaries may not be classed with the nondenominational and faith missions but is included here because Crowther was one of the first of the missionaries to go inland to the Niger River.

62. Bingham, *Seven Sevens of Years*, 14.

63. Johnstone, *Operation World*, 422.

64. Johnstone, *Operation World*, 423.

65. It should be noted that, among them, EMS of ECWA started earlier in the 1950s.

All, with its charismatic leader the late evangelist Paul Gindiri, and Food for the Total Man's Ministry of evangelist Matthew Owojaiye. Most of these mission societies and evangelism ministries are in northern Nigeria. Today, the Middle Belt is predominantly Christian, while the gospel is making serious inroads into the Muslim core in the north.[66]

Mainline Christian denominations in Nigeria practiced the separation of church and state as taught by Western missionaries. The political and economic spheres belonging to this world were seen as a restricted area for Christians who want to enter heaven. In postcolonial Nigeria, the Christians were the most educated—a gap that Muslims have not been able to close, but the Muslims continue to dominate the economic and political sphere. Religion, economics, and politics are inseparable for Muslims.

Christians in Nigeria began to see the need to participate in the socioeconomic and political life of Nigeria for several reasons, but the most important in my opinion is the oppression and marginalization of Christians, especially the Christian minority of northern Nigeria, which requires the involvement of Christians in politics to break off the yoke of bondage laid on them by colonial masters who ran a government with policies that favored the Hausa-Fulani Muslims.[67] The struggle for the emancipation of the minority Christian and non-Muslim groups started in the colonial era. Ibrahim James writes, "The discrimination meted to these mission-trained elements in employment, in admissions into government schools for their wards, etc. provided the generating impulse for the formation of political associations for channeling their discontent with the colonial administration."[68] Today there are many Christians in politics for the purpose of providing leadership to the nation with Christian principles and the emancipation of the Christian minorities of northern Nigeria. For example, Professor Jerry Gana is a respected Christian elder from the north who is prominent in the political arena. His effort to contest the presidency in the 2019 general elections in Nigeria was commendable.

Summary

Christians and Muslims are almost equal in strength in Nigeria—the south predominantly Christian and the north predominantly Muslim. Fairness in political or government appointments is defined by a balanced representation of both Christians and Muslims and any form of imbalance can be a source of conflict. Christians go into politics to have representatives

---

66. Johnstone, *Operation World*, 423.
67. Turaki, *Tainted Legacy*, 8.
68. James, *Studies in the History*, 155.

in all spheres of public domain, and to have political leaders who promote and defend policies that are favorable to Christians and the Christian religion. The nonexistence of the separation of mosque and state in Islam, especially in the use of public resources for the causes of Islam, causes Christians who live in the more affluent, more blessed southern part of the country feel cheated. Hence the need to have Christian leaders who will use the same resources for Christian causes. Therefore, the government uses public funds to sponsor Christians to Jerusalem, as Muslims are sent to Mecca for pilgrimages with public funds.

The emergence of the Pentecostal movement in Nigeria in the 1970s arrived with a prophetic mandate that God will transfer power and wealth from unbelievers to believers, thus one of the important reasons Christians became involved in politics. Pentecostal pastors in Nigeria have on many occasions prophesied the transfer of wealth and the change of power from unbelievers to believers. This is evidenced by a popular caption of a program, "Power Must Change Hands."[69] For the prophecies to be realized, Christians must be involved in politics. At the time of this writing, Professor Yemi Osinbajo, a Pentecostal pastor, is the vice president of Nigeria. M. A. Ojo says in a statement about the Pentecostals of Nigeria and politics, "Certainly, charismatic and Pentecostals have utilized their religious capacity to manipulate the public sphere to their advantage. Unlike the situation in Ghana and Zambia in the 1990s, when countries' presidents Jerry Rawlings and Frederick Chiluba, attempted to manipulate Pentecostal sentiments to their own political advantage . . . in the Nigerian case, it was the Pentecostal movements that made such attempts."[70] In Nigeria, there are Pentecostal prophets who pray, fast, and prophesy for key political leaders.

Christian persecution and the threat of Islamization have increased Christian involvement in politics. Persecution and the threat of Islam have caused Christians in Nigeria to politically resist the attempt by Muslim leaders to Islamize Nigeria. Boko Haram and Fulani herdsmen are seen as tools that are used to try to achieve the goal of Islamization. Christian involvement in politics is seen as one of the key factors in trying to resist the Muslim Islamization agenda. To buttress this point, the *Global Update Magazine* writes in an editorial:

> There are two categories of believers that God is looking for in this end time: Number one; the Elijahs and number two; the Davids. The Elijahs are the prophetic voices for Nigeria while the Davids are those whom God will entrust leadership in their

---

69. Igboyin and Adedibu, "Power Must Change Hands," 2.
70. Ojo, "Pentecostal Movements," 186.

hands. That is the only way Islamization can be stopped. The current uninformed, weak, and materialistic church cannot stop the Islamization of our country.[71]

By becoming involved in politics in Nigeria, Christians see themselves as the Christian David fighting the Goliath of Islam to liberate Christians from the oppression of Hausa-Fulani Muslims.

ISLAMIC FUNDAMENTALISM AND RADICALISM

The problem of safety in the northern part of Nigeria has been of great concern, especially since it involves mass destruction of lives and property. Added to this concern are the untold hardships of refugees and internally displaced people. One of the major causes of this problem is Islamic fundamentalism. This work traces the Islamic history of fundamentalism in Nigeria from the jihad of Uthman Dan Fodio to other emerging fundamentalist groups in northern Nigeria today. This section also discusses how fundamentalism has affected Islam internally and how it affects non-Muslims. Political power, the institution of Shari'a law, and the quest for an Islamic state have been at the heart of the fundamentalist struggles (jihad). Influenced by these factors, jihad works to purge Islam and the Islamic society of the influences of the West and paganism. Their actions have been a major source of conflict in northern Nigeria. This section first discusses the rise of Islamic fundamentalism and radicalization. Then the emergence of radical Islamic groups. Finally, this section explores Shari'a law and jihad as a means of creating an Islamic state.

Islamic Fundamentalism

The origin of Islamic fundamentalism can be traced back to the political struggle that brought about the first split within Islam, which resulted in the Sunni-Shi'a unresolved conflicts. The Shi'a believe that Ali, the cousin, and son-in-law of Muhammad, is the legitimate successor of the prophet and the leader of the Islamic community, while branding the first three caliphs as mere usurpers. It is not possible within the scope of this book to trace all the fundamentalist groups since the Sunni-Shi'a split because they are so numerous.[72] Most fundamentalist groups are either regional or a local cultural expression of Islamic fundamentalism and radicalism.

The common assumption that motivates and continues to breed fundamentalists and their groups is that the Muslim world is in a state of political

---

71. *Global Christian Update*, "Exposing and Truncating," 4.
72. Lapidus, *History of Islamic Societies*, 58.

and moral decay, caused by the intrusion of Western cultural, political, and economic ideologies. The fundamentalists view these as paganism akin to the pre-Islamic community. According to Muslim fundamentalists, "There is need to purge western cultural and political influence and to do so, the Muslim world 'must be re-Islamized,' through 're-politicizing' Islam. To do this effectively, the reintroduction of Shari'a is inevitable."[73]

Regarding fundamentalism and radicalism in northern Nigeria, I believe that while reformations such as the Iranian Revolution in 1979 impacted fundamentalism in northern Nigeria, the reformation of Dan Fodio in the early nineteenth century was most significant. Dan Fodio has remained a model for new fundamentalists and reformists in northern Nigeria, which this work will further discuss.

Uthman Dan Fodio was born in Maratta in 1754 in the family of Musa Jokollo and reared at *Degel* in the far north of Nigeria. His father was a Fulani man who migrated from Futa Toro, Senegal. He descended from the *Toronkawa* clan of the Fulani. Dan Fodio's father schooled him thoroughly in Islamic theology and jurisprudence.[74] There were other influences on his education and scholarship. As an Islamic scholar, his reformation ideologies were influenced by the writings of *al-Maghili* and *al-Yahsubi*, who classify unbelievers into three categories: "First those born into unbelief (Christians, Jews, and others); second, apostates who renounce their religion; and, third, those who are 'adjudged unbelievers on account of their actions.'"[75] Based on the third classification, Dan Fodio justified his jihad against the Hausa states that had already embraced Islam as both a reformation and a jihad against pagan tribes. The jihad sought to reform what Dan Fodio believed to be heretical Muslim governments of the Hausa states and to eradicate non-Islamic titles, practices, and systems of taxation from governance in the region.[76] According to Laremont, "The 1804–1810 jihad transformed the political landscape. The seven Hausa states before the jihad became one Muslim caliphate led by Usman dan Fodio as an *emir al mu'minnin*."[77] The jihad was also instrumental in the spread of Islam to Nupe, Ebirra, Yoruba, and other areas of present-day Nigeria. Fundamentalist ideology of this nature is a source of intra-religious and interreligious conflict, found not only in Islam but also in the Christian fold.

---

73. Davidson, *Islamic Fundamentalism*, 10–11.
74. Laremont, *Islamic Law and Politics*, 48.
75. Laremont, *Islamic Law and Politics*, 46.
76. Laremont, *Islamic Law and Politics*, 59.
77. Laremont, *Islamic Law and Politics*, 68.

Ousmane Kane observes that "up till the 1950s, the Islamic field of northern Nigeria . . . was dominated by two Sufi brotherhoods: the *Qadiriyya* and the *Tijaniyya*."[78] The *Qadiriyya* Sufi Order had enjoyed popularity since the jihad of Dan Fodio. The *Tijaniyya* Sufi Order was introduced to the Sokoto caliphate by Shaykh Umar Tall between 1831 and 1837. Internal modifications were introduced by new groups within the *Qadiriyya* and *Tijaniyya*, and as Kane writes, "Whereas the earlier *Tijaniyya* of *Umarian* and the *Qadiriyya* of *Dan Fodio's* inspiration were both elitists, *Tijaniyya Ibrahimiyya* (*Ibrahim Niasse's* sect) and *Qadiriyya Nasiriyya* (of *Nasiru Kabara*) were open to grassroots participation, especially youth and women, which partly accounts for their success."[79]

The *Qadiriyya* and *Tijaniyya* encountered a new movement that has Dan Fodio's fundamentalist ideology, which claimed that the Islam practiced by the Sufi in northern Nigeria needed reformation. In the late 1970s, the *Jama'at Izalatul Bid'a wa Iqamatu al Sunna* began reformations based on the Wahhabi ideologies of Islam practiced in Nigeria.[80] The movement is popularly called Yan Izala in northern Nigeria. They considered themselves as *ahl al-Sunna* (followers of the tradition of the prophet) and advocates for the eradication of innovation (*bid'a*). The reformation by the *Izala* group is centered on four main points: Unitarianism (*tawhid*) is preferred over associationism (*shirk*). Second is the denunciation of Sufism, which guarantees their followers happiness in this world and salvation in the hereafter. Central to this point is the polemics surrounding Tijani's prayer, the *salal al-fatih*, a prayer written by Ahmad *al-Tijani* that is revered by followers of the *Tijaniyya* sect and believed to have some magical powers.[81] Third is advocacy for egalitarianism in religion and in society. The fourth point is an attempt to restrict adherents of reform in their interactions with the larger community of Muslims.[82] The most important figure in this reformation is the late Shaykh Abubakar Mahmoud Gumi, whose sermons and teachings, mostly polemics against the Sufi order both in the Sultan Bello Mosque and Radio Nigeria Kaduna, were unrivaled. There were also counterreformations by the Sufi orders to maintain their relevance.[83]

Politically, Gumi was one of the key Islamic fundamentalists in Nigeria and the key leader of the *Izala* group. He advocated that Nigeria should

---

78. Kane, *Muslim Modernity*, 70.
79. Kane, *Muslim Modernity*, 72,
80. Laremont, *Islamic Law and Politics*, 154.
81. Laremont, *Islamic Law and Politics*, 143.
82. Kane, *Muslim Modernity*, 131.
83. Kane, *Muslim Modernity*, 82.

be divided if Christians refuse to accept Muslim leadership. In response to Gumi's suggestion, Azumah comments, "*Gumi's* political agendas and views played a significant role in polarizing Christian-Muslim relations in Nigeria as he consistently hyped up and exploited Muslim fears of Christian domination."[84] He was a key motivator of violence in northern Nigeria through his fundamentalist views of both non-Muslims and Muslims of other sects.

Rise of Fundamentalist Groups

Fundamentalist and radical Islam found a breeding ground in Nigerian institutions. The Muslim Student Society of Nigeria, with branches in Nigerian institutions of learning, served a crucial role in Islamic reformations in Nigeria. It is one of the earliest religious associations to recruit a nationwide following. To a large extent, most of the Islamist and reformist groups are splinter groups of this society.[85] The Shari'a debate of 1977–78 advocated for the inclusion of Shari'a in the constitution of Nigeria. The subsequent declaration of Shari'a in twelve of the nineteen states of northern Nigeria in 2000 was a direct result of the ideologies inspired by the Iranian revolution of the 1970s.

Another fundamentalist group that emerged in northern Nigeria is the Muslim Brothers, known in northern Nigeria as '*Yan Shi'a* (the Shi'ite group) and led by Shaykh Ibrahim *El-Zakzaky*. This group was inspired by the Iranian Revolution of 1979 and often associated with Shi'ism to seek the overthrow of the Nigerian Constitution, which the Shi'ite group considers a creation of infidels. The group led several civil disobediences and riots in the 1980s and 90s and is still a potential threat to peace in northern Nigeria.[86] At the time of this writing, the leader of the Muslim Brothers, *El-Zakzaky*, was in prison for actions considered to be a threat to national security. Some see the undertone of the Sunni persecution of the Shiites since both the president of Nigeria and the governor in Kaduna State are Sunni Muslims.

In addition to the Muslim Student Society of Nigeria and the Muslim Brothers, the *Maitatsine* group ('Yan Tatsine) fought for reforming Islam in northern Nigeria. This group instigated the worst riot in Kano in the 1980s, which spread to other parts of northern Nigeria. '*Yan Tatsine* leader Muhammadu Marwa came to Kano, Nigeria, from Cameroon. He was nicknamed *Maitatsine*, meaning one who curses, because his preaching was filled with curses on the Nigerian government and those who do not embrace his

---

84. Azumah, *Legacy of Arab-Islam*, 37.
85. Azumah, *Legacy of Arab-Islam*, 73.
86. Kane, *Muslim Modernity*, 95–96.

ideology. Kukah writes, "As far back as 1962, *Maitatsine's* intransigence had angered the authorities in Kano and so led to his deportation from Kano."[87] How he was able to come back to the city of Kano and become so influential is unknown. Kukah quotes Raymond Hickey, who made this objective observation: "Maitatsine sought to sweep away the accretions, which, he believed polluted Islam in the new materialistic Nigeria."[88] He had an idea and zealously pursued it though in the wrong way. Although the Maitatsine violence was supposed to be intra-religious within Islam, churches and businesses of Christians also suffered in the attack.

The height of fundamentalism and radicalism came with the emergence of terrorist groups such as Boko Haram, Islamic State West Africa Province (ISWAP),[89] and Fulani herdsmen. However, some of their activities were noticeable as early as 2002 when they began in Yobe State as the Nigerian Taliban.[90] In 2009, the group started attacking churches and government institutions because they are a product of the West. They were in opposition to the West, including Western education, to the extent that they were nicknamed Boko Haram, meaning Western education is forbidden.[91] Their real name is *Ahl-al Sunna wa Lidda'awati wa al-jihad*, or "people of the tradition of the prophet who propagate Islam through jihad."[92] The group became more violent after their leader Muhammad Yusuf was arrested and killed by security agents without trial. After the death of Yusuf, Abubakar Shekau became the leader of Boko Haram.[93] He has posted several videos threatening to kill Christians and Muslims who do not accept their ideology. Boko Haram has a manifesto of establishing an Islamic state, and their connection with ISIS further reinforces that ideology.

In his study of the Boko Haram phenomena, John Azumah attempted to trace the roots of Maitatsine, Boko Haram, and other splinter terrorist groups to *Izala* and its Wahhabi ideology. Azumah discovered that "Maitatsine's teaching, and activities filled into the broader pattern of dissent and activities of the Yan *Izala* and *Salafi* groups founded by *Izala* alumni." He further traced the similarities between Maitatsine and Boko Haram in their views and modus operandi. Azumah found that "Maitatsine, like

87. Kukah, *Religion, Politics and Power*, 154.
88. Kukah, *Religion, Politics and Power*, 155.
89. ISWAP is a breakaway group from Boko Haram. Because of ISWAP's nature as a terrorist group from the same roots, discussion on Boko Haram includes ISWAP.
90. Ukanah, *In God's Name*, 255–57.
91. Ukanah, *In God's Name*, 249.
92. Mohammed and Haruna, *Paradox of Boko Haram*, 27.
93. Britannica, "Boko Haram," para. 3.

Boko Haram, established a separate community, had a particular dislike for the police and started a campaign of violence after their leader was killed in a police raid." Boko Haram also created their own community within Maiduguri, and they became very violent after the death of their leader. They disliked the police and anything Western, including education. Commenting on the role of *Izala* and *Salafi* on the birthing of terrorism in Nigeria, Azuma writes, "One can safely conclude, therefore, that the *Yan Izala* created the environment for the rise of *Maitatsine* in the 1980s just as *Ahlus Sunna* did for Boko Haram."[94] I am of the opinion that the introduction of Shari'a in the twelve northern states in the year 2000 formed the bedrock for the emergence of Boko Haram, because the introduction of Shari'a in an entire region could be an inspiration that the creation and emergence of an Islamic state was a possibility.

In trying to establish the root cause of the emergence of Boko Haram, Abdulkareem Mohammed in *Paradox of Boko Haram* links the growth and development of Boko Haram to economic deprivation. In other words, Mohammed believes that poverty and unemployment among youths is the underlying cause of the terrorism in northern Nigeria. However, Yusufu Turaki argues that "it is wrong for some analysts to interpret Boko Haram as a product of economic underdevelopment of the North."[95] He sees Boko Haram and Fulani herdsmen as militant groups being sponsored by the elites to serve political, ethnic, and religious aims. I agree with Turaki in the sense that Boko Haram does not fight with sticks and clubs but with automatic and sophisticated weapons, which cannot be acquired by poor people. This shows evidence of strong support from either inside or outside Nigeria. Another factor that supports Turaki's view is the inability of the Nigerian army to defeat Boko Haram all these years. Since the Nigerian army has fought gallantly in international and continental peacekeeping, it is surprising that Boko Haram is too difficult for them to defeat.

The negative impact of Boko Haram on Christians, Muslims, and worshipers of the African traditional religion can only be estimated because instances of violence have not been reported. This is partly due to the media's inability to access some of the places where violence has occurred. In the *Voice of America News Online* on December 10, 2018, Agence France-Presse reported that "Boko Haram's Islamist insurgency has killed more than 27,000 people and left 1.8 million homeless in northeast Nigeria since 2009, triggering a humanitarian crisis in the wider

---

94. Azumah, *Legacy of Arab-Islam*, 39.
95. Turaki, *Historical Roots*, 128.

region."⁹⁶ The kind of inhuman treatment of Boko Haram against its victims is described by the UN High Commissioner for Human Rights in a report to the United Nations General Assembly.

> Boko Haram has used stones, machetes, knives, sophisticated and high-caliber weapons, improvised explosive devices, landmines, guns mounted on pickup trucks, military helicopters, armored vehicles, and motorcycles to perpetrate killings. Men and boys who refused to adopt the beliefs professed by Boko Haram were specifically targeted in killings, as were law enforcement officials, teachers, health-care workers, and members of civilian self-defense group.⁹⁷

The report further indicates that "the killings were often preceded by death threats or an invitation from Boko Haram 'inviting' men and boys to join them in 'the work of Allah.' Those who refused to join were killed, and their bodies often left to rot in the streets, in wells or riverbeds."⁹⁸ In addition, Boko Haram also beat their victims and forced them to recite the Qur'an, the Muslim scripture. They abducted Chibok and Dapchi girls, and there are numerous other unreported abductions of women who suffered severe forms of abuse, "including sexual slavery, sexual violence, forced marriages, forced pregnancies and forced conversions."⁹⁹ The original intention of Boko Haram, as perceived by Christians in Nigeria, was to persecute Christians. Because the West is perceived by Muslims in Nigeria as Christian, anything Western is rejected. The current menace of Boko Haram is a problem not only for Christians but for all Nigeria.

Another fundamentalist group in northern Nigeria is the Fulani herdsmen, whose persecution agenda can be understood side by side with Boko Haram. The origin of the Fulani has been discussed in the background information of Uthman Dan Fodio, who was a Fulani man. Christians and other people of northern Nigeria have always had farmer-herder conflicts, which were usually minor conflicts settled by the ward head or the local chief. Life between the farmers and the Fulani herdsmen had been peaceful until recent violent happenings began to occur.

Beginning in 2010, Fulani herdsmen escalated conflict violence. In 2010, *Dogon Nahawa* was attacked, resulting in an estimated four hundred deaths as well as multiple injuries and loss of houses and property.¹⁰⁰ Since

96. France-Presse, "Amnesty Calls on ICC," para. 5.
97. UN High Commissioner for Human Rights, *Violations and Abuses*, 6.
98. UN High Commissioner for Human Rights, *Violations and Abuses*, 6.
99. UN High Commissioner for Human Rights, *Violations and Abuses*, 8–9.
100. Akinyele and Igwe, "Villagers Bury Their Dead," para. 1.

then, the Fulani herdsmen attacks have continued in different parts of the Middle Belt of Nigeria. Emeka Umeagbalasi summarized the atrocities of the Fulani herdsmen:

> Terrorist Fulani Herdsmen are the second largest killers of Christians in Nigeria, accounting for an estimated 12,000 Christian deaths since 1999, including 2,500 killed between 2013 and 2014, 1,229 killed in Benue State between 2013 and July 2016. The terror agro-jihadists also killed not less than 1000 Christian and destroyed over 20 churches in Southern Kaduna in 2016 alone and cumulatively, killed over 4300 Christians since June 2015 when the Buhari administration came to power. In less than five months, between December 2017 and April 2018, terrorist Fulani herdsmen have killed a total of over 800, if not 1000 Christians, in Kogi (over 120), Benue (over 200), Taraba (over 200), Adamawa (over 80), Plateau (over 60) and Southern Kaduna (over 40). There are also other pockets of killings of Christians in different parts of Nigeria by the jihadists leading to the deaths of scores of defenseless citizens.[101]

To buttress Umeagbalasi's point, Obadiah Mailafiya adds, "What the peoples of the Middle Belt today face is a tragedy that can best be described as genocide. Fulani militias in the thousands have been rampaging across the primeval savannah, killing, pillaging, and burning down entire villages. Not only do they maim and kill, but they also destroy farmsteads and repopulate them with their own people."[102]

The identities of the Fulani herdsmen were initially difficult to establish because of the guerilla warfare tactics adopted in their operation. Initially, they were called "unknown gunmen," but later were identified as Fulani because the local people they attacked saw their faces and heard them speak Fulfulde, the Fulani language. Their identity was clearly revealed when they started carrying out some of their attacks during the day. One of the survivors from *Zargwok* village in Plateau State testified that "some of them were speaking French and others Arabic while the local Fulani herdsmen living around were the ones leading them. This was well coordinated jihad with both local and foreign support."[103]

Fulani herdsmen leadership is not as clearly defined as is Boko Haram—with Shekau as their leader and spokesman and Sambisa Forest as their primary base. However, there is suspicion about some form of

---

101. Umeagbalasi, "Imminent Extinction of Christianity," 30.
102. Mailafiya, "Fulanis," 16.
103. *Global Christian Update*, "Update of Bloody Jihad," 15.

leadership of the Fulani herdsmen provided by the *Miyetti* Allah Cattle Breeders Association of Nigeria, of which the Nigerian president Muhammadu Buhari is said to be their life patron. The suspicion is substantiated by the ways the leadership of *Miyetti* Allah speaks in defense of the terrorists instead of condemning their actions. In such defense, the leaders argue that the Fulani have been denied herding space, and as such, space should be created for them to freely graze so there could be peace. The reason why the *Miyetti* Allah leaders have not been arrested by the government and held responsible for their heinous crimes in the Middle Belt cannot be explained. A former military head of state in Nigeria and an elder statesman, Yakubu Gowon, expressed this concern when he visited to commiserate with the governor of Benue State over the attacks of the Fulani herdsmen in his state. He said, "Security agencies should invite and question the leadership of *Miyetti* Allah *Kautal Hore*, who had threatened to unleash violence on Benue State and later justified the killings and their roles."[104] He further lamented, "I am sad and worried at the religious dimension the killings are assuming."[105] The response of *Miyetti* Allah leadership in Plateau State that the elder statesman is speaking nonsense under the influence of old age is disturbing, disrespectful, and arrogant.

What Christians and non-Muslims of the Middle Belt and southerners have not been able to comprehend is the open support of this criminality by the leadership of the government of Nigeria and northern Nigerian political leaders, especially those of Fulani heritage. The governor of Kaduna State, in a show of such support, claimed to have paid the Fulani herdsmen money so that they would stop the killings in Kaduna State.[106] The killings have not stopped. The Federal Government of Nigeria has been accused of meeting with the *Miyetti* Allah leaders and paying them billions of Naira to stop the killings,[107] yet the situation is getting worse. In addition to this support, the federal government is pushing for the creation of grazing fields, specifically targeting the lands of the Christians in the Middle Belt and the southern part of Nigeria. This move has been resisted by locals in the targeted areas.[108]

---

104. Faroye, "Old Age," para. 4. Yakubu Gowon, who is now in his eighties, ruled Nigeria from 1966 to 1975 as military head of state. He fought the Nigerian civil war of 1967–70 for the unity of Nigeria. He is one of the most respected elder statesmen in Nigeria.

105. Faroye, "Old Age," para. 6.

106. "We've Paid Some Fulani to Stop Killings in Southern Kaduna—El-Rufai," *Vanguard*, Dec. 3, 2016 (https://www.Vanguardngr.com/2016/weve-paid-fulani-stop-killings-southern-kaduna-el-rufai/).

107. Sesan, "Miyetti Allah Admits," para. 1, 6.

108. Laah, "Call for Christian Communities," 28.

The fact that the perpetrators of these attacks have not been arrested and prosecuted is more worrisome. In my opinion, the attacks of the Fulani herdsmen are a jihad waged on the Christians and non-Muslims of the Middle Belt of Nigeria, while aiming at the southern part of Nigeria. This is part of the jihadist manifesto of their great-grandfather Uthman Dan Fodio and the vision of Ahmadu Bello, who promised to "dip the Qur'an in the Atlantic Ocean."[109] Bello was targeting the Islamization of Nigeria from the north to the coastal areas in the south. Christians suspect that the Fulani herdsmen attacks are a step towards fulfilling the visions of both Dan Fodio and Bello. This is evident by the fact that the Fulani herdsmen attacks are selective of Christian villages. Where they have completely taken over villages, they quickly repopulate with Fulani.[110] The Christians who have been displaced must search for places in other villages to resettle. Now refugees, some victims are in internally displaced persons camps. The terrorist activities of the Fulani herdsmen are a major source of conflict in northern Nigeria.

The Desire for an Islamic State

The main ideology of Islamic fundamentalists is to have an Islamic state or a state where the ruler is a Muslim and governs according to the dictates of Shari'a. This ideology underlies radicalized Islam, not only in Nigeria but in many parts of the world where Islamic groups are actively involved in terrorism. Examples include Syria, Iraq, and Pakistan. Jihad is a means of actualizing the Islamic state, whether in the form of armed struggle, personal struggle to live a good life as a Muslim, or stealth jihad—the use of political power available to Muslims for the advantage of Islam. The following section describes the interrelationship among the Islamic state, Shari'a and jihad, the core ideologies that inspire radical groups such as Boko Haram, Fulani herdsmen, and other radical Islamic groups operating in other parts of the world.

Shari'a

Shari'a is the Islamic legal code practiced in Islamic states. Among the core ideologies of fundamentalist Muslims, it is important to recognize that Shari'a is a combination of both divine law and politics. There can be no true Shari'a without an Islamic state, and jihad in all its ramifications

---

109. Boer, *Why This Muslim Violence*, 41. Dipping the Koran in the Atlantic Ocean means Bello had a goal of converting the entire country to Islam from the semidesert of northern Nigeria to the coast of the Atlantic Ocean in southern Nigeria.

110. Ishaku, "Herdsmen's Violence," 34.

is an instrument used to actualize an Islamic state.[111] Doi quotes Sayyed Hossein Nasr on the importance of Shari'a to Muslims: "To a Muslim [it] is essentially the divine law which includes not only universal moral principles but details of how man should conduct his life and deal with his neighbours and with God; it includes all aspects of human life and contains in it tenets and guide for a Muslim to conduct his life in harmony with the divine will."[112] Nasr's claim above underscores the importance of Shari'a to a Muslim. The Shari'a functions as a guide to a Muslim as to what is religiously lawful, unlawful, and desirable.[113]

The advocation for Shari'a has been a source of conflict in northern Nigeria because Christians are resisting it. They do so for the following reasons: Shari'a is religiously biased in favor of Muslims, it is oppressive to non-Muslims (Christians inclusive), and it is incompatible with democracy, under which Christians have enjoyed freedom, rights, and privileges.

The politics of Shari'a in Nigeria is traceable from its full implementation in the Uthmanic caliphate of the early nineteenth century to its mixture in the politics of northern Nigeria by Bello in the 1960s. It took a new shape when northern Nigerian Muslims began to agitate for its inclusion in the Nigerian constitution during the Shari'a debate of 1977 and 1989.[114] Shari'a advocation accelerated with the introduction of Shari'a law in twelve of the nineteen states of northern Nigeria in 1999–2000. The president of Nigeria at the time, Olusegun Obasanjo, argued that it was a political Shari'a and would eventually die naturally. However, Shari'a is not dead in Nigeria. It is a strong political ideology that defines Islamic politics in the country.

The National Christian Elders Forum (NCEF) expressed concerns of Shari'a as a major source of conflict in Nigeria:

> The above facts notwithstanding, the National Christian Elders Forum has come to the conclusion that Nigeria's major problem is the conflict of ideologies of Democracy and Shari'a, two incompatible ideologies one visible (democracy) and the other (Sharia) by a few militant Islamic Jihadists based on the teaching of the Muslim Brotherhood of Egypt founded in 1928 and exported by Saudi Arabia throughout the world to counter secularism.[115]

The first noticeable conflict is that, according to Islam, Shari'a is a divine law from Allah and by implication cannot be amended. Conversely,

111. Nwedo, *Church, Colonialism and Islam*, 10.
112. Doi, *Islam in Nigeria*, 204.
113. Doi, *Islam in Nigeria*, 207.
114. Gwamna, *Religion and Politics*, 102–3.
115. Asemota, "Testimony of Hope," para. 5.

democracy operates based on a constitution, which can be amended to conform to changing values that may occur in society.[116] The second is that the practice of Shari'a assumes an Islamic state, and Nigeria is a not an Islamic state. The Constitution of the Federal Republic of Nigeria clearly states that the nation shall not adopt a particular religion as a state religion given the religious plurality of Nigeria.[117] The third conflict is the second-class (*dhimmi*) status given to non-Muslims in an Islamic state, which Nigerian non-Muslims have been fighting.[118] Non-Muslims cannot become second-class citizens in their ancestral land without being conquered by war, which was the context of such subjugation in Islamic empires. The fourth conflict is that Islamic state laws mandate the payment of *jizya*, a tax paid by non-Muslims for being protected. These heavy taxes were used by Islamic empires to convert to Islam those who could not afford to pay the tax.[119]

Several have conveyed the connection between Shari'a and the creation of an Islamic state. Dogara Gwamna emphasizes Shari'a and its importance to the politics of northern Nigerian Muslims: "Shariah provided the legal framework upon which feudal political hegemony of the North was based."[120] This concern is further echoed by Yusufu Turaki and quoted by Gwamna, "Shariah, by its nature, creates an Islamic state, which denies Christians and non-Muslims the right of state because the state is religiously Islamic and therefore theocratic."[121] This is the concern of Christians in northern Nigeria that led them to sternly resist the implementation of Shari'a law in Kaduna State, which led to a blood bath in the year 2000.

Shari'a is an Islamic political structure that reinforces and justifies the domination and persecution of non-Muslims, especially Christians. Christianity is targeted because it is the world religion that is missionary in nature and poses threats to the existence and expansion of Islam. Islamic law, as stated above, recognizes non-Muslims as second-class citizens, especially in an Islamic state. The colonial government in its ladder of priorities recognized the emirs first, then the Muslim communities, and the bottom of the

---

116. Asemota, "Testimony of Hope," para. 60 (under "Experimenting with Democracy and Sharia").

117. See http://www.nigeria-law.org/ConstitutionOfTheFederalRepublicOfNigeria.htm, ch. 1, pt. 2, §10.

118. The *dhimmi* status in Islam is the status accorded Christians, Jews, and Sabians who are followers of religions that were given Holy Books before Islam was founded. These religions are to be tolerated. They have to pay heavy taxes for the privilege of living in and being protected by an Islamic state.

119. Levy-Rubin, *Non-Muslims*, 42–43.

120. Gwamna, *Religion and Politics*, 127.

121. Gwamna, *Religion and Politics*, 114.

ladder was occupied by non-Muslims.¹²² This classification proves the claim that Muslims were favored by the British colonialists. I wish to disagree with John Paden who claims, "During the colonial and post-colonial eras non-Muslim populations were not subject to Muslim law."¹²³ Contrary to that claim, non-Muslims in northern Nigeria in both colonial and postcolonial periods have been oppressed under Islamic laws. They are rated as second-class citizens, persecuted, discriminated against when attempting admission and employment in public institutions, denied social amenities, and more because they are not Muslims. In matters of justice, the court of law has favored Muslims. An example is the case of a church that we planted in *Tsoro* village, Kano State. Muslims fanatics destroyed the church building in 2004. The matter was taken to court, but the Muslim judge ruled the case in favor of the fanatics who destroyed the church building. Cases that demonstrate such injustices to Christians in northern Nigeria are excessively numerous.

Jihad

Of the three ideologies, the second to be discussed is jihad. Jihad is defined as a "struggle in the path of God."¹²⁴ Jihad is so important to Islam to the extent that some scholars see it as the sixth pillar of Islam.¹²⁵ The struggle to meet this Islamic injunction of fighting a jihad is a source of conflict in northern Nigeria, which the reader of this work should be aware of. The leader of the *Tijaniyya* Sufi Order, an influential Islamic sect in northern Nigeria, categorizes jihad into two types. The leader, Ibrahim Niass, "emphasized the *jihad al-nafsi* (interior *jihad* or conquest of the personality)" and "*jihad al-kharij* (exterior *jihad* or conquest of the infidel or apostate)."¹²⁶ The Sufi are a more pacifist Islamic sect, and as such Niass prefers the first over the latter. Lamin Sanneh makes the following observation about jihad: "The idea of 'holy war' was not only alien to the gospel but profoundly damaging to the church and society. No such scruples attend the idea of jihad in Islam, whether of jihad as 'the greater jihad' of spiritual struggle or as 'the lesser jihad' of divinely sanctioned military combat. Islam is not a pacifist religion or a creed of the fainthearted."¹²⁷

---

122. Kukah and Falola, *Religious Militancy and Self-Assertion*, 103.

123. Paden, "Unity in Diversity," 33.

124. Hashmi, "Jihad," 1:377.

125. The pillars of Islam include prayer, fasting, almsgiving, and pilgrimage to Mecca and Shahada.

126. Laremont, *Islamic Law and Politics*, 164.

127. Sanneh, *Translating the Message*, 48.

The two kinds of jihad portray the inner struggles of the Muslim to live his/her life according to dictates of the Qur'an, Hadith, and the Shari'a as opposed to confrontational jihad, which may involve armed conflict to expand the frontiers of Islam. Sanneh concludes that Islam is not a pacifist religion, which contradicts the claim of pacifism by the *Tijjaniyya* Sufi. Norman Geisler and Abdul Saleeb argue that Muhammad, the prophet of Islam, believed in jihad and commanded his followers to fight wars.

> Muhammad, by divine revelation, commands his followers: "fight in the cause Of God" (2:244). He adds, "Fight and slay The Pagans wherever you find them" (9:5). And "when ye meet The Unbelievers (in fight) Smite at their necks" (47:4). In general, they were to "Fight those who believe not In God nor the Last Day" (9:29). Indeed, Paradise is promised for those who fight for God: "Those who have left their homes . . . Or fought or been slain,—Verily, I will blot out From them their iniquities, and Admit them into Gardens With rivers flowing beneath;—A reward from the Presence Of God, and from His Presence Is the best of rewards" (3:195; cf. 2:244; 4:95).[128]

Passages like the ones quoted above often drive conflict, depending on how they are interpreted. A committed Muslim wants to do what will earn him/her eternal reward, so these kinds of verses are often used to mobilize Muslims to violence. It may be argued that Muslims are commanded to fight only the nonreligious, but Qur'an 9:29 includes the People of the Book, that is Christians, Jews, and Sabians, among those to be smitten if they do not believe what Islam believes. Jihad has been practiced by Muslims since the inception of Islam as a means of the expansion of the vast Islamic empire from Muhammad's time to the end of the Ottoman Empire in 1922. Modern jihad is fought through migration, terrorism, and acquisition of land and property in their target nations. The West is a target of jihad, and there has been significant spread of Islam in the West.[129]

A powerful tool used in the fight of modern jihad is *taqiyya*, which has to do with deception. The doctrine of *taqiyya* originates with the Shi'a sect because of persecution from the Sunni sect of Islam. "Interspersed among the much numerous Sunnis, who currently make up approximately 90 percent of the Islamic world, the Shi'a often performed *taqiyya* by pretending to be Sunnis externally, while maintaining Shi'a beliefs internally,

---

128. Geisler and Saleeb, *Answering Islam*, 174. The reader is encouraged to read the texts provided by Geisler and Saleeb in Yusuf Ali's English translation of the Holy Qur'an.

129. Fregosi, *Jihad in the West*, 25–26.

as permitted by Quranic verse 16:106."[130] Shi'a are often persecuted by the Sunni as heretics.

On *taqiyya*, the NCEF claims that the doctrine of *taqiyya* is not limited to Shi'a but widely practiced by Muslims: "*Taqiyya* [deception] is of fundamental importance in Islam. Practically every Islamic sect practices it."[131] *Al-Tabari's Tafsir* (Quranic exegesis) has the following comments on 3:28, which is a major text on *taqiyya*: "If you [Muslims] are under their [infidel] authority, fearing for yourselves, behave loyally to them, with your tongue, while harboring inner animosity for them . . . Allah has forbidden believers from being friendly or on intimate terms with the infidels in place of believers—except when infidels are above them [in authority]. In such a scenario, let them act friendly."[132] Muslims have used this doctrine when they are in the minority but change their behavior when they have significant strength or are in the majority. In northern Nigeria, experience with *taqiyya* is evidenced by politicians and top government officials, who swear to uphold the Constitution of the Federal Republic of Nigeria, just to betray it later in favor of an Islamic agenda. For example, in 2000, although they swore to uphold a democratic constitution 1999, the governors of twelve northern states declared that they are Shari'a states (states that operate on the Shari'a law).[133]

Christians in northern Nigeria have identified two types of jihads, conventional and stealth, that are waged against Christians in Nigeria. Christian elders articulated this in a statement to the United Kingdom Parliament: "It is clear that it is stealth jihad to have a Constitution that prohibits State Police even as money in billions of dollars is voted for vigilantes and religious police, thus rendering the Police weakened by stealth jihad while Boko Haram and Fulani herdsmen execute the conventional jihad."[134] Conventional jihad is waged by groups such as Boko Haram, Fulani herdsmen, and other Islamic mercenaries who kill, unleash terror, and destroy the lives and property of Christians. Those in power and top government officials fighting by stealth jihad use government means at their disposal to provide cover for those groups fighting for Islam. This frustrates Christians by denying their rights and promoting all forms of injustices against them.

---

130. Ibrahim, "Islam's Doctrines of Deception," para. 5. Al-Tabari (838–923) is one of the most respected Quranic exegetes throughout the Islamic world.

131. Asemota, "Project Nigeria 2018," para. 10.

132. Ibrahim, "Islam's Doctrines of Deception," para. 11.

133. Christian Elders Forum, "Fulani Herdsmen Are Foot-Soldiers."

134. Ndujihe and Eyoboka, "Insecurity," para. 20 (under "Evidence of Collusion").

Christians in Nigeria view the attacks on Christians and Christianity in Nigeria as a declaration of jihad on them. This complaint was evidenced in a communique released by Islam in Africa after their Abuja Declarations 1989 conference and quoted by Solomon Asemota in the article "Jihad in Nigeria: Burying the Head in Sand," affirming that the purpose of the organization was to "eradicate in all its forms and ramifications all non-Muslim religions in member nations. Such religions shall include Christianity, Ahmadiyya and other tribal religions."[135] It is further observed that the word "Christianity" in the original document was underlined, which makes Christianity a priority target for the jihad.

The question that needs an urgent answer about jihad is whether the attacks on Christians in northern Nigeria are an effort to actualize the mandate of the 1989 declaration cited above by waging a jihad against Christians. To buttress this point, Asemota quotes a research report conducted by Arne Mulder in 2015 that affirmed "over 13,000 Christian places of worship (churches) have been destroyed in northern Nigeria as of December 2014."[136] The question that must be asked is: "Under what condition do Muslim insurgents destroy Churches if not jihad?"[137] Jihad is a major tool for Christian persecution, and it is used effectively in all its ramifications to persecute Christians in northern Nigeria.

The quest for an Islamic state has been the dream of every Muslim, whether fanatic or moderate. In northern Nigeria, members of Boko Haram have clearly told Nigerians that they are fighting for an Islamic state.[138] They demonstrated that when they captured some areas in the northeast of Nigeria and hoisted their flag of an Islamic state. Shari'a, jihad, and an Islamic state are three elements that are interrelated in Islam. Interpretations and how to go about them may differ, but the three are the dream of many practicing Muslims.[139]

Results

Conflicts in northern Nigeria are often complex. There is not one way of interpreting them. Most of the time, they are a multilayered mix of several deep-rooted issues that may not be easily discernible by outsiders. Other than religion, politics, and colonial legacies, factors that cause conflicts in northern Nigeria include the poor economy owing to the corruption

135. Asemota, "Jihad in Nigeria," §8.2.
136. Asemota, "Jihad in Nigeria," §8.3.
137. Asemota, "Jihad in Nigeria," §8.3.
138. Asemota, "Jihad in Nigeria," §8.1.
139. Turaki, *Historical Roots*, 30–31.

of government officials, corporate organizations and businesses, population explosion, Islamic education popularly known as *almajiri* schools, unemployment, illiteracy, ethnicity, migration, contest for space, poverty, and many others.[140] Although there are contributing factors for potential conflicts, many view their origin as religious. Nigeria has the largest populations of Christians and Muslims living side by side, so it is inevitable for conflicts to take on religious tones.[141]

The nation of Nigeria has gone through over thirty years of military rule, a system which has injected corruption into the nation and now pervades every aspect of public life. The church is not spared as it, too, struggles with the issue of corruption. Nigerians blame this corruption for the unemployment, hunger, and backwardness they experience. They also blame it for the substandard power supply, closing of industries, poor education in public institutions, inadequate or lack of health facilities, bad roads, and unproductive workforce.[142] In summary, corruption has affected almost every system to the extent that Nigeria operates as a failed state. Many conflicts arise because the needs and aspirations of the citizens are not met. It is not news that Nigerian workers go on strike because of unpaid salaries or allowances due them for several months. Sometimes because of the rage and anger from unmet needs, government buildings and facilities are set ablaze. In the core north, Islamic fundamentalists use such occasion to burn down churches and kill Christians.

Nigeria has one of the fastest growing populations in the world. It is estimated that Nigeria will be the third most populous country in the world by the year 2050.[143] Northern Nigeria, dominated by Muslims who are allowed to marry up to four wives, is where the population is growing fastest. There are men who boast of having thirty, forty, or fifty biological children, but unfortunately, most of the men who mass-produce these children do not have the resources to properly feed, clothe, and educate them.

An example of how population explosion contributes to the problem of violence in Nigeria could be seen in my discussion with a taxi driver and a Muslim. As we were driving to a particular destination in the city of Kaduna, I began discussing sources of conflict in northern Nigeria with him. The driver was angry with Muslims who give birth to so many children and are not able to take care of them. He commented, "These people do not even know where some of these children eat or sleep. Why wouldn't

140. Adamu et al., "Nigeria," 18.
141. Akinade, "Sacred Rumblings."
142. Mbachirin, "Responses of the Church," 237–38.
143. Provost, "Nigeria Expected."

we have problems in northern Nigeria?"[144] Many of these children in their early childhood are left to struggle and find food for themselves. These vulnerable children are destitute of food, clothes, and shelter, so when paid a little amount of money, they are often used as tools for violence. Most young people are either not employed or not employable. It is said that an idle mind is the devil's workshop.

The Islamic system of education in northern Nigeria, popularly known as *almajiri* school, though religious, is a social problem and a major source of conflict. At the early age of five or six, boys are denied parental care and taken far away from their parents and entrusted into the hands of a Qur'anic teacher. The parents may occasionally visit. These children live by begging for alms—food, clothes, money. They also work for their teacher as a form of compensation for the training they are being given. Because of the destitution, these children are easily mobilized for political, religious, or ethnic violence. John Yahaya confirms this manipulation of *almajiri* and the poor in his work "Ethnic and Religious Conflicts in Kaduna and Plateau States: Implications for Development in Nigeria." He notes that in most of the ethno-religious or political violence, the *almajiri* (students) are always victims because the elite mobilize them for violence.[145]

The vulnerability of youths in northern Nigeria toward violence can also be connected to illiteracy. "More than 50 percent of Nigerians are illiterate, one of the highest rates in Africa."[146] The lowest level of literacy in Nigeria is in the north. Northern Muslims openly show preference for their Qur'anic schools over Western education. The former president of Nigeria, Dr. Goodluck Jonathan, attempted to address this imbalance in the north by establishing *almajiri* schools where Muslim children have the Qur'anic education alongside Western education in a suitable environment funded by the government, but this effort did not yield fruit. The buildings were left to rot while the Qur'anic education continued in the traditional way.[147]

Ethnicity and contesting public space are also issues that cause conflict in northern Nigeria. Yusufu Turaki writes, "The ethnic factor, its history and identity are major factors in ethno-religious crises and conflicts in northern Nigeria."[148] The current Fulani herdsmen invasion of the Christian Middle Belt of Nigeria provides a useful example of ethnicity and contest for space, mixed with religion. The continuous desertification

---

144. Informal discussion with a taxi driver, Kaduna, Nov. 5, 2018.
145. Yahaya, "Ethnic and Religious Conflicts," 99.
146. Mbachirin, "Responses of the Church," 247–48.
147. Adeyemi, "Left to Ruin."
148. Turaki, *Historical Roots*, 10.

of northern Nigeria and countries bordering that region is causing mass migration, especially of nomads in search of fertile grasslands for grazing.[149] The Fulani intentionally want to displace some of the minority tribes of the Middle Belt who are Christians, and these people groups are not ready to let go of their historical, ancestral lands. Many lives and properties have been lost on account of the conflicts between Fulani herdsmen and indigenous Christian communities.

CONCLUSION

Uthman Dan Fodio, the key figure in the Islamic reformation in northern Nigeria, remains a model to many fundamentalists. The first problem Dan Fodio's jihadist ideology presents is conflict within Islam. Since Dan Fodio did not accept Hausa Muslims as proper Muslims, reformist groups who follow his ideology have conflicts with other sects within Islam. The Boko Haram attacks on fellow Muslims can also be seen in this context, as they refer to all Muslims who do not accept their view of Islam as "unbelievers." There was no Christian influence yet in northern Nigeria at the time of Dan Fodio's jihad. Non-Muslims were pagans he fought to Islamize. Today in Nigeria, although the Qur'an makes a distinction between pagans and Christians and the way they should be treated, this distinction and priority treatment given to Christians over pagans exists only in theory. Practically, many fundamentalists of northern Nigeria see every non-Muslim as a pagan and object of attack.

Politically, the ideological blueprint for many northern Nigerian Muslim leaders can be traced back to Dan Fodio. Dan Fodio waged jihad against the Hausa states, formed a caliphate, and became the caliph. His lineage through the sultanate of Sokoto continues to exert significant political influence in northern Nigeria. His grandson, Ahmadu Bello, who became the first premier of the northern region of Nigeria, remains the political mentor of Muslim politicians in northern Nigeria who seek to fulfill his Islamic ideology. With the help of the colonial masters, Bello tried to suppress Middle Belt tribes his grandfather was unable to conquer. With education and Western influence, it has not been easy for the Muslim oligarchy to suppress the Middle Belt tribes. This has been a major source of conflict between the mostly Christian minority tribes and the Muslim Hausa-Fulani in northern Nigeria.

The impetus for introduction and/or full implementation of the Shari'a in a multireligious and secular nation like Nigeria by fundamentalists has been a source of concern. The non-Muslims in northern Nigeria,

149. Adamu et al., "Nigeria," 18.

who are mostly Christian, do not want to be governed by the laws of another religion. It is for that reason the NCEF insists that the major source of conflict in northern Nigeria is the incompatibility of democracy and Shari'a. The Christians prefer democracy with its freedoms and rights over Islamic laws, which will reduce every non-Muslim to the status of a *dhimmi*, or second-class citizen.[150]

The recent conflicts in Nigeria have a complex and multifaceted background. The indirect rule of the British, politicization of religion, the rise of fundamentalism, and the desire for an Islamic state have all contributed to the persecution that Christians in northern Nigeria currently endure. The next chapter explores the persecution of Christians and their responses to this persecution.

---

150. Asemota, "Testimony of Hope," para. 1 (under "Sharia Revival").

3

Responses to Persecution

Northern Nigerian Experience

INTRODUCTION

THE PERSECUTION OF CHRISTIANS in modern times is a reality in many communities of the world. Northern Nigeria has had many horrific conflicts that have left thousands of people dead, and property worth billions of dollars destroyed. The conflicts have also destroyed precious interethnic, interreligious, and social relationships that have been formed in the past three decades. There are several questions that have been raised by this violence. For instance, with the political, economic, ethnic, and religious dimensions of violence in northern Nigeria, can the suffering experienced by the Christians be described as Christian persecution? If so, how should Christians respond and what is the effect of their responses on discipleship and evangelism?

To answer these questions, I have discussed how Christians in northern Nigeria are being persecuted, arguing for acknowledgement that the persecution is because of their faith. The types of persecution experienced by Christians in the region are also considered, as they were shared with me during the field research. It is important in this discussion that the reader understand the plight of Christians in the affected region, and the importance of proper responses to persecution. Proper response to persecution will aid Christian witness and discipleship in Nigeria. This chapter also features the impact of the responses to the persecution of Christians in northern Nigeria on community relationships, evangelism, and discipleship as further evidence of the need for proper response to persecution by Christians in northern Nigeria and around the world. The reader should note that the first names and initials of the subjects interviewed, and those who responded to the questionnaires, were changed to guarantee the security of their identities. Therefore, the names used in this research are not their real names.

THE REALITY OF RELIGIOUS PERSECUTION IN NORTHERN NIGERIA

The discussion on Christian persecution in northern Nigeria attempts to answer one of the major questions asked in this chapter introduction, that is, whether the treatment that Christians are experiencing in northern Nigeria can be labeled Christian persecution. Further, are Christians in northern Nigeria being persecuted by Muslims for being Christians? What about the Muslims who are also suffering alongside the Christians in northern Nigeria because of the activities of terrorists? Before any discussion on responses can be meaningful, answering these questions is important for the reader to have facts that prove Christians are experiencing persecution because of their faith.

In relation to the questions above, Christians in Nigeria, particularly in the north, feel strongly that they are being persecuted. This opinion is evident in the actions of some eminent Nigerian Christian leaders under the aegis of NCEF, who took the case of Christian persecution in Nigeria to the United Kingdom Parliament. They reported that "President Muhammadu Buhari the Nigerian President was pursuing a jihad or Islamization agenda and he is not serious about tackling insecurity arising from Boko Haram insurgency and herdsmen-farmers crises in the country."[1] However, while responding to this case of persecution in an article titled "Don't Politicise Religion in Nigeria," the president of Nigeria claims that the causes of the conflict with Fulani herdsmen are not religious or theological but caused by climate change and population growth.[2] To buttress this point, there was a paper written by the Nigerian government and signed by the Nigeria High Commissioner to the United Kingdom to counter the claim that Nigerian Christians are being persecuted for their religion. The paper stressed that the country's challenges had no ethnic and religious coloration.[3] David R., a local chief, in an interview also concluded that the attacks on some villages in his chiefdom by Fulani herdsmen were herder-farmer conflicts. However, he quickly observed that the attacks were only

1. Ndujihe and Eyaboka, "Insecurity," para. 1.
2. Buhari, "Don't Politicise Religion," para. 16.
3. "Aftermath of Danjuma's Petition on Persecution of Christians," *Africa News Circle*, June 28, 2019 (https://www.africanewscircle.com/?p=34961).

on Christian villages. The Muslim villages in the chiefdom remain intact, which gives the attack a religious coloration.

Having listened to the view that denies the existence of the persecution of Christians in northern Nigeria, the following arguments will help the reader understand that Christians in northern Nigeria definitely are being persecuted for being Christians: First, the definition of Christian persecution by Tieszen as "any unjust action of varying levels of hostility perpetrated primarily on the basis of religion and directed at Christians, resulting in varying levels of harm as it is considered from the victim's perspective"[4] is in agreement with the thinking and perspective of Christians in northern Nigeria who are the victims studied in this research.

In the research questionnaire that was administered, the victims were asked whether Christians in northern Nigeria are being persecuted for their faith. Appendix D, table 1, shows results for Kaduna State. Out of eighty-five respondents to this question, sixty-nine *strongly agree* that Christians are suffering persecution in northern Nigeria for their faith in Christ, representing 80 percent of the total responses. Sixteen *agree*, representing 20 percent. There was no disagreement with this question. Appendix E, table 1, presents the results for Borno State for these questions. It shows that out of seventy-eight respondents, sixty-three *strongly agree* that Christians are being persecuted for their faith, representing 80.2 percent. Fourteen *agree*, representing 17.4 percent. There was only one response each for *disagree* and *strongly disagree* and none for neutral. This shows that the victims in northern Nigeria perceive the attacks they are suffering as persecution for their faith.

Sometimes when discussing persecution, many assume that the violent attacks by Boko Haram, the Fulani herdsmen, and other bloodletting violence are the only forms of persecution being experienced without consideration of other forms of injustice suffered by Christians in northern Nigeria. This research suggests that persecution in northern Nigeria is not only violent persecution, but it ranges from mild to extreme. In the questionnaire, Christians in northern Nigeria were asked to respond as to what degree they are persecuted, and these were the responses. As shown in appendix D, table 2, two responded in Kaduna State that the persecution is mild, representing 2.4 percent; thirty-three said extreme persecution, representing 39.8 percent; and forty-eight respondents stated both mild and extreme, representing 57.8 percent. There was no response for no persecution, which indicates that respondents from Kaduna State agree that

---

4. Tieszen, *Re-Examining Religious Persecution*, 41.

Christians in northern Nigeria suffer persecution to varying degrees from mild to extreme.

Responses to the same question above by Christian leaders in Borno State were similar, found in appendix E, table 2. Only four out of seventy-six respondents said that the persecution is mild, representing 5.2 percent; thirty-two responded that the persecution is extreme persecution, representing 42.1 percent. Thirty-nine respondents said both mild and extreme persecution, representing 51.3 percent; one respondent replied no persecution, which represents 1.3 percent of the respondents. Both the results of Kaduna and Borno States agree that Christians in northern Nigeria are and have been suffering persecution to varying degrees. Persecution of Christians in northern Nigeria should not be limited only to attacks of Boko Haram and Fulani herdsmen but include other forms as well. The results above clearly show that from the victim perspective, Christians in northern Nigeria are suffering persecution to varying degrees.

Second, some Nigerians argue that the conflict in northern Nigeria is merely economic, political, and ethnic violence just as the president of Nigeria, Muhammadu Buhari, claimed that the conflicts in Nigeria are not religious or theological but arose from climate change and population growth.[5] There is no denying the role these factors play in exacerbating the violence in the region. However, Islam is "a total way of life,"[6] which means that Islam links religion, economy, culture, and politics. Islam does not practice the separation of church and state, so therefore, even though all forms of attacks from Muslims against non-Muslims are primarily religious, they may take the dimension of politics, the economy, or ethnicity. To buttress this point, Muhammadu Buhari, a Muslim, lost the presidential elections in 2011 to Jonathan Goodluck, a Christian, and the political violence that ensued quickly turned religious with several churches burned, Christians killed, and Christian houses and businesses destroyed.[7] Why? Because the political battle was seen by Muslims as primarily religious.

Third, the question as to why Muslims also suffer attacks by the terrorists raises questions to the claim that Christians are suffering persecution in northern Nigeria because of their faith. The theory of Islam versus Islamism may be helpful in explaining this phenomenon. Solomon Asemota states in his executive summary of the "Christian Elders Project Nigeria 2018: Message for All Nigerians": "While Islam is a religion, Islamism otherwise called 'political Islam' is not a religion but a political ideology that holds

5. Buhari, "Don't Politicise Religion," para. 16.
6. Stefanos Foundation, *Religious Intolerance*, 44.
7. Adamu et al., "Nigeria," 30.

that Islam must dominate the society."[8] The paper further states that the activity of the Islamists, which they called jihad, "affects not only Christians and traditionalists, but also moderate Muslims who are not Islamists."[9] The Muslims who do not adhere to their ideology are labeled "unbelievers," and as such, they become subjects of attack. This is evidenced by the video message Abubakar Shekau, the leader of Boko Haram, posted in 2012 and is quoted by Asemota as saying, "I warn all Muslims at this juncture that any Muslim who assists an unbeliever in this war should consider himself an unbeliever and should consider himself dead."[10]

Unfortunately, rural Muslims who are ignorant of this have become victims of raids for food and women by the Islamist fighters such as Boko Haram. I wish to propose primary and secondary targets of persecution to further explain why some Muslims also suffer attacks from radical Islamists. The primary target is the actual person(s) targeted while the secondary target is those who suffer along with the primary target, whether directly or indirectly. In the case of northern Nigeria, Christians and Christianity are the primary target because it is the major threat to Islam and a major barrier to achieving the Muslim ideological goal of establishing an Islamic state ruled by the Shari'a in Nigeria, while Muslims who also suffer in the hands of the terrorists are the secondary target.

TYPES OF PERSECUTION EXPERIENCED BY CHRISTIANS IN NORTHERN NIGERIA

From the data, this section discusses different types of persecution experienced by Christians in northern Nigeria. The experiences range from mild to extreme. The first category is *mild* persecution, which has to do with all forms of discrimination, denial of rights, and oppression. There are non-Muslim minorities who later embraced Christianity in northern Nigeria who have been suffering since the time of Islamic colonization and slavery, which predates British and post-British colonialism. The second category is *extreme* persecution, with mass destruction of lives and property resulting from mob violence to terrorism.

Mild Persecution

Christians in postcolonial northern Nigeria have suffered *mild* persecution to varying degrees from the Muslims who predominate the region. Reading

8. Asemota, "Project Nigeria 2018," Executive Summary, para. 5.
9. Asemota, "Project Nigeria 2018," Executive Summary, para. 6.
10. Asemota, "Jihad in Nigeria," §8.10.

about the experiences of Christians in northern Nigeria in relation to persecution is important in understanding the ongoing discussion of Christian responses to persecution. The connection between the experiences and the responses is very important. To authenticate and establish the reality of the experiences of Christians in northern Nigeria, the Christian leaders were interviewed during field research and asked to share their experiences of Christian persecution as it affects them, their families, places of work, communities in which they live, interethnic and interreligious relationships, and economic activities. These experiences of Christian persecution across Kaduna and Borno States show that Christians in northern Nigeria suffer discrimination and other forms of injustice. It is a known fact that Christians and non-Muslim minorities of northern Nigeria are beneficiaries of mission education, which should have elevated their status in business and public service, but the Islamic forces have used discrimination to frustrate the region's highly trained work force based on religion and ethnicity.

Discrimination in Places of Work

To investigate cases of various forms of discrimination suffered by Christians in northern Nigeria, Christian leaders who suffer discrimination in their places of work were interviewed. Individuals interviewed included Kenneth C., the pioneer general secretary of CAN and a church elder of his denomination, who does not mind being identified and who was also a lecturer in an influential college in northern Nigeria. He was once due for promotion as a senior lecturer in the institution. The panel that was constituted to recommend those for promotion gathered for the meeting. When his documents were brought forward, he was commended as one who had done his work well. His students had performed well in both internal and external examinations, and he was recommended to be promoted. The director of the College of Engineering, who was his immediate boss and a Muslim, raised objection to his promotion on the grounds of his Christian activities. If not for the timely intervention of one of the members of the panel, who was a Christian, Kenneth would have been denied the promotion. Later Kenneth was again to be promoted to the rank of principal lecturer in the same college. He was interviewed, and the committee selected him for the promotion. However, because he is a Christian, his name was substituted overnight with the name of a Muslim who was less qualified than him. He further shared how his wife was fired from her job because of her faith from the same college, and his son was denied a scholarship to study abroad because he is a Christian.

Kenneth is not alone in this kind of experience of discrimination. Another person interviewed with the experience of discrimination in his workplace is Caleb K., who is an ordained pastor and a professor in one of the foremost public universities in northern Nigeria. Because he is a Christian and from an ethnic minority of the southern part of Kaduna State, he was not given cooperation by his colleagues. Even the vice chancellor did not cooperate. He was told by his Muslim colleagues that if he only had a Muslim name, he would have received cooperation. Because of his religion and ethnic background, he was unceremoniously removed as director of a center in the University.

Another case is Judith M., who was one of those interviewed from Borno State. She is a deaconess in the local church. Judith is a PhD holder who still teaches at a high school in Borno State. Borno is one of the educationally disadvantaged states in northern Nigeria and should have appreciated having Judith teach in the university, an indigenous woman with a PhD. But she was denied such a privilege because of her Christian faith. Presently she works under people she taught in high school. As her students graduated and went to university, some came back to be her colleagues. Some former students have been promoted to the rank of principal because they are Muslims, and she must work under them. Her crime is that she is a Christian.

Suleiman B., a leader of his denomination and pastor of a local church from Borno State who was interviewed, confirms the claims of Judith, saying, "I have witnessed where a Christian teacher will teach a student who will complete high school, go to the university and graduate and come back to be the principal of his teacher simply because the teacher is a Christian." Suleiman further reiterated that the persecution of Christians in northern Nigeria is in every sector of the government. "If your name is identified with Christianity, you are in for it. You may never be promoted; in some cases, you may never even be employed. My wife was denied promotion for ten years because of her Christian identity."

Larai U. had a similar experience of discrimination in the workplace. She suffered discrimination of unpaid retirement benefits after leaving the civil service and continues the struggle to receive her paid entitlements, while her Muslim colleagues who retired at the same time have long been paid. At the time of the interview, she had yet to be paid and did not know when that would take place.

Gregory J. from Mbalala in Chibok local government represents Christians from rural areas and was also interviewed. He is a parent of one of the abducted Christian girls from Chibok who lamented that "everywhere in Chibok local government in the field of employment, we find it very difficult, when there are positions from the state government, it is only Muslims that are employed. In terms of leadership, you will discover that Muslims with lower qualifications are employed to head Christians with higher qualifications."

Reinforcing the claim of discrimination against Christians in northern Nigeria, Jeremy W., the chairman of a chapter of CAN and a pastor, described all forms of discrimination as persecution. He said, "People are being persecuted because of their faith when it comes to employment, promotions, business even on their own properties. Kaduna State has experienced a lot of these because there is a high level of competition between Christians and Muslims."

Discrimination is suffered by both the young and old as evidenced in the interview with Mark J., who lamented that his children were denied the university courses they wanted to take and for which they are qualified. The reason? Courses that are marketable are not given to Christians. Many young men and women in the north who are Christians are "reading" courses they never wanted because they were not permitted to take the courses that would lead to their desired life career.

Oppression of Ethnic-Christian Minority

The foundation for oppression of non-Muslim minorities can be traced back to the precolonial, colonial, and postcolonial era in northern Nigeria. The Hausa-Fulani Muslim rulers plundered the minority tribes before the coming of Christianity, and such a relationship continues even as the northern minorities have embraced Christianity and Western education.

Charles W., a local church elder who was interviewed, lamented the inhuman treatment of non-Muslims in northern Nigeria who suffered under the Muslim emirate system. He claims that their parents and grandparents were forced to farm for the Muslim rulers and had their farmlands and harvest forcefully taken. Those who refused to be converted to Islam were made to pay heavy "taxes with their farm produce, animals and even sometimes with their young men and women who are forcefully taken by the Zaria or *Zazzau* emirate to work and farm in Zaria; some of those young people never came back to their families."

As an insider who comes from one of the Christian minority tribes in Kaduna State, I have heard such stories passed orally from parents and grandparents about the agonies and sufferings experienced under the emirate rule. Yusufu Turaki in his book *Tainted Legacy: Islam, Colonialism and Slavery in Northern Nigeria* reinforces Charles's claim of the oppression of the non-Muslim minority in the Middle Belt.

> For the non-Muslim of the Middle Belt, jihad and shari'a would always equate to brutal colonization, slave raids, slave trading and slavery. The theological justification for a 'holy war' against them and the imposition of Muslim shari'a on them can be evaluated only with reference to their experience of inhuman treatment and the dehumanizing effects of slavery upon them, as individuals and as a group.[11]

The claim of oppression of non-Muslim minorities by Muslim rulers from precolonial to postcolonial era form the bedrock of the continued oppression and persecution of the Christian minority in northern Nigeria. The Hausa-Fulani seek to continue this oppression while the Christian minorities are fighting for emancipation. The tension, in my opinion, is one of the major causes of violence in the region.

Denial of Government Services

Another dimension of mild persecution experienced by Christians in northern Nigeria is in the form of using political power at the disposal of Muslim leaders to deny Christians and Christian communities the government services due them. These kinds of actions show clearly that the denial of such services is because the individual or community belong to the Christian faith.

The trip to Chibok for field research exposed me to some of the worst treatment of Christians in that part of Nigeria. The road to Chibok revealed one of the most neglected local governments in Borno by the state government. For over forty years of the existence of Chibok local government, the roads have never been tarred. One of my informants, Gregory J., who is in his sixties, said he has been hearing rumors about the construction of Chibok Road since he was fifteen years old, and until now it has not been constructed. Some Muslim politicians have used the construction of the roads all these years as campaign promises to get votes from the people of Chibok but have never fulfilled those promises. In an informal discussion, a friend from Chibok said that the current president of the Federal Republic of Nigeria, Muhammadu Buhari, came to Chibok in 1983 when he was the military head of the state of Nigeria. He promised to construct the road, but it was never done.

The Christian leaders in Chibok feel that they are treated this way because Chibok local government in Borno State is predominantly Christian. Therefore, the Muslim leaders at the state level do not want to aid the progress of the Christians. When interviewed, Michael Y., a pastor and an indigene of

---

11. Turaki, *Tainted Legacy*, 73.

Chibok, said that he was aware of the rumor of the construction of Chibok Road at the time Ibrahim Babangida was the military head of state. He remarked: "The secretary to the government wrote that the road to Chibok has been constructed and completed, but that wasn't true."

In addition, a pastor of a Pentecostal church in Chibok, Balarabe T., was interviewed and lamented, "You can see the terrain where we are, you can see our roads, all these things are as a result of our faith. There are a lot of things that are supposed to come to us, because these people do not want those things to come to us so they divert them."

As an insider, to buttress the claim of Balarabe, I can testify of such marginalization and denial of rights. While I was serving as an evangelist in Kano State, the village of *Mairomo* in that state was denied electric services because they are Christians. When the services were to be provided for some rural communities, such as *Mairomo*, the electric poles were deliberately diverted, and this village was left out. Even today, the community has not enjoyed electric services because of their Christian faith.

Another case of denial of services was experienced by Adamu F., a pastor in Kaduna city, who shared that he is finding it difficult to get an indigene form (residency form) for his children in Kaduna North local government because of his religion and ethnicity. Added to the experience above, he also shared an experience of discrimination in a public hospital dominated by staff that are Muslims. Muslims who came behind him were attended to while he was left in the queue, because by his appearance he was identified as a Christian.

Another experience of denial of government services in some Christian communities is no schools. Christian children must walk several miles to attend school in Muslim communities. In addition, clinics and hospitals are rarely built in Christian communities, and such communities often have no roads, no water, and no electricity. During electioneering campaigns, these communities are wooed with promises, but the politicians forget about those communities once they win the election. The only hope of most of these communities has been the efforts of missionaries, churches, and Christian organizations who go to such rural communities to sink wells, build schools, provide teachers, train them in new techniques of farming, and build clinics, hospitals, or other health services. The good thing about the Christian community services is that they do not discriminate. The services are often provided for both Christians and Muslims.

Denial of Rights

Christians in northern Nigeria experience denial of rights as part of persecution. These denials of rights contravene the constitution of Nigeria, which in section 38, subsection 1, guarantees religious freedom to Nigerian citizens. The constitution says, "Every person shall be entitled to freedom of thought, conscience, and religion, including freedom to change his religion or belief, and freedom (either alone or in community with others, and in public or in private) to manifest and propagate his religion or belief in worship, teaching, practice, and observance."[12]

Contrary to the provision of the constitution, Christians in many states in northern Nigeria are often denied lands and places of worship. According to Mark J., it is considered a crime to sell lands to Christians for the purpose of building a church. In places where the converted indigenous person owns inherited lands, he or she is not allowed to sell or donate such land for the purpose of building a church.[13] Christians must buy houses and begin to worship in them amid hostility. Sometimes they are chased out, or beaten, and sometimes dragged to the authorities. After several repeated experiences, some of the churches survive but some do not. I also had these experiences in Kano State in my own church planting work in Hatsai and Banaka villages. Christian churches are destroyed, sometimes at will, by Muslim fundamentalists and sometimes with the help of government security agents.[14]

In 2003, related to the difficulty of building churches and the destruction of same, Ibrahim Shekarau won the governorship election in Kano State. One of the campaign promises to his immediate community of Giginyu was to remove an ECWA church, the only church surviving in the community, so that there would no longer be a church in the Giginyu community. The ECWA church in question was in a police barrack. First, the Muslim youth of the community were directed to attack, loot, and destroy the church. Some of the youths were found wearing choir robes on the streets of Giginyu, and no one arrested them. The next step was to propose relocating the police barrack in which the church was situated to another community within Kano city and to build a hospital on that property, which Shekarau did. No church is allowed in Kano State health institutions. That is how he got rid of that church.[15] Giginyu and Badawa

---

12. See http://www.nigeria-law.org/ConstitutionOfTheFederalRepublicOfNigeria.htm, §38.1.
13. Stefanos Foundation, *Religious Intolerance*, 65.
14. Stefanos Foundation, *Religious Intolerance*, 67.
15. Stefanos Foundation, *Religious Intolerance*, 68–69.

are neighboring communities, and I was pastor of Glory Land Baptist Church Badawa, the closest neighbor to the ECWA Giginyu where this incidence occurred. Such experiences of the demolition of churches are found in almost all the core northern states of Nigeria. The Muslims have some level of restraint in demolishing churches at will in the Middle Belt region because of its Christian population.

Another dimension to the persecution is in the denial of certificates of occupancy for church buildings, which is a right for all citizens, except if used for illegal activities. Christians are denied the certificate of occupancy even when they own the piece of land on which they want to build the church. In some cases, according to Mark J., the certificates of occupancy that were issued during the colonial period are revoked. Christian churches occupy lands without lawful government permission because they were denied legal documents. As such, the Muslims in authority feel free to attack and destroy them without any compensation. Some of those churches whose certificates are denied or revoked were, most of the time, the first to occupy those lands. This is because the Muslim authorities were in the habit of sending the Christians to build churches on the outskirts of the cities. Eventually, those places get developed and become the envy of the town or city—Sabon Gari in the city of Kano, for example.[16]

Another form of denial of rights is in the provision of religious education. The government of Nigeria permits primary and secondary institutions teaching Christian or Islamic religious knowledge to students who come from either background. In northern Nigeria, the authorities will normally employ teachers to teach Islamic religion and refuse to employ teachers to teach the Christian religious knowledge. In some cases, the Christian students are forced to attend Islamic religious knowledge classes, which is in violation of their constitutional rights.[17] In tertiary institutions, Christian students are denied land to build chapels for worship while there are gigantic mosques and smaller ones all over such campuses, for example, Bayero University, Kano. In some places where Christian chapels were built for worship, the students and Christian teachers and professors must fight both legal and physical battles to build and sustain those places of worship, such as the chapels in Ahmadu Bello University Zaria and Kaduna Polytechnic, Kaduna.

Nuhu Z., a Christian youth leader interviewed, shared his experience in the struggle to build the chapel at Ahmadu Bello University Kongo campus,

---

16. Crampton, *Christianity in Northern Nigeria*, 133.

17. Christian Association of Nigeria, Borno State Chapter, *Christianity in Crisis*, 38–39.

which needed both physical and legal battles to actualize. The Kaduna Polytechnic Chapel, where I was once a student and a member of the Christian community, was named Chapel of Victory because of the victory won in the physical fight between the Christians and Muslims over its construction.

Constitutional rights of Christians are also violated when it comes to religious conversion. The freedom to change one's religion is enshrined in the Constitution of the Federal Republic of Nigeria as a right for all Nigerians, but this is not applicable in northern Nigeria. There has been a lot of evangelistic effort by Christians targeting the Muslims, and there have been conversions, but when people become Christians, they do so at the risk of their lives. The Islamic law prescribes a death sentence for any apostate. Three days are given to anyone who leaves Islam to recant his/her new faith and return to Islam, after which if he/she does not, the person can be killed. Many former Muslim believers remain in hiding after several years of conversion. Those who are not killed are stripped of all they possess, including inheritance, wives, children, houses, businesses, and jobs. The difficulties these converts experience forces some of them to return to Islam. Missionaries working in northern Nigeria are considering several strategies that will help sustain those who come to Christ from the religion of Islam.

Extreme Persecution

Christians in northern Nigeria experience both mild and extreme persecution. Having discussed mild persecution in the form of marginalization, discrimination, and denial of constitutional rights, I will now discuss *extreme* persecution. This persecution should be understood as the type that results in the loss of many lives and a lot of property. Extreme persecution started on a large scale in the 1980s with mob violence that later transformed into terrorism in the 2000s, where the key players are Boko Haram and Fulani herdsmen.

Mob Violence

Violent religious and ethnic crises in postcolonial Nigeria began earnestly in the 1980s with mob violence. The first was the *Maitatsine* violence in 1980 in the city of Kano, Nigeria. The *Maitatsine* saga continued in some parts of the north like Bulunkutu, Jimeta Yola, Bauchi, and Kaduna. *Maitatsine* riots were more of intra-religious violence within Islam that involved security agents, although some Christians and churches also suffered.[18] The next large-scale violence between Christians and Muslims took place in 1987

18. Ukanah, *In God's Name*, 70–76.

at Kafanchan. Then in 1992, there was the Zangon Kataf violence, which was ethno-religious and involved the Hausa-Fulani who are Muslims and the Kataf people group in Southern Kaduna who are Christians. The violence spread to Kaduna city and Zaria, and many churches were destroyed, and many lives lost.[19] The resistance of the Muslims of Kano in 1991 to the planned Great Gospel Crusade of German evangelist Reinhard Bonnke also resulted in the loss of lives and property.[20] Ethno-religious crises continued to increase and spread to many other parts of northern Nigeria to the extent that it is difficult to chronicle all of them.

The introduction of Shari'a in the year 2000 opened a new chapter of religious violence. In 2000, Christians in Kaduna protested the introduction of Shari'a (the Islamic legal system), which was to be used in the state. They were attacked by violent Muslims, and this fiasco ended in some of the worst religious violence in the history of Nigeria as thousands of people—both Christians and Muslims—were massacred. It was during this violence that the Baptist Theological Seminary, Kaduna, where I am a faculty member, was completely burned down by the Muslims. Another terrible attack on the Christians that started as political violence and ended up religious was the postelection violence of 2011 when Jonathan Goodluck, who is a Christian, won the presidential election in Nigeria, and Patrick Yakowa, a Christian, won the governorship election in Kaduna State. Violence erupted, hundreds of lives perished, and several churches and businesses were looted and burned.[21]

Discussing the extreme persecution experiences of Christians in northern Nigeria from mob violence begins with Caleb K., who was interviewed by the author. Caleb was at the center of the 1987 religious violence that took place in Kafanchan when he was a lecturer and Christian chaplain of the College of Education Kafanchan. In the incident, part of his house was burned. He also escaped a staged accident and a hired assassin who was sent to kill him. The assassin later confessed that he was close to stabbing Caleb, but he saw fire around him, which showed God's power protecting him from being stabbed. During the same event, some Christian leaders were targeted to be killed by the Muslims. Caleb was one of those on the list, but God spared his life.

Sharing the experience of the 1987 Kafanchan violence, Mike C. told me that at that time he was a young pastor of an Assemblies of God church, leading a local congregation in a Muslim community of *Maraban* Jos. He

---

19. Adamu et al., "Nigeria," 22–24.
20. Ukanah, *In God's Name*, 140–44.
21. Adamu et al., "Nigeria," 29.

told of suffering from persecution due to the violent crisis that spread to different parts of Kaduna State. The owner of the property his congregation was renting was a Muslim. The landlady was forced by some fanatical Muslims to evict the church with a threat to burn down the house if she did not comply. A Baptist church graciously shared their property with the Assemblies of God church until Mike was transferred to Kafanchan in 1994. In Kafanchan, he aired a radio program that attracted persecution. Muslims with guns, daggers, sticks, and other dangerous weapons went to the church he was pastoring, looking to kill him. They did this three times, and three times they missed him. The denominational leadership had to quickly transfer him out of town for his safety.

Another interview was with Pastor Suleiman B., who shared his experience with mob violence as an instrument of persecution by Muslims in the northeast. His first direct encounter with violent persecution was in September 1994 at Potiskum, Yobe State. While in the pulpit as a leader of worship in a COCIN service, they were informed that violence had broken out in Potiskum. With Baptist and ECWA churches already in flames, some of the hoodlums moved to the Anglican church to burn it down, and the COCIN church was next. They had to quickly end the church service that day and ask members to go home. About fifteen of the members remained to put up some resistance, but they were overpowered by the mob. The Muslims came in and gathered all the pews and set them ablaze, but the fire from the pews could not reach the roof. So, they climbed up and poured gas, but the roof did not catch fire. They also tried pulling down the pillars of the building, but the building was still standing. After the crisis, the COCIN church in Potiskum was nicknamed *shegiyar* church, meaning "stupid church," because it refused to be burned. Eleven churches were burned in the rampage, two pastors were killed, and many Christians were wounded.

Jeremy W., a pastor and an ecumenical leader, shared his experience with mob violence during the Shari'a violent crisis in the city of Kaduna in the year 2000. At the time of the crisis, Jeremy was the pastor of a Baptist church. The church building was burgled and property destroyed. He was fortunate that the building was not burned, since it was situated amid houses belonging to Muslims and burning it would impact the adjoining houses. On February 20, 2000, when the violence started, Jeremy ran to his house and Muslim youths came and surrounded the house. It took the intervention of another Muslim who persuaded them with money to go away. That is how his life was spared. He and his family had to move to a military barrack for security. What is interesting in Jeremy's experience is what prevented the Muslims from burning the church building. This reflection was the challenge that led him into deeper Christian-Muslim dialogue with a desire of finding a lasting solution to religious violence in northern Nigeria.

The Shari'a 2000 crisis discussed above was the first encounter that Ezra M., a Christian youth leader interviewed, had with violent persecution. Three close relations were killed in that crisis. This was a bitter experience for him that has lingered for many years.

The experience of the Zangon Kataf crisis of 1992, which spilled over to Kaduna and Zaria and involved mob violence, was shared by Nuhu Z., a Christian youth leader who was interviewed. Zangon Kataf is a town in Zangon Kataf local government, Kaduna State. This ethno-religious violence took place between the Kataf people group, who are mainly Christians, and the Hausa-Fulani, who are mainly Muslims, as previously mentioned. In the crisis, Nuhu's family house in Anguwar Rimi, Kaduna, was attacked. There was loss of property but no loss of life in his family. However, some of his friends died, even Muslim friends. He also lamented the loss of his pastor, Rev. B. B. Bije. Nuhu still lives and works in Kaduna.

Mob violence against Christians also occurred when a man from Denmark by the name of Kurt Westergaard drew a cartoon of Muhammad, the prophet of Islam.[22] Most people from Borno State, both Christians and Muslims, did not know his name or whether he was a Christian or not. There were protests in the Muslim world about the cartoon, but it was a different thing for Christians in northern Nigeria. Informants in Borno State shared their experiences of what happened on February 18, 2006. I interviewed Mark J., a chairman of a CAN chapter, about the crisis, and he said that during the cartoon violence, fifty-six churches were burned within forty-five minutes and families were burned alive in their homes. This figure is confirmed by *Christianity in Crisis*, a report published on the Danish cartoon violence by CAN, Borno State Chapter. This report stated that fifty-six churches were burned, fifty-one Christians killed, and about N1.5 billion (one-and-a-half-billion Naira) worth of property destroyed.[23]

Another person interviewed who shared his experience of the Danish cartoon violence was Collins T. He said that in Maiduguri, some young Muslim men came to his house with a gun to shoot him. Fortunately for him, he was not at home. He had to relocate his residence from that area for security reasons and the safety of his family.

In the case of Desmond B., a young pastor who was interviewed, he was a young boy when the Danish cartoon crisis took place, and what he

---

22. Barron, "Artist Who Set Off," para. 2.

23. Christian Association of Nigeria, Borno State Chapter, *Christianity in Crisis*, 109–10.

saw was very traumatic. The fact that fifty-six churches were burned within the period of forty-five minutes suggested a planned, well-coordinated attack. Christians were being attacked and killed for what one may consider unreasonable and unthinkable excuses.

In the year 2011, a political crisis in Nigeria that became bloody religious violence was the postelection violence. As mentioned, Jonathan Goodluck, a Christian, had just won the presidential election and Patrick Yakowa the governorship election in Kaduna State. The political victory did not go well with the Muslims. Many towns and cities in Kaduna State, including Kafanchan, where Ezra M. was interviewed and shared his experience, were affected. Ezra and his friends were locked up in a house for one week because of the incident. Many Christians lost their lives and their businesses, and houses and church buildings were burned or destroyed. Ezra is a pastor, and his church was closed and had to move to another part of the town for safety because it was close to a danger zone. Ezra confessed that many of his members were traumatized, including himself, and they have had to live with the trauma for several years.

Boko Haram

The persecution of Christians in northern Nigeria, as has been discussed, began with mild persecution, like discrimination and denial of rights and privileges, and deteriorated into mob violence, resulting in the destruction of lives and property. From 2009, the persecution had developed to full-scale terrorism with Boko Haram and Fulani herdsmen as key players. In 2009 a group called *Ahlal Sunna wa lidda'awati wa al-Jihad*, popularly known by the given nickname "Boko Haram," appeared in Maiduguri, the Borno State capital. The group began their initial attacks on Christians, security agents, and government institutions—the latter two classed as products of the West, and by implication, considered Christian. Today, because of the lack of cooperation of other Muslims with their ideology of an Islamic state, these Muslims have also become subjects of attack. Several Christian leaders interviewed from the northeast shared their experiences of Boko Haram attacks.

One of those interviewed was Bishara L., who is a pastor of the EYN. Bishara's encounter with Boko Haram began when he was transferred to *Ashigashiya* in Gwoza to work. Boko Haram made several attempts to kill him. "They hunted me in the Gwoza area as an animal because they wanted to kill me." He was transferred to Michika in Adamawa State, and they still followed him. He said that they wrote and dispatched letters, searching to kill him. His crime was that the medicine man who used to give them vexing charms was converted to Christianity under his ministry, so the Boko Haram members could no longer receive diabolical powers from the former medicine man. Within three days of his transfer to *Kautikari*, which is his present place of ministry, Boko Haram launched an attack. For eight hours they killed people and destroyed houses without military intervention. Bishara suspected that because "the army commanding officer was a Muslim, he deliberately allowed Boko Haram to destroy the community because we are Christians." For eight months they suffered constant attacks from Boko Haram, and three times they attempted killing him, but the Lord saved him.

Commenting further on what happened at *Kautikari*, Elisha O., a church elder from *Kautikari*, confirmed that Boko Haram attacked the village seven times, and in the first attack, seventy people were killed. He personally suffered loss. His shop was looted and burned down, and they burned the food stuff he had gathered for the use of his family. He had to relocate his family to stay with his sister in Kano while he remained at *Kautikari*. Any time the Boko Haram come to attack the village, they always run to the bush. The pastor of their local church, who was not an indigene, could not endure the attacks, so he left. The elders continued to lead the church, meeting at five in the morning for Sunday services in the open air. They were compelled to worship in the open because their church building was destroyed by Boko Haram.

In an interview, Suleiman B. further narrated some experiences when Boko Haram started in 2009. It was in the night when he saw a team of about fifty members of Boko Haram passing through the street where he lived. They walked past his house and the church where he was pastor to neighboring churches, and they burned down several churches. He climbed on his roof to watch what was happening. The sight was so devastating and traumatizing to him.

Another experience with violence by Boko Haram was described by Desmond B., who is a young pastor of a Pentecostal church. In his residence at *Bintu* Sudan in Maiduguri, Desmond shared an experience about one day when returning from church, he heard the loud sound of a bomb blast that lifted the roof of the house where he lived. After about five minutes, there was another explosion. The two explosions claimed about one hundred lives. There was also a day during the midweek service, while people were worshipping in the church where he is a pastor, when they heard gunshots. It was an exchange of gunshots between Boko Haram and the security personnel posted at the church. Though the security personnel experienced some injuries, they were able to repel the attack.

Larai U. also shared a traumatic experience about a family encounter with Boko Haram. She had traveled to the headquarters of the EYN in Mubi on October 29, 2014. While there, she had her first encounter with Boko Haram attack, and she and her family had to immediately flee to Cameroon Republic for safety, returning to Nigeria two weeks later. The second experience came three weeks after the Mubi experience in Chibok. On November 13, 2014, Larai had just exited the bathroom when she heard gunshots. She and her husband quickly jumped into the car and rushed for their lives, while Boko Haram members were following and shooting. At one point their car got stuck in a hole, and they quickly jumped out and ran on foot. They spent the night in the bush and were able to arrive in Maiduguri, the Borno State capital, the following day. Meanwhile, their son had a gunshot wound and was later able to be taken to the hospital in Maiduguri for treatment. When they were finally able to return to their house on January 20, 2016, they saw that Boko Haram had taken away everything but had not burned it down.

In addition, Saleh F., a retired pastor and former leader in COCIN, was interviewed about his experiences with Boko Haram. His son, a soldier, went missing in Gwoza when the town was captured by Boko Haram and made the capital of their "caliphate." At the time of the interview, it had already been four years since his parents had seen him or received any news of his whereabouts. This is a traumatic experience for the family. Saleh confirmed that the people of Maiduguri live in fear because when any member of the family goes out, they are not certain the person will come back. There are bomb blasts almost every day in Maiduguri. "You don't sleep well, and when you do sleep, you are not sure of waking up alive the following day."

Collins T. shared in the interview how he was pursued six times by members of Boko Haram to kill him. These attempts were made on him because he was a Christian leader. In one of the incidences, both he and his secretary were chased, and his secretary was shot and killed. Collins narrowly escaped death.

The painful experience with extreme persecution by Boko Haram can best be shared by the parents of the abducted Chibok girls. I had the privilege of meeting with thirty-two parents of the abducted girls during the research time in Chibok, as well as interviewing Gregory J., a leader of the Chibok girls' parents who is at the forefront of guiding others to share their story about the abduction of their children. Although there were a few Muslims whose daughters were abducted, Gregory is of the opinion that the abduction was targeted at Christians. In defense of this claim, Gregory says,

> Out of 219 schoolgirls abducted by Boko Haram on April 14, 2014, only 18 were Muslim girls. All 201 are Christians so the difference is clear, the reason why I say this is that, even before

the night of the abduction, some of the Muslim parents sent to withdraw their daughters back home, not exposing the secret since the principal and the vice principal of administration were Muslims, so they knew about the abduction and withdrew their daughters and left our own. Only 18 Muslim girls were involved but 201, can you imagine all Christian daughters? So, it is Christian persecution.

If Gregory's claim to Christian persecution is true, why were Muslim girls involved? The following possible reasons may be suggested. Perhaps the parents of these girls were not reached with the information about the planned abduction of the Christian girls, or they heard the information and made light of it and, as such, did not withdraw their children the night before the abduction.

Saratu Z., one of the mothers of the abducted girls interviewed, shared her experience:

> We had struggle, sorrow, and pain when they abducted our children, we lost hope that we will ever see any of them. This thing that happened is new to us. It has caused sorrow and pain to us, but people all over the world have been praying and fasting for us. God in His mercies brought back our daughters. We are glad, but our joy is not complete because there are still others in the hands of Boko Haram that are not yet released. Whenever we see those parents whose children are not yet released we are still in pain. We enjoin Christians the world over to keep praying for them and to do whatever effort they can to secure the release of the remaining girls in the hands of Boko Haram.

Saratu is one of the fortunate parents whose daughter has been released, but she confesses that her joy is incomplete without the release of other girls in the hands of Boko Haram.

Abduction of Christian girls is not limited to the incidence of the Chibok girls. The incidence of Dapchi girls in Yobe State is still fresh in our memory where 110 girls were abducted. The federal government was able to negotiate for the release of all of them except Leah Sharibu, a Christian girl who refused to renounce her faith in the Lord Jesus Christ.[24] The case of Leah Sharibu further strengthens the fact of Christian persecution in the attacks of Boko Haram.

Abduction of Christian girls and marrying them to Muslims predates the Chibok girls' abduction. Mike C., an ecumenical leader in Chibok who was interviewed, confirms such abductions: "We have had cases of Christian

---

24. See https://www.uscirf.gov/leah-sharibu-0.

girls who are abducted, forcefully converted to Islam, and married to Muslims and the parents of the girls are warned not to say anything. If they should say anything, it could cost their lives."

An example is that of Mr. Jonathan and his daughter.

> On 15 November 2016, Mr. Jonathan Usman, a member of ECWA Church Abadawa in Saminaka town, Lere Local Government was scheduled to appear before a Shari'a Court. He was being forced to appear before this court by the abductors of his 15-year-old daughter, Sarah Jonathan. She was abducted and taken to the Emir of Saminaka's Palace on 16 August 2016. Her abductors stated that they had married her off to an unknown person, on the pretext that she had converted to Islam. Yet according to the laws of the land she was a minor who was subject to parental religion until reaching the age of maturity, and who should not marry without parental consent.[25]

This incident took place in my hometown, though I was not an eyewitness because I was not in Nigeria at the time of the incidence. Most Christian parents could not do anything about their abducted children, either because of poverty being unable to go to court, or because they went to court and were denied justice because the judge was a Muslim.

It should be noted that at this time, the experience of the attacks of Boko Haram is not limited to Christians alone. Muslims are also being attacked by Boko Haram. The first reason for attacking Muslims may be their refusal to cooperate and accept Boko Haram ideology of an Islamic state, so they are therefore considered infidels. The second possible reason may be when the Boko Haram runs out of food supplies and other necessities, they raid villages indiscriminately, and this might account for some of the attacks on Muslim villages and communities. The third possibility is shared by Christians in the northeast that since the Christians have been attacked and they refuse to take vengeance, because of answered prayer, God has turned the Muslims against each other.

Fulani Herdsmen

A few years after the appearance of Boko Haram in the northeast of Nigeria, a strange but deadly terrorist group of Fulani herdsmen also appeared. The Fulani are roving nomadic people found in most countries of West Africa. These people invade villages overnight, wake the villagers with gunshots, kill whoever they see, loot, and burn down villages. While the informants

---

25. *Global Christian Update*, "Demands of ECWA," 16.

in Borno State shared their experiences with Boko Haram in the northeast, those in Kaduna shared the experiences they have been having with Fulani herdsmen in the Middle Belt of Nigeria. Unlike Boko Haram, the Fulani herdsmen do not target Muslims, but Christian villages only.

In the Fulani attack on Godogodo village, Benjamin Y., an ordained pastor interviewed, narrowly escaped death. The experiences were so traumatic to him and his family that he had to temporarily leave Godogodo to his hometown. The Fulani used their own cattle to destroy farmlands, and on his farm, everything was destroyed, which affected him economically. Most pastors in rural areas in his context are paid poorly, so they must augment with farming to support themselves and their families. One of the greatest challenges at this period was that his parents and relations feared for his life and that of his family, so they tried to persuade him not to return to ministry. The Lord helped him to cross that hurdle. He is back and actively serving the Lord amid security and economic challenges.

Raymond D., an elder in the local church where he is a member, was interviewed and shared his experience of the attack on Godogodo on October 14, 2015. When the village was attacked by Fulani herdsmen, their farmlands were also destroyed, and they had to run from their homes and sleep in the bush. There was no harvest that year, caused by the destruction at the hands of the Fulani herdsmen. In his opinion, "The Muslims have ganged up against Christians—they try to take away our homes, use their cattle to destroy our farmlands, they even raped our women because they want to drive us away from the fertile land which God has given us." Raymond concluded that, apart from the effort to displace the community, this attack mainly on Christians is an attempt to deprive Christians of their right to worship God.

Concerned about happenings in Southern Kaduna and the Middle Belt of northern Nigeria, Charles W., a church elder who was interviewed, said that the experiences in the past few years in the region have been very horrific because villages and communities have been violently annihilated by Fulani herdsmen. Examples of such communities in southern Kaduna include Ninte, Gidan Waya, Godogodo, Tafan, Zankan, Bakin Kogi, and many others. He claims these persecutions are a systematic attempt at uprooting the indigenous people from their ancestral lands by use of violent force which is ongoing in different Christian communities in the Middle Belt. The attack on his own village, Bakin Kogin Kaninkong, on February 19, 2016, provides a good example. He said the village was eclipsed completely by Muslim Fulani fighters, who were determined to wipe out the village and possibly take over but were repelled by the courage and fighting determination of the Christian youth of the community, after a six- to seven-hour gun battle with the marauders. As a Christian, Charles believe that the victory was not won ordinarily because of the fighting skill and determination of the youth of the community, but that the God of the Christians showed his omnipotent power over the force that came to annihilate the Bakin Kogi community. The presence of the Fulani killers is still around the community, and many farmers have been killed while working their farms. Charles claims that "the number of people being assassinated on their farms outnumber those from the attack of February 19, 2016." There have not been reasonable measures put in place by the government to protect these vulnerable Christians, which is the reason why most of them resort to self-defense.

Another case is that of Gwantu and surrounding villages that have had their own measure of the Fulani herdsman attacks. Abraham G. in an interview with me shared the experiences of June–July 2014 when the Fulani herdsmen carried out the calculated massacre of Christian men, women, and children in villages like Gobi, Ambei, Nandu, Fadan Karshi, Karshi, and Daji. He said hundreds of dead bodies were brought to the General Hospital in Gwantu. Reverend Jonathan of the Evangelical Reformed Church Gobi lost his wife in one of the attacks. Pastor Abraham described the experience as moving and traumatic.

In a related experience, Pastor Adamu F. also shared in an interview with the author about the attempts to kill him. He stated that he escaped gunshots three times. July and August of 2016 were the period of attacks on the communities of the Godogodo area. The attacks were so intense that everybody, including the pastor, had to run for their lives. They became displaced people, depending on the goodwill of Christians for food and shelter from other villages that were not attacked. Adamu reported that when he returned to his house two days after they had escaped, the police commandant who was posted to the community showed him empty bullet shells of ammunition. He said, "The Fulani came in the night and shot guns thinking that my family and I were in the pastorium, but we weren't there. I saw the 320 bullet shells." The pastor shared the pain of losing three church members, and the crops on the farm were both stolen and vandalized by the Fulani herdsmen.

Summary

The experiences of persecution that Christians in northern Nigeria are experiencing can be summarized in the words of Bishop Joseph D. Bagobiri thus:

> Christians of different traditions experience various forms of hostility from governments, organized militia terrorist groups and individuals merely as a result of their faith in Jesus Christ. They are driven out from their villages and towns while their houses and possessions are very often confiscated, their places of worship are destroyed, and the symbols of their Christian affiliation are destroyed or removed from public view. They are kidnapped, subjected to forced marriage, sold for ransom, imprisoned, tortured, and murdered only because they are Christians. Despite the fact that Christians make up roughly a third of the world's population, there are still large pockets of the planet where they are targeted and hunted down simply because of their faith in Jesus Christ.[26]

Having heard from Christian leaders in northern Nigeria about what they are experiencing, there is proof that Christian persecution is a reality in northern Nigeria. Thus, this work will now proceed to examine the types of responses to the persecution of Christians in northern Nigeria. These responses intersect two regions, the northeast, which Borno represents, and Middle Belt, which Kaduna represents. These two regions have experienced more of extreme Christian persecution in northern Nigeria. Responses in these two areas will represent Christians there.

RESPONSES TO PERSECUTION IN NORTHERN NIGERIA

Considering the subject of persecution of Christians in northern Nigeria, I used the theoretical framework of Glenn Penner's fight, flight, and fortitude to discuss Christian responses to persecution in the region. The data gathered from northern Nigeria is processed and opinions of Christians in northern Nigeria examined concerning fight, self-defense, and pacifism as valid Christian responses to persecution. Also discussed is the impact of the responses to persecution of Christians in northern Nigeria on evangelism and discipleship.

Christian responses to persecution that should be considered valid must be the type that agrees with the teachings of the Bible. In pursuance of that, Christian leaders in northern Nigeria were asked what they consider to be biblical Christian responses to persecution. Responses from Christian leaders in Kaduna State, displayed in appendix D, table 5, indicate that thirty-five out of the seventy-nine respondents to this question consider pacifism to be the biblical response to persecution, representing 44.3 percent. Self-defense was responded to by thirty-four persons,

---

26. Bagobiri, *Seed of Another Humanity*, 3.

representing 43 percent. Two responses were for revenge, which represented 2.6 percent, and eight responded "all of the above," representing 10.1 percent. The responses above show that pacifism is the most biblical form of response to persecution, though the margin in Kaduna State between pacifism and self-defense is very small.

In Borno State, the Christian leaders were asked the same question as to what they consider to be biblical Christian responses to persecution. The results in appendix E, table 5, are as follows: forty-nine out of the seventy-three respondents to this question consider pacifism to be the biblical response to persecution, representing 67.2 percent. Self-defense was responded to by six persons, representing 8.2 percent. Three responses were for revenge, which represents 4.1 percent. Fifteen responded "all of the above," representing 20.5 percent. The responses of the Christian leaders in Kaduna State representing the Middle Belt, and the responses from Borno representing the northeast, show that Christians in northern Nigeria consider pacifism the most biblical form of Christian response to persecution.

The persecution of Christians in northern Nigeria is largely coming from Islam, which is the most dominant religion in the region. Both Christians and some peace-loving Muslims have shared concerns about the spate of violence and have proposed the use of interreligious dialogue as a means of resolving the problem of violence in northern Nigeria and in the country. There are several groups in Nigeria, both those formed and supported by the federal government of Nigeria and nongovernmental organizations, that are working to bring Muslims and Christians in Nigeria to the dialogue table to discuss how to overcome religious violence in Nigeria. Such groups include the Nigeria Inter-Religious Council (NIREC), which was formed by the Nigeria Supreme Council for Islamic Affairs (the largest Muslim ecumenical group in Nigeria) and CAN (the largest ecumenical Christian body in Nigeria). The formation of NIREC in 2000 had strong support from the then-president of Nigeria, Olusegun Obasanjo.[27] An example of nongovernmental organizations engaged in dialogue and peace-building in northern Nigeria includes the Interfaith Mediation Center in Kaduna run by Pastor James Wuyeh and Imam Ashafa. Another organization with a similar goal is the Global Peace Foundation, Nigeria.

The church should look critically at the value and importance of dialogue, which has the potential to offer preventive and curative measures to violence. As a matter of necessity, Christian dialogue groups should begin to engage the Muslims in northern Nigeria to have ongoing discussions towards peaceful coexistence. In this section, responses to persecution

---

27. Onaiyekan, *Seeking Common Grounds*, 111.

are examined, relative to the views and practical responses of Christians in northern Nigeria, as shared by the leaders. Glenn Penner's theoretical framework of fight, flight, and fortitude is used in the discussion.

Fight

Christians are followers of the Prince of Peace and, as such, are expected in every place to be ambassadors of peace. That is why it is an unpopular opinion among believers in Christ to advocate fighting or vengeance. However, this research discusses whether attacks and/or vengeance are or should be practiced by Christians in northern Nigeria. There is further inquiry as to why, in response to persecution, some Christians resort to vengeance against or attack their persecutors. Again, answered in the discussion, is whether Christians in northern Nigeria approve of vengeance and attacks as valid Christian responses to persecution.

Looking at the issue of attacks, Christians do not encourage fighting back, but when pushed completely, some have carried out vengeful attacks against their persecutors. Instances of such vengeful attacks can be found in the responses of Christians in the Middle Belt states where the Christian population is very significant. During or after an attack, some Christian youths gather and mount reprisal attacks on Muslims and their communities, killing, maiming, and destroying houses and mosques. To buttress this point, David R., a Christian traditional ruler, said in an interview: "Like these herdsmen attacks, sometimes because the tension is high, when the youths hear that herdsmen have attacked a certain community, and since they expect the herdsmen to be Fulani or Muslims, the youths react by attacking any Fulani or Muslim who may be innocent and may not be aware that such an attack has been carried out."

Mike C., another Christian leader who was interviewed, confirmed that in the city of Kaduna there has been a kind of vengeance on the Muslims by Christians that has made it difficult for Christians and Muslims to live together in certain communities.

This kind of fighting back or vengeance has been carried out in places like Kaduna, southern Kaduna, Plateau, southern Bauchi, and a few other places in the north. Brown O., a member of the NCEF and a foremost evangelist in northern Nigeria, lamented that in Plateau State, the youths not only killed their victims but even ate the flesh of some of the victims, which is detestable, evil, and unacceptable to the Christian faith.

In an informal conversation, a friend of mine who lives in Jos confirmed this claim. In one of the attacks in Jos, he happened to meet these youths, and they offered him some human flesh to eat, which he rejected.

In further discussion on Christians fighting back or taking vengeance, I came across an article written by Emeka Ibemere that claims to have discovered a Christian militia called *Akhwat Akwop* in Kaduna in 2011 that vowed to match Boko Haram blood for blood.[28] I am a resident of the city of Kaduna with a vast network of relatives, friends, and ministry colleagues and partners. I have never heard of such a group. If they have existed since 2011 in the city of Kaduna or any part of the state, I should have heard about them or an attack on Muslims by them. All information I have about this group comes from Ibemere's article or from materials that referred to it. I am not denying but doubt the existence of such a Christian militia in Kaduna and even in northern Nigeria.

Christian leaders across Borno and Kaduna States discourage and/or condemn attacks and vengeance on the persecutors. Brown O. said in an interview, "We are against revenge attacks because revenge attacks means that any Muslim you see, you attack even if the person knows nothing about the evil that has been committed. That we feel is not biblical and it is very wrong."

However, Kenneth C., a Christian elder and leader interviewed, argues that Christians should not quickly condemn such people who use revenge. He said, "Of course, there are people in the churches who say, 'we have had enough of these nonsense' so they resist. Of course, the pastors call such carnal Christians, but even the so-called carnal Christians have their own use in the Bible. The Lord prepares them for a time like that." This claim by Kenneth does not have a solid footing, and he did not provide any biblical reference to back up his claim of God using carnal Christians this way. He concludes that one should not condemn those whom God raises to deal with the Muslim fanatics, just as one wouldn't condemn others God raises to pray.

Why should Christian people resort to vengeance? In response to this question, as Kenneth said above, many Christians are weary of the killings and are looking for strategies to stop. Such Christians feel that the Muslims are taking the pacifism of Christians for granted, and if Christians fight back, it might reduce or stop the attacks.

Another reason for vengeance came from an informal discussion with a friend who is of the opinion that most of the Christian youths who are easily mobilized for reprisal attacks are orphans whose parents were killed in previous violent attacks while they were young children. These children witnessed their parents being killed and their houses burned, and they were

---

28. Ibemere, "Christian Group Vows."

left as young orphans to fend for themselves. The deep-seated anger in them easily makes them ready tools for counterattack.

It should be noted that the Christian youths involved in those counterattacks are often nominal Christians. However, there are many who do not agree with responding with vengeance. For instance, Brown O. stated in his interview that true Christians will not kill Muslims. Because of the fact that they bear Christian names and come from Christian families, the Christian fold must take responsibility for their misdeeds. Just as the Crusades were not fought by all Christians but Christianity is blamed for it, so it is with the Muslims. Even though not all Muslims in Nigeria are Boko Haram, Islam is blamed for their attacks because members of Boko Haram are Muslims. In most cases when Christians are hard pressed and carry out reprisal attacks, they do not initiate the attacks themselves.

Except for Kenneth and Charles, the Christian leaders interviewed rejected the idea of attacks or vengeance as a Christian response to persecution. If such happens, it is considered a product of human weakness and not a biblically approved method as a response to persecution.

Flight

Pacifism is the age-old, agreed-upon response to persecution known to Christians. This understanding has its roots in the Christian interpretation of the pacifist passages of Jesus in the Gospels, pacifism in the treatment of the enemy in the Pauline epistles, and other New Testament passages that speak to Christians' responses to persecution. The stories of early Christian persecution and martyrdom contributed to this thinking.

Using qualitative research data for the discussions, the interviews contain abundant data in support of pacifism as a more biblical way of responding to persecution by Christians that will impact evangelism and discipleship more positively. Bishara L., who was interviewed, is a pastor of the EYN church. He is a down-to-earth pacifist coming from the pacifist background of the Church of the Brethren. He said, "God did not allow humans to kill." As such, he believes that Christians can only pray—they cannot even defend themselves. He insisted, "If they are killing us, the highest thing we can do is to leave the place for them and flee." He has demonstrated this belief by fleeing to different places as he is being chased by Boko Haram.

Collins T., another Christian leader in Borno State, said in an interview that he responds to persecution by showing love to the Muslims and sharing the gospel of love with them. He said, "I have not personally gone out to defend myself physically, but I trust God, depend on him, and ask him to help me." He added, "The fact that they are violent sometimes it shows that if we are not violent is an indication, that we have something they do not have."

The general type of response to persecution in Borno State as garnered in the interviews is not retaliation, but prayer and leaving everything to God. Another pastor interviewed, Michael Y., stated that when you look at Scripture, persecution of Christians is to be expected, and when it happens, a Christian should commit oneself to God and not repay evil for evil.

Judith M. added when interviewed, "I only pray, because our Lord has taught us not to retaliate, and our warfare is not carnal, we are only to pray and ask God to give us the grace to continue in the race."

In Kaduna State, the response is slightly different. There are those who believe in pacifism, and there are those who do not. The discussion in this section will center on those responses that have to do with pacifism. Self-defense will be discussed later. Some respondents from Kaduna State started with bitterness and hatred towards Muslims but later had a change of attitude, and their actions and reactions were changed to love. This led them to seek dialogue and the welfare of the Muslims. One such is Caleb K., a Christian leader and university professor who confessed that he initially responded to the persecutions with "aggression and hatred." In the interview he stated that he hated Muslims with a passion until he went to the seminary to study Islam and Muslim evangelism, and the knowledge he gained was instrumental in his change of attitude from hatred to love.

Jeremy W. shared a similar experience, saying that he felt bitter about the Muslims and thought of fighting back during the attacks. What first transformed Jeremy was that the Scriptures taught him to love his enemies, and second was the reason his church was not burned in the 2000 crisis in Kaduna. He felt that if the church could be spared because it was in the midst of the Muslim houses, then something positive could come from Christians relating closely with the Muslims.

Another person interviewed was Ezra M.: "I was actually a pacifist as far as response is concerned, the reason being that the opponent is coming with arms and I do not have one and my Christian principle did not warrant me to buy and keep one as a way of defense, so I became defenseless. I was looking for a place to hide but with bitterness in my heart."

As in the case of Ezra, there are many who practice pacifism simply because they can do nothing. This can easily happen where Christians are in the minority. It should be noted that interview respondents from Kaduna State who believe in pacifism also believe that a Christian can defend oneself.

If pacifism is the only valid option for Christian response to persecution, should Christians in northern Nigeria flee? Where will over thirty million Christians flee to? One of the places the people of northeast found as a place of safety to where they could run is Plateau State, where the Christians have been defending themselves. However, if they too were fleeing, to where would the northeast Christians run? The question is whether self-defense is a valid option for Christian response to persecution, which leads the discussion to self-defense as fortitude.

Fortitude

Fortitude is the courage, brevity, and strength to face problems in life. The courage to defend oneself in the face of aggression is considered fortitude in this book. Self-defense in Nigeria is a constitutional right, and Christians as citizens of Nigeria have the right to defend themselves. Self-defense in the context of mass murder and wanton destruction of property is not only self-defense but defense of the defenseless. The violence experienced by Christians in Nigeria, be it mob violence or a terrorist attack, does not follow the rules of war. Children and women, even pregnant women, are ripped open and killed. Self-defense is primarily considered in the face of extreme persecution. While Christians are encouraged to endure mild persecutions as part of their Christian experience, they are also encouraged to defend themselves against genocide.

The analysis of the questionnaire data on the type of response that is most biblical (see appendices D and E, tables 5, respectively) indicates that nearly all respondents from Borno State agree that pacifism is the most biblical way to respond to persecution. In Kaduna State, responses for pacifism and self-defense were almost equal. This shows that a large population of Christians in Kaduna State, representing the Middle Belt, believe that Christians can defend themselves against Islamic aggression that is annihilating Christian communities in the region. In the interviews conducted by the author, about 90 percent of those interviewed in Kaduna State agree that Christians can defend themselves, while in Borno State there are a significant number who still leave a window for possibilities of self-defense when pressed.

One person who expressed the view of self-defense is Nuhu Z., a young Christian leader who has been a leader of Christian youth in the north. In an interview, he clearly stated that when and if he is persecuted, he will defend himself physically, legally, socially, and in whatever way possible. He was one of those who fought for a place of worship in the Ahmadu Bello University Zaria Congo Campus mentioned previously. For him, these battles are to be fought spiritually and physically.

Another person who shared this position was Kenneth C. When interviewed, he expressed the opinion that it would be irresponsible to stand and watch another man walk into his house to slaughter his wife and rape his daughter without putting up some resistance, especially since the constitution of Nigeria gives him the right to defend himself. He believes that pacifism should not be taken to the extreme. Kenneth has been a leader of CAN and, as a northerner living in Kaduna, has experienced much persecution since the 1970s.

Darrell M. shared another perspective on the response of fortitude in his interview. Darrell is a pastor and a practicing lawyer who, like me, has observed responses to persecution by Christians move from pacifism to violent resistance. He said,

> It came much later, when they discovered that their patience and desire to allow peace to reign meant they were going to be slaughtered more and more and Christians had to assert their rights since they have constitutional rights both to their lives and their right to worship and properties and so and so. They rose in defense of those rights which includes religious rights and we have observed in the past twenty years or more, that Christians have resisted quiet very violently which was not the initial reaction earlier.

Darrell lamented that Christians in northern Nigerian have not effectively used legal means to defend themselves. He has seen a lot of violations of constitutional rights, wherein Christians should have sought redress in courts of law. He commented that Christians should get more organized and be involved in what he called "judicial activism." Christian self-defense should lead to the enforcement of fundamental rights of citizens guaranteed by the Constitution of the Federal Republic of Nigeria and by all human rights laws.

The Christian traditional chief David R. opined in an interview that self-defense is sometimes necessary because if you do not do so, you will just be killed. He cautioned that Christians should not attack, because attacking would violate the central teaching of Christianity.

Charles W., a local church elder who was also interviewed, is more radical in his views on self-defense. He said, "I am a complete believer in self-defense of Christians. Even if the self-defense means someday, I will have to stop the attacker before he attacks, I will do it. The saying that the best form of defense is to attack makes sense to me, so sometimes if in defense you must attack then you attack." Here Charles seems to contradict most respondents who rejected the idea of Christians attacking the persecutor first. Can Charles be dismissed as unchristian with this idea? Can there be a critical situation that could warrant attack as a form of self-defense? A thorough study of the situation is needed with context in the light of the Scriptures before any evaluation.

Caleb K. in an interview expressed the opinion that the way Muslims carry out attacks on Christians in northern Nigeria is a declaration of war. When war is declared, he said, you have no option but to defend yourself. Caleb encourages defense rather than offense and further said, "When they attack us and we defend ourselves, we are justified to do so." Caleb raised the issue of weapons for defense and rejects the idea of churches stockpiling weapons in anticipation of attack. However, he feels that individual Christians can legally own registered guns for self-defense and protection against all attackers, including armed robbers and dangerous wild animals.

The constitutionality of self-defense was again emphasized by Jeremy W. in an interview. He said that even natural laws teach self-defense. "If I see danger coming, I do not have to look for the police to come and stop it. I should be the one to either run away from the danger or block the danger and the police can take care of the rest." As much as he encourages self-defense, he discourages the idea of Christians being the first to attack the persecutors.

While the respondents from the northeast overwhelmingly rejected the idea of self-defense by Christians, some respondents believe that some extreme situations could warrant self-defense. After a good argument in favor of pacifism, Balarabe T., a Pentecostal pastor who was interviewed, concluded, "You know, when a person is pushed to the wall, there is nothing he cannot do, that is the thing." He is saying that there are people who had to defend themselves because that was the only option for them to survive or to help others survive.

At *Mbalala*, Gregory J. in his interview admitted that in their community they have young men with weapons who keep watch over their churches to ensure that the churches are not burned or overpowered by Boko Haram.

Collins T., a Christian leader in Borno State and an indigene of Chibok, revealed that the strategy they used in Chibok town for self-defense was to dig a deep ditch around the town, leaving only three gates into the town through which people go in and out with vigilante or security agents manning those gates to prevent attacks from Boko Haram.

About *Kautikari* in Chibok, Borno State, Elisha O., a church elder interviewed, said that in their village they defend themselves. He said, "We have a vigilante group that have been doing a good job, their efforts have strengthened us. Probably if not for their efforts, Boko Haram would have taken over our village."

In another interview, Michael Y., an ecumenical Christian leader, stated, "I know even in Chibok, there are people who will not tolerate nonsense for the sake of Christ. Anything bad done to them, they will retaliate."

Why are the stories of self-defense or some form of resistance more prominent from the Chibok area? Suleiman B., a pastor in Maiduguri, Borno State, who was interviewed, shed some light when he said that the reason the people of Borno were not defending themselves is probably because of the Christian population. He argued that if they had the Christian population strength of Kaduna or Plateau, they probably would have been defending themselves. Though some Christian leaders in Borno State would argue otherwise, this claim makes some sense.

Why is self-defense an important discussion as a response to persecution and violence in northern Nigeria? First, there may not be a need to discuss self-defense because security issues are adequately managed by government security agents. This is the situation in places or communities where the government truly guarantees the security of lives and the property of its citizens. However, where security agents are suspected to have colluded with criminals to destroy Christians, I am in support of the opinion of those who advocate the option of self-defense when faced with destruction. This issue of collusion of security agents is substantiated by the alert raised by Theophilus Danjuma, a retired military general, who said that the Christian and ethnic populations of the Middle Belt would be wasting their time if they are waiting for the military or police to protect them. He stated that "the military collude with the terror groups and facilitate their carrying out the killings across the land."[29] The only measure for survival, if they are able, is self-defense. It should be noted that the persecution of Christians in northern Nigeria is not an official government policy. Christians are not officially hunted by the government, although government means have been used indirectly in northern Nigeria to persecute Christians in some cases. If it were a direct government policy, then protests and nonviolent resistance could be used to persuade the government to revoke such policies.

The impossibility of nonviolent resistance in most of the Nigerian cases of violence is evidenced in the case of Shari'a violence in Kaduna in the year 2000. When there was an official government policy to introduce Shari'a in the state, Christians gathered, prayed, and marched to the capitol to present a protest letter to the governor. Muslims attacked the Christians, and it resulted in the most deadly and destructive religious violence ever

---

29. Oborji, "Is Christianity on Trial," 7.

experienced in the state. The Christians had to fight hard to defend themselves against the aggressors.[30] Where nonviolent action works, I believe Christians in northern Nigeria will prefer it.

The second reason why the discussion on self-defense is an important response is when genocide is involved. If Christians can afford it, they should be able to defend themselves to prevent mass destruction of lives. In most of the attacks by both Boko Haram and Fulani herdsmen, there has been mass destruction of lives of men, women, and children. Communities have conducted mass burials of hundreds of victims of such attacks. Elisha O. described the genocide in *Kautikari* where Boko Haram killed seventy people in the first attack on the village.

Abraham G., a pastor, testified in an interview that in the attacks in the Gwantu Area, "hundreds of dead bodies were brought to the General Hospital in Gwantu."

There are dozens of such heartbreaking stories of genocide and attempts to wipe out Christian communities, both in northeast Nigeria and the Middle Belt, causing me to question whether it is ethical to have the means of stopping such genocide and yet refuse to do so under the pretext of Christian principles. This ethical question needs to be explored further by Christian scholars and theologians.

The third reason for advocating self-defense concerns the defense of the weak and vulnerable, which is a Christian duty. As mentioned above, the persecution attacks do not spare women and children. Using self-defense, Christians should rise and protect women from rape and all forms of abuse and death. The abducted Chibok girls provide an example of such abuse. If Christians can provide a resistance that could avert such occurrences, such action will be a great service to the church and humanity.

The problem with self-defense is the difficulty of drawing the boundary line between self-defense and vengeance. This is evidenced in the answers of the respondents in both the interviews and the questionnaires. Many respondents see vengeance and self-defense as the same, hence the rejection of self-defense. Vengeance in the name of self-defense, the other way around, is engaged by many Christian youth. The question is, who determines what is self-defense and what is vengeance? Christian leaders and scholars should be able to engage the study of the Scriptures and their context to provide solutions to such problems.

It is very important to look at types of self-defenses I proposed, which in my opinion will help explain the meaning and importance of self-defense and how it should be carried out in a proper manner. First is

---

30. Ukanah, *In God's Name*, 203.

confrontational self-defense. In this type of defense, the persecuted confronts the aggressor with or without weapons to repel the impending attack. This confrontation may result in loss of lives, especially if it involves armed conflict. In some cases, it is a mere threat that will send the enemy away. For example, when I was a Christian student leader at Kaduna Polytechnic, Nigeria in the early 90s together with other leaders of Christian groups, we grew weary of yearly attacks on Christians on campus by a fanatical group of Muslim students during the Ramadan fasting period. I invited all Christian students prior to the fasting in 1993 and instructed them to be ready to defend themselves in case of any aggression. The Muslim students heard of the plan and could not carry out any attack that year, and the Christian students enjoyed peace in subsequent years on campus.

I do not subscribe to the attack-first idea, as Charles W. believes, as an acceptable Christian form of self-defense, when necessary, nor do I agree that Christians should stockpile weapons in their churches, waiting for anticipated attacks from Muslims. Rather, I believe that when Christians are confronted with evil, such as that which will cause genocide, they should resist it with whatever is available to them—be it stones, sticks, cutlasses, or legally acquired guns.

When interviewed, Brown O. testified that God has been giving victory to Christians even when they resist with inferior weapons. Confrontational self-defense, especially if it involves armed struggle, should always be the last option to a Christian after all other options fail to achieve the desired goal. If possible, avoiding self-defense by armed struggle is the best option.

Second is apologetic self-defense. In some cases, Christians are persecuted because of false information about the Christian faith, sometimes publicized by enemies of the cross. While in Kano, Nigeria, I was reasoning with a Muslim group, attempting to enlighten them about Christianity and began to discuss the subject of being born again. One of the participants quickly responded that they were told that Christians sometimes gather for meetings in the church at night and commit adultery and fornication. Some of the women will get pregnant. The children born of these pregnancies come out with unusually curly hair. These kinds of children, he said, are the "born again." This kind of misinformation can create hatred for Christians and make them vulnerable to unnecessary attacks. As a result, Christians are attacked as the cause when there are natural disasters because of their alleged immoral lives. I had to educate the Muslim group on what Christians teach about being born again to clear the air. Christian apologetics should go beyond just educating Christians on how to defend the faith against the attacks of the enemy and focus on the explanation of the Christian message and doctrines to those who are not Christians, especially those who find themselves in the context of persecution. Good apologetics of this type will reduce persecution that arises from ignorance or misinformation.

Third is legal activism and advocacy as a type of self-defense that Christians can use. Christians should study the Constitution of the Federal Republic of Nigeria thoroughly and be acquainted with their rights and privileges as individuals and as a group. As a form of self-defense, they should seek redress in courts of law. Darrell M. in an interview lamented that Christians in northern Nigeria have been experiencing persecution in violation of their fundamental human rights as citizens of Nigeria but have not "seriously sought redress in courts of law."

Some Christians avoid going to court because they argue the Scripture forbids Christians to go to court (1 Cor 6:1–6). Paul taught that a Christian should not take a fellow Christian brother or sister to court because they have the leadership of the church to settle disputes among Christian brethren. However, unbelievers cannot be judged by the elders of the church and unbelievers can be taken to court. The fear that judgment may be overturned in favor of Muslim attackers is real. I have experienced such injustice as mentioned earlier, but there are also cases, though rare, where justice has been upheld by courts of law in the region. Christians in northern Nigeria should consider forming Christian activism and advocacy groups that will engage in defending Christians and the Christian cause within the context of the law.

In the foregoing discussion, self-defense is not limited to armed struggle with the opponent. There are other options, as suggested above, to where the use of armed force would be the last option for a believer when all other options fail.

IMPACT OF RESPONSES TO PERSECUTION ON EVANGELISM AND DISCIPLESHIP

Understanding how the responses of Christians to persecution impact evangelism and discipleship is helpful in recognizing that responses to persecution can produce either a positive impact or negative impact on evangelism and discipleship. Understanding the results of negative and positive responses to persecution provide a guide to believers in focusing on responses that will be more beneficial for spiritual kingdom purposes. The field research data of both interviews and questionnaires reveal the impact that different types of responses to persecution by Christians in northern Nigeria have on evangelism and discipleship. The data on the impact of responses to persecution is categorized into positive responses that promote evangelism and discipleship and negative responses that inhibit evangelism and discipleship.

Impact of Positive Responses to Persecution on Evangelism and Discipleship

In both the interviews and the questionnaires, there were responses that were considered positive that impact and promote evangelism and discipleship in the context of persecution, evidenced in the data and discussions below. There were several people interviewed who described how proper response to persecution could aid in evangelism. Darrell M. shared the opinion that Christians, when persecuted, should be prayerful and maintain a right relationship with God. In response to persecution, Christians should be good to their persecutors, pray for them, and protect them when they are in trouble. These Christians, he believes, will keep open the door of dialogue and be a possible continuous witness to them.

Building on the discussion above, Caleb K. insisted that the best response that will impact evangelism and discipleship is to show love, respond to the persecutors with care, and show understanding. He commented, "There is nothing that pleases the Muslim like showing understanding to him/her as a person and then as a Muslim." He also emphasized the need for Christians to stop mocking and demonizing the religion of Islam. He said these actions close the doors for evangelism. Dialogue is another way of responding that will open doors for evangelism and further discipleship, but in dialogue, Christians should engage the Muslims in a respectful manner. Caleb is a living testimony to the importance of such relational efforts in reaching Muslims, even in the context of persecution. While I was in Caleb's house for this interview, a Muslim couple walked in who have adopted him as their father because of the kind relationship he maintains with Muslims.

In the same spirit, Collins T., a Christian leader in Borno State, maintains that Christians should show love, friendship, care, and openness to the Muslims. When you show them love, you will be able to attract them. He recommends that you "give them gifts, visit them when they are sick, take them to the hospital, and pay their bills if you can afford to, and correct their children if they are misbehaving."[31]

This recommendation shows the importance of being involved in the life of the persecutor to win him/her to Christ. Collins testified of a

---

31. In African context, a child is a child of the community; you are showing love to parents when you meet a child misbehaving and you correct or even discipline him/her on behalf of the parents. When you do so and report to the parents, they are expected to thank you for the good you have done to their child.

Muslim couple naming their daughter Rahab after his wife, not minding the Christian name because of the impact of the relationship they have had with them. Gregory J. said, "Be truthful, be factual, and do not fear persecution. Don't involve yourself in cheating. Let your yes be yes and your no be no. When you do good to them, you are spreading the gospel."

Larai U., a Christian women's leader interviewed, added that Christians should not stop preaching the gospel even in times of persecution. She emphasized that those preaching the gospel should live the gospel and share with those in need. Instead of using guns to respond to persecution, Christians should take the Bible and respond.

To effectively use the Bible to respond to persecution, Audu K. recommended in a questionnaire the development of strategic evangelism and discipleship is needed using biblical wisdom and principles to reach and penetrate the so-called no-go areas, despite persecution and tendencies. This recommendation is very important because traditional ways of evangelism are becoming increasingly dangerous in northern Nigeria, due to terrorist activities.

Practical Christian living shatters the wall of hatred and opens doors for the communication of the gospel. Thomas P., a church elder responding to the questionnaires, buttressed this point by saying, "Christian reaction speaks silently to unbelievers, because the extent of endurance and patience of Christians surprises other religions. The unbeliever's interaction with Christians in day-to-day living can be a door for evangelism." Christians are called to be the salt and light of the world and, by this, lighten the dark places of the earth with the gospel.

Impact of Negative Response to Persecution on Evangelism and Discipleship

It should be noted that responses to persecution in northern Nigeria have both positive and negative impact on evangelism and discipleship, depending on the type of response. Having seen the positive impact above, it is important to discuss areas where the responses are impacting evangelism and discipleship negatively. Relationship is of primary importance when it comes to evangelism and discipleship. Good relationships open doors for Christian witness while bad relationships can close doors. In the questionnaire administered to Christian leaders in both Kaduna and Borno State, the leaders were asked what they thought has been the result of Christian responses to persecution in terms of relationship with their religious neighbors in northern Nigeria.

Responses from Kaduna State found in appendix D, table 7, reveal that twenty-one respondents are of the opinion that the responses have resulted in peaceful co-existence, which represents 25.6 percent of the eighty-two that responded. Forty-two answered that the responses to persecution have generated enmity and suspicion, which represents 51.2 percent. Nineteen respondents are of the view that the responses have brought broken relationships between Christians and their religious neighbors, which represents 23.2 percent of the responses. The interview responses above show that responses to persecution by Christians in northern Nigeria have brought enmity and suspicion in community relationships in some or most parts of northern Nigeria.

The same item did not have the same result in Borno State. The results on relationships with religious neighbors because of responses to persecution shown in appendix E, table 7, about Borno indicate that thirty-four respondents are of the opinion that the responses have resulted in peaceful co-existence, which represents 45.4 percent of the seventy-five persons who responded. Eleven who participated agreed that the responses to persecution have generated enmity and suspicion, which represents 14.6 percent. Thirty respondents are of the view that the responses have resulted in broken relationships between Christians and their religious neighbors, which represents 40.0 percent of the responses. The research above show that responses to persecution by Christians in northern Nigeria have brought peaceful co-existence in community relationship in some or most parts of northern Nigeria.

If interview results from Kaduna and Borno States are compared, it can be deduced that the Christians in Borno State are living more peacefully with their Muslim neighbors. Their problem is with Boko Haram terrorists, who also attack Muslims for not agreeing with their ideology. In Kaduna State, where experiences with religious crises since the 1980s have forced Christians to relocate to the southern part of the city for safety, Muslims have also been forced to move to the northern part of the city for safety. Today, there are communities in the southern part of the city where no Muslims live and communities in the northern part where no Christians live. The results show that the religious violence and persecution have impacted community and personal relationships negatively, and that relationships with the Muslims come with suspicion and enmity. With these kinds of relationships, evangelism and discipleship become difficult and even when presented, are often not effective. In one of my summer trips to Nigeria, I went to preach in a church in the southern part of the city. Upon crossing the Kaduna River which is the boundary of the northern and southern part of the city, the Christian church member who gave me a ride back home said, "You people living in this part of the city are trying. Whenever I cross this river to the northern part, I feel I am in the enemy's territory." This is an example of a response to persecution that has degenerated to vengeance.

In the questionnaire, respondents were asked what impact the responses to persecution of Christians in northern Nigeria have had on evangelism and discipleship. The general response has been that the persecution has reduced or rendered almost impossible the work of evangelism and discipleship. Lawrence A. said, "Such nasty and horrible action stopped mission work in Gwoza badly."

There are now no-go areas for Christians to preach the gospel. In some areas, whole Christian communities have been destroyed and the believers have moved as refugees in the city of Maiduguri and other places that are safe. I had an informal visit to one of the internal displaced persons camps managed by CAN. What I saw was a pathetic situation. Commenting on the negative impact of the responses of Christians in northern Nigeria, Ruth R. a women's leader who responded to the questionnaire, is of the opinion that defensive responses to persecution have made unbelievers unable to see Christians as the true light. This indicates that self-defense, as understood by the respondent, has portrayed Christianity in a bad image and is affecting evangelism.

Patrick L. also responded to the questionnaire and opined that responses to persecution in his context have a negative impact on evangelism because the relationships with Muslims have degenerated to suspicion and acrimony.

In response to the questionnaire, Dora H., a young Christian leader, said that movement to places of safety as a response to persecution has affected evangelism in areas where the Christians are leaving, while the church is growing in the places of safety to where the Christians have fled.

Tanimu A., a pastor who also responded to the questionnaire, addressed the issue of fear as a response that has hindered evangelism and discipleship. He also looked critically at the money and other resources spent on security apparatuses in northern Nigeria. These resources, he said, would have been directed to missions and evangelism, but the churches are forced to devise means of defense to protect lives and property against terrorist attacks.

The interview data also shows that there is a negative impact to evangelism and discipleship in some types of responses to persecution. The kinds of responses generally rejected and condemned by the respondents are attacks and vengeance, which they believe will produce a negative impact on evangelism and discipleship because they do not give the Christian faith a positive image.

To buttress this point, Christian leader Michael Y. said, "When Christians react to persecution by taking revenge, by the time normalcy returns, you cannot evangelize them because what you have done contradicts your preaching, so you have no message for them."

Caleb K. in an interview also condemned attacks on Muslims as a Christian response to persecution since it would be counterproductive in evangelism and discipleship. He said, "I see Christians go to burn Muslim places of worship in reaction to the burning of churches. We don't have that pattern in the Bible. I see Christians respond to Muslims with abusive language just as Muslims also abuse us. This does not promote evangelism and discipleship." Caleb recommends that Christians should study the Muslim scriptures so that they will learn more about them and be able to respond appropriately.

Another form of response to persecution that is impacting evangelism and discipleship negatively is that of some Christians who are weak in faith. These Christians are returning to African traditional religion and occultism for power to protect themselves and protect the church. Brown O., an evangelist in northern Nigeria, gave an example of people in Plateau State who were eating the human flesh of their victims. This is not an acceptable form of Christian response to persecution.

I was shocked that the eating of human flesh was not limited to the Christians in Plateau State but was also in Borno State. Judith M. claims that some Christians in southern Borno and parts of Adamawa "have become diabolic in trying to protect themselves from persecution. Some have taken even to eating human beings in the name of protecting themselves." When Christians are turning to fetish practices and becoming cannibals, then those Christians should first be evangelized and discipled.

There are also some weak Christians whose response is to leave the faith. Some have become Muslims for fear of persecution. The unfortunate thing is that Boko Haram does not spare Muslims unless a convert to Islam joins them or accepts their ideology. There are those who renounce Christ, and the persecutors see them as hypocrites and execute them.

In support of the claim that some Christians respond by converting to Islam, Bishara L., an interviewed pastor, lamented, "Some Christians because of worldly things have converted to Islam. Some get converted for fear of death, while others compromise and claim that since they were forced to be converted to Islam, God will understand." In some cases, the persecutors provide some incentives to lure Christians, especially the rural poor, to Islam, and sometimes the incentive is a promise to spare their lives if they will convert to Islam. Many weak Christians have fallen for that kind of deception.

Summary

This section on the impact of the responses to persecution includes the beautiful comment of John B., a church elder. In response to the questionnaire, he is of the opinion that responses to persecution have both negative and positive impacts on evangelism and discipleship. He looked at it from the angle of migration and mass movement, either as refugees or those looking for places of safety. This type of response in some cases tends to hinder evangelism and discipleship since the community is scattering, and in some cases, the scattered believers result in further spread of the gospel and multiplication of disciples and churches. Joseph Bagobiri observed:

> While the blood of the martyrs had been the seed of the Church in some places, we have seen also that in many other places, discrimination, violence, and martyrdom have been the reason for the death of the church and Christian communities. While the persecution of Christians has led to the birth of the Church in some parts of the World such as ancient Rome and Albania, the same persecution has led to the extinction of the Church in many parts of the world.[32]

Bagobiri's comment is the reality we are facing as we reflect on the strength of the church in North Africa and how Islam, with both mild and extreme persecution, almost wiped out the church in that region of Africa. I draw strength from the optimism of Christians in northern Nigeria who believe that the church will survive the storm of persecution and grow stronger.

Appendix D, table 6, reveals that Christians in Kaduna share this optimism as they responded to what Christians in northern Nigeria think of the future of Christianity in the region if the persecution continues. Nineteen of the eighty-three who responded to the question believed the Christian faith will survive the storm of the persecution, representing 22.9 percent. Thirty-one were optimistic that Christianity will grow even stronger, which represents 37.4 percent. Four respondents believed Christianity will be wiped out, which represents 4.8 percent. Twenty-nine responded that Christianity will be weakened and will remain weak if the persecutions continue, which represents 34.9 percent. The responses for item 6 in table 6 indicate that Christians in northern Nigeria are optimistic that the Christian faith will survive the storm and even grow stronger.

The Christians in the northeast, represented by Borno, also expressed their faith and confidence that the church in Nigeria will survive the storm

---

32. Bagobiri, *Seed of Another Humanity*, 8.

and grow stronger. Appendix E, item 6, sought to understand what Christians in northern Nigeria think of the future of Christianity in the region if the persecutions continue. Thirty-four of the seventy-six who responded to the question in Borno State believed the Christian faith will survive the storm of the persecution, representing 44.8 percent. Twenty-two were optimistic that Christianity will grow even stronger, which represents 28.9 percent. Seven respondents believed Christianity will be wiped out, which represents 9.2 percent. Thirteen responded that Christianity will be weakened and will remain weak if the persecutions continue, which represents 17.1 percent. The responses for item 6 in table 6 indicate that Christians in northern Nigeria are optimistic that the Christian faith will survive the storm and even grow stronger.

Christians in both the Middle Belt and the northeast believe that though there are negative responses that inhibit evangelism and discipleship, there are also positive responses that are opening doors for evangelism and discipleship. They believe that the church in Nigeria will survive the storm and be stronger. I hold the strong opinion that proper responses to persecution by Christians are key to the survival of the church through the storm.

CONCLUSION

In this chapter, it has been established that the suffering which Christians are experiencing in northern Nigeria can be termed Christian persecution despite the number of Muslims who are also affected due to their refusal to align with the Islamist terrorists. Christians have suffered persecution to varying degrees. It started with mild persecution of discrimination and denial of rights and deteriorated to violent, destructive persecution now inflicted by Islamist terrorists. Christians see value in enduring persecution as pacifists and do encourage that response, but in the wake of genocide and mass waste of lives, Christians are encouraged to defend themselves since the government of Nigeria is not proactive in defending the Christians. Responses to persecution have both positive and negative impact. Pacifism is highly recommended for its positive impact on evangelism and discipleship, while vengeance and attacks are rejected because of their negative impact on evangelism and discipleship. Self-defense as an option for Christians is still in the developmental stage. Because of mass murder and genocide and the Christian duty and responsibility to defend the weak and poor, some Christians now see value in adopting self-defense as an option for Christians facing persecution. As I studied responses to persecution in northern Nigeria, there was great encouragement from the optimism that the church will overcome the storm of persecution and emerge a stronger church. The next chapter will examine the responses of the early church to persecution to gain insights for Christians in northern Nigeria and to develop a response to persecution that has a positive effect on evangelism and discipleship.

4

Biblical and Historical Responses to Persecution

INTRODUCTION

RESPONSES TO PERSECUTION MAY differ from person to person. Even church communities may differ from others on how to respond to forms of persecution. To provide a balanced view on Christian responses to persecution, there is need to look at the example of Jesus, the teachings of Christ, and the apostles in the New Testament. Also needed is an historical understanding of early Christians to balance and appropriately respond to persecution in the contemporary milieu. This chapter explores the biblical and historical responses to persecution in providing that balance.

BIBLICAL RESPONSES TO PERSECUTION

For Christians in northern Nigeria to develop the right kind of response to persecution, they must consider the examples provided in the Scriptures. Jesus provides the primary example of all Christian action and behavior. His experiences with persecution and his teachings about persecution provide the foundation for developing an appropriate response to persecution. This section examines each—the persecution of Jesus, his predictions about the future persecution of the disciples, and the biblical passages that are most used to justify responses to persecution by churches in northern Nigeria.

Persecution of Jesus

Fulfilling the suffering servant prophecies of Isaiah (42:1–4; 52:13–15; 53:1–12), Jesus suffered persecution from the beginning of his ministry to the end on the cross. This section looks at the persecutions of Jesus, why he was persecuted, the acceptance-rejection tension, and blessings from the persecutions. From childhood, Jesus began to experience persecution when Herod ordered the killing of infants in Bethlehem (Matt 2:16). The flight to Egypt marked the beginning of Jesus' experience with persecution (Matt 2:13–18). In Luke, Simeon predicted the rejection of Jesus, saying that the "child is destined for the fall and rising of many in Israel" (Luke 2:34). Jesus further predicted the Jews' rejection of himself and his subsequent death (Luke 9:22, 44; 17:25; 18:31–33). The whole of his life and ministry are put in the context of persecution, culminating in his death.[1] As part of the fulfillment of Simeon's prophecy, the first sermon of Jesus in the synagogue in Nazareth was met with bitter resistance from the Jews who were intent on killing him (Luke 4:16–30),[2] "but he walked right through the crowd and went on his way" (v. 30).

The four Gospels contain many examples of the persecutions that Jesus experienced, ranging from mild to extreme, and record his responses to them. Glenn M. Penner outlines an overview of the hatred towards and persecution of Jesus in the Gospel of John. These include rejection by Jesus' own immediate family (John 7:1–10). His family members did not initially believe him. His siblings, the children of Mary born after Jesus, rather mocked him. In another development, Jesus was threatened with arrest (John 7:30, 44–52) by leaders of the Jews who even sent officers to arrest him, but they couldn't lay hands on him. He was further threatened with stoning (Jesus 8:59; 10:31). This time, he hid himself and escaped. John also pointed out that his reputation was besmirched (John 9:24–29), he was slandered (John 10:19–21), and finally he was arrested and killed on the cross (John 18:1—19:37).[3]

Jesus suffered opposition from the leaders of the Jews—the scribes, the Pharisees, the Sadducees, and lawyers—who set traps with their questions and planned continually how they might arrest and kill him. He stood up as a witness to the truth during his questioning before the judges who passed a death sentence on him. To Jesus, the crucifixion was not a tragic failure of his mission but rather its fulfillment.[4] Christians in northern Nigeria need to develop this kind of attitude to persecution, which acknowledges that persecution does not portray the Christian as a failure, but a step toward maturity and success in Christian life and ministry. Scott Cunningham adds, "Luke

---

1. Penner, *In the Shadow*, 146.
2. Sauer, "Theology of Persecution," 269.
3. Penner, *In the Shadow*, 151.
4. Sauer, "Theology of Persecution," 269.

legitimates Jesus as an agent of God's salvation through the persecution that he experienced." Therefore, the suffering of Jesus proves him to be a true prophet, suffering as the Old Testament prophets suffered.[5]

Jesus experienced both acceptance and rejection, and this tension is portrayed by John in his Gospel. He wrote, "Jesus came to his own but his own did not receive him" (John 1:11). However, it was not every Jew who rejected him; there were those who accepted him (John 1:12–13). Penner writes that "John sees people in one of two camps: the disciples who accept Jesus and abide in Him in one camp, and the 'world' which includes all those who reject, oppose, or are indifferent to Him in another camp."[6] In like manner, the disciples of Jesus will also experience this tension—they will be accepted and rejected by Jews and gentiles (Matt 10:24–25).

There were several reasons why Jesus was persecuted. John R. Philips in *Risk and Suffering in Church and Mission* outlines the reasons from the Gospels, including first, Jesus' call to absolute obedience to the will of the Father. There is agreement of the four evangelists that the cause of Christ's suffering was his obedience to the will of the Father (Matt 26:42; Mark 14:35; Luke 22:42; John 17:4). Second, the identity of Jesus seemed to raise questions, confusion, and misunderstanding, which resulted in his suffering and persecution. His claim to be the Son of God, the Messiah, the Eternal One, and the I AM created confusion and controversies among the Jews (Mark 3:20–35; John 8:54–58; 10:22–39). Third, Jesus confronted evil with truth, and the leaders of the Jews were not ready to hear that type of message. The teaching of Jesus was sometimes misunderstood or misinterpreted by his hearers (Mark 1:15; John 6:60), which also became a source of persecution. Fourth, his actions, which were always unique, created antagonism (Mark 5:1–17). These actions included his healing on the Sabbath day, mingling with tax collectors and sinners, and eating with unwashed hands. Jesus broke many Jewish protocols and established rabbi standards, which caused him to be persecuted. Fifth, the mission of Jesus also attracted persecution—his declaration in the synagogue in Nazareth brought immediate persecution. Even his disciples expressed disapproval when he declared that his mission was to die, and Peter rebuked him outright for saying it (Luke 4:16–30; Matt 17:22–23).[7]

The suffering of Christ was part of his mission on earth. There was no way he could have accomplished his mission without suffering. At Gethsemane, he prayed to the Father, "Abba, Father . . . everything is possible

---

5. Cunningham, *Through Many Tribulations*, 62.
6. Cunningham, *Through Many Tribulations*, 150.
7. Philip, "Theology of Risk," 13.

with you. Take this cup from me. Yet not what I will, but what you will" (Mark 14:35). This shows that there was a correlation between his mission and his suffering.

Persecution of the Disciples

During the earthly ministry of Christ, Jesus taught the apostles about the persecution they were going to face after his death and resurrection as his followers. To use the words of Christ: "When the bridegroom is taken from them . . ." (Mark 2:19–20). Jesus began to indicate to his disciples the future persecution they would suffer when he sent them out on mission. Penner compares the disciples being sent as "sheep among wolves" in Matt 10:16, which compares with the experience of the suffering servant prophesied in Isa 53:7:

> Jesus is putting His disciples in exactly the same position in the world. They will be defenseless to stop the onslaught that awaits them. They will be attacked, just as surely as a pack of wolves will set upon a flock of sheep. Survival, however, is not their prime concern. They are to be committed to accomplishing the purpose of God, even if it means their death.[8]

In Scott Cunningham's discussion of Luke's theology of persecution, he notes that the persecution of the apostles must be interpreted in the light of Christ's comments about suffering—"I will suffer" Jesus says, "and therefore, you also must be willing to suffer."[9] The disciples were to prepare to face persecution from government authorities, families, friends, and religious leaders (Matt 10:21–22). Luke added that the disciples would be hated, ostracized, reviled face to face, and their reputation defamed on "account of the Son of Man" (Luke 6:22). There would be temptation to apostatize to escape danger (Luke 10:22), but Jesus continued to encourage his disciples to endure to the end.[10] The expected persecution would be both local and universal. The disciples of Christ were to expect persecution locally from the Jewish leaders, as Jesus said, "You will be handed over to the local councils and be flogged in the synagogues" (Matt 10:17). Beyond the Jewish authorities, they would be taken to kings and governors to become "witnesses" both to the Jews and gentiles (v. 18). James Kelhoffer pictures the universal persecution not only of the apostles but all followers of Christ. Thus, "the Matthean discourse predicts that 'all nations will hate and persecute Jesus' followers, apparently it

---

8. Penner, *In the Shadow*, 120.
9. Cunningham, *Through Many Tribulations*, 87.
10. Penner, *In the Shadow*, 130.

will be while the Matthean community carries out missionary work among the Gentiles (Matthew 24:9–14)."[11]

The call for discipleship is a call to follow Jesus, as he beckoned, "Come, follow me" (Mark 1:17). This call to "follow" means sharing the life of Christ, and this sharing includes his joy and pain. Penner says, "Jesus knew that persecution and suffering—not prosperity, power or influence—would be the norm for those who receive him and found life in his name."[12] That was why he was explicit about the cost of following him as it would include persecution.

The call to discipleship is a call to carry one's cross, the cross being a symbol of shame, suffering, ridicule, and even death. In the Synoptic Gospels, disciples are called to carry their cross and follow Jesus. Reflecting on Luke 9:23, Christof Sauer says, "The core meaning of taking up one's cross in discipleship . . . is witnessing to Jesus Christ, even in a situation of persecution and martyrdom."[13] Cunningham adds that "suffering is an integral part of discipleship. Bearing one's cross is closely linked to following Jesus."[14] Penner calls believers to understand that "Jesus does not call us to carry his cross. He calls us to bend over and pick up our own cross and follow him."[15]

In the book of John, the equivalent of "carrying the cross" in the Synoptic Gospels (Matt 10:38; 16:21–28; Mark 8:34–38; Luke 9:23–27; 14:27) is the death of a seed for fruitfulness (John 12:23–26). Jesus exemplified death as fruitfulness with his life, and he expects his followers to "lose their lives" to gain their lives. Penner says, "If the hostile, hateful world is to hear the truth of Jesus, His messengers must hate their own lives for the world's sake" (Matt 16:24).[16]

Commitment to discipleship and suffering is a lifelong commitment. In Luke 9:57–62, Jesus laid out the conditions of discipleship to would-be disciples who wanted to follow him. To the last person who wanted to follow him, he said, "No one who puts a hand to the plow and looks back is fit for service in the kingdom" (v. 62). There is a tendency for disciples to turn back when faced with persecution. Penner outlines from the book of Matthew four dangers that could face a believer when persecuted. These dangers include the danger of denying Christ. To those who deny him, Jesus said he will deny them before his Father; they will be among those of whom he will say,

11. Kelhoffer, "Withstanding Persecution," 123.
12. Penner, *In the Shadow*, 151.
13. Sauer, "Theology of Persecution," 270.
14. Cunningham, *Through Many Tribulations*, 87.
15. Penner, *In the Shadow*, 136.
16. Penner, *In the Shadow*, 153.

"I do not know you" (Matt 10:33; 7:21–23). There is also the danger of loving one's family more than Christ. Anyone claiming to be a disciple who has any preference or priority more than Christ is committing idolatry, which God detests (Matt 10:34–37). Another danger is that of not being prepared to lose family for Christ's sake. Some people have not been able to truly follow Christ because of their attachment to family—family values, honor, inheritance (Matt 10:38–39). Finally, Penner says there is the danger of refusing to be a disciple because of fear of accepting those who, because of their witness for Christ, are wanted by authorities or mobs (Matt 10:40–42). Penner adds, "Persecution is dangerous ground, yet more perilous is the possibility of failing to be what God expects us to be by denying Him."[17]

The question these verses raise is, what about "secret disciples" who keep their faith secret because of extreme persecution? For example, have some secret converts to Christianity from Islam in northern Nigeria denied Christ? In answer to this question, the Gospel of John tells us of two secret disciples, Nicodemus and Joseph of Arimathea (John 7:50–52; 19:38), who as leaders of the Jews could not confess their faith openly. The two came out openly after the death of Christ and championed the cause of his burial—they "were now willingly and openly confessing their faith no matter the cost."[18] I therefore argue that the stories of Nicodemus and Joseph of Arimathea provide room for missionaries in areas of extreme persecution like northern Nigeria to grow secret disciples who, as they mature, may someday disregard the consequences and make public confession. Bob Bryant quotes a tradition that says that both Joseph and Nicodemus "did suffer for their confession. According to the tradition, Nicodemus is said to have been removed from his office in the Sanhedrin and banished from Jerusalem, while Joseph was cast into prison."[19] The underground churches and Christians in Muslim and communist countries are legitimized by this narration in the Gospel of John.

RESPONSES TO PERSECUTION

The Gospels present different kinds of responses to persecution. This section focuses on the response of Jesus and the responses required of the disciples in their future persecution. The persecution of Jesus has been discussed. Jesus responded to persecution in several ways.

First, he was confrontational and apologetic in his response to persecution. In John 8, he confronted his persecutors, saying, "I know that you are

---

17. Penner, *In the Shadow*, 135.
18. Bryant, "Secret Believer," 71.
19. Bryant, "Secret Believer," 71.

Abraham's descendants. Yet you are looking for a way to kill me" (v. 37). He went further to tell them, "You belong to your father, the devil, and you want to carry out your father's desire" (v. 44). Jesus was not always running away from his persecutors—there were times he confronted his persecutors.

Second, Jesus defended himself on accusations levied against him by the religious leaders of his day. He defended his position on why he healed on the Sabbath day by questioning whether they would help their animal if it fell in a pit on the Sabbath day. Therefore, he declared, a human being is more valuable than an animal. He told them that the Sabbath is made for doing good (Matt 12:9–14). When accused of why he ate with sinners, Jesus replied that it is only the sick who need a doctor (Luke 5:27–31). The authority for his ministry was also questioned by the leaders of the Jews, and he defended himself (Mark 11:27–33; Luke 20:1–8). He defended his messiahship (Mark 12:35–37; Matt 22:41–45; Luke 20:41–44) and defended himself against the attacks of the leaders of the Jews on his many other claims and identity.

Third, in his response to persecution, there were times Jesus withdrew and hid himself temporarily from his persecutors (John 10:39–40). John 11:54 states that "Jesus no longer moved about publicly among the people of Judea. Instead, he withdrew to a region near the wilderness, to a village called Ephraim, where he stayed with his disciples."

When he was arrested and on trial, Jesus stood as a defenseless lamb of God in the face of false accusations, cruel mockery, and scourging. In all these experiences, he did not fight back. Josef Tson frames the action of Jesus this way: "God cannot respond to hate with hate, because if he did, he would borrow not only the method, but also the nature of the one who is the originator of hate, the evil one. God can only respond with love, because he is love, and by suffering and sacrificing Himself for the ones who hate him, he expresses the essence of his own nature."[20] The climax of Jesus' response to persecution was his prayer on the cross for his persecutors: "Father, forgive them, for they do not know what they are doing" (Luke 23:34).

As discussed above, the persecution of the disciples of Christ in the Gospels was still in the future. As they learned from the master who forgave even on the cross, they would respond to persecution in numerous ways, including rejoicing because their reward in heaven is great and leaping for joy for being counted worthy to share in the experience of the prophets (Matt 5:12; Luke 6:23).[21] The apostles demonstrated this joy when they were beaten by the leaders of the Jews: "So, they departed from

20. Tson, "Suffering and Martyrdom," 182.
21. Cunningham, *Through Many Tribulations*, 74.

the presence of the council, rejoicing that they were counted worthy to suffer shame for His name" (Acts 5:40–41). The disciples of Christ were to respond to persecution fearlessly even if it meant dying. They should not "fear those who kill the body and after that can do no more" (Luke 12:4), but they should fear God who can both kill the body and throw the soul in hellfire (12:5).[22] Another way they were to respond was by praying for their persecutors (Matt 5:44; Luke 6:27–28). The prayer of Jesus for those who crucified him is a model for the disciples in times of persecution.[23] In Acts 7, Stephen followed the steps of the Master as he prayed for his persecutors while they were stoning him (v. 60).

Jesus permitted his followers to also flee when necessary. The main purpose for fleeing is not out of fear but for mission. He told them, "You will not finish going through the towns of Israel before the Son of Man comes" (Matt 10:23). When there was persecution of Christians in Judea, the disciples, less the apostles, scattered to gentile nations, which resulted in the planting of the missionary church of Antioch (Acts 11:19–21). They were taught not to resist their persecutors. They should be ready to "turn the other cheek" (Matt 5:38–42). Turning the other cheek is a critical issue among Christians in northern Nigeria, therefore more attention will be given to this passage. Jesus told the apostles that when they are arrested and they stand before authorities, they should depend on the Holy Spirit to give them the words to say (Matt 10:19). When responding to persecution, believers are to carefully listen to the Holy Spirit and discern how to properly respond to persecution, as was required of the apostles.

CRITICAL NEW TESTAMENT PASSAGES ON RESPONSES TO PERSECUTION

Believers in Nigeria learn not only from the example of Jesus but also what he taught about responses to persecution. Christians from northern Nigeria often appeal to the Bible for validation of their responses. Some base their arguments on passages from the Old Testament, while some who argue for the proper Christian response use passages in the New Testament. It is pertinent in this work to attempt the interpretation of passages in the New Testament that are most used as justification for responses to help the reader understand the context and usage in Scripture. This section examines Matt 5:38–42, 43–45b; Rom 12:14, 17–21; and Matt 10:23, which are the most-used passages by Christians in northern Nigeria to legitimize their kinds of response to persecution.

22. Cunningham, *Through Many Tribulations*, 106.
23. Schirrmacher, "Persecution," 286.

Matthew 5:38–42

> You have heard it was said, "Eye for eye, and tooth for tooth." But I tell you, do not resist an evil person. If anyone slaps you on the right cheek, turn to them the other cheek also. And if anyone wants to sue you and take your shirt, hand over your coat as well. If anyone forces you to go one mile, go with them two miles. Give to the one who asks you, and do not turn away from the one who wants to borrow from you.

In northern Nigeria, some Christians see this passage as validating pacifism in all ramifications, while others are of the opinion that proper interpretation of the passage limits its pacifism to interpersonal relationships and minor conflicts but not war and genocide. The background of this passage is from the *Lex talionis*, the law of retribution found in Exod 21:24; Lev 24:20; and Deut 19:21. Craig Keener states, "The 'eye for an eye' and 'tooth for a tooth' are part of the widespread ancient Near Eastern law of retaliation."[24] The *Pulpit Commentary* adds that the expression of "eye for an eye" and "tooth for a tooth" had already become proverbial in the Greek language even before the translation of the Septuagint.[25] This buttresses Keener's point on how widespread the law of retribution was at the time the passage was written.

The key phrase that has to do with response to persecution is *me antistenai to ponero* (not to resist the evil person). *Ponero* (evil, bad, wicked, malicious, slothful) describes the kind of aggressor that should not be resisted.[26] Different translations of the Bible render *me antistenai to ponero* as "ye resist not evil" (KJV), "don't resist an evil doer" (HCSB), "do not resist an evil person" (NASB), and "resist not him that is evil" (ASV). Using the King James rendering "ye resist not evil," *Gill's Exposition of the Entire Bible* argues that resisting evil "is not to be understood of any sort of evil, not of evil of sin, of bad actions, and false doctrines, which are to be opposed; nor of the evil one, Satan, who is to be resisted, but of an evil man, an injurious one, who has done us an injury."[27] This argument confirms that the KJV rendering refers to an evil person, not a thing.

---

24. Keener, *New Testament*, 58–59.

25. See *Pulpit Commentary* on Matt 5:38 at biblehub.com/commentaries/matthew/5-38.htm.

26. See *Greek Interlinear* of Matt 5:39 at biblehub.com/interlinear/matthew/5-39.htm.

27. See *Gill's Exposition of the Entire Bible* at biblehub.com/commentaries/matthew/5-39.htm.

What was the interest of Jesus in the law of retribution? *Barnes' Notes on the Bible*, commenting on Matt 5:38–42, contends that the Jews "were to take eye for eye, and tooth for tooth and to inflict burning for burning. As a judicial rule it is not unjust. Christ finds no fault with the rule as applied to magistrates and does not take upon himself to repeal it. But instead of confining it to magistrates, the Jews had extended it to private conduct, and made it the rule by which to revenge."[28] Keener reinforces the claim above when he says that the principle of retribution in Israel and other cultures was "enforced by a court and refers to legalized vengeance; personal vengeance was never accepted in the law of Moses, except as a concession for a relative's murder (Numbers 35:18–21)."[29] According to this evidence above, Jesus cut the excesses of the Jews and affirmed that the law of retribution does not include personal vengeance without recourse to the law courts.

John MacArthur contends that the instruction not to resist an evil person "deals only with matters of personal retaliation, not criminal offenses or acts of military aggression."[30] He goes on to say about Matt 5, "Jesus applied the principle of non-retaliation to affronts against one's dignity (v. 39), lawsuits to gain one's personal assets (v. 40), infringements on one's liberty (v. 41), and violations of property rights (v. 42). He was calling for a full surrender of all personal rights."[31] *Matthew Henry's Commentary* reveals that Christ's instruction on not resisting evil is to "suffer any injury that can be borne, for the sake of peace, committing your concerns to the Lord's keeping."[32] As much as there is agreement of scholars on the issue of nonresistance for personal injuries and rights, Barnes advocates self-defense as he writes, "The law of nature, and all law, human and divine, justify self-defense when life is in danger. It cannot surely be the intention to teach that a father should sit by coolly and see his family butchered by savages, and not be allowed to defend them. Neither natural nor revealed religion ever did, or even can, inculcate this doctrine."[33]

---

28. See *Barnes' Notes on the Bible* at biblehub.com/commentaries/matthew/5-41.htm.

29. Keener, *New Testament*, 59.

30. MacArthur, *MacArthur Study Bible NKJV*, 1402.

31. MacArthur, *MacArthur Study Bible NKJV*, 1402. The blow on the right cheek, Keener writes, was the most grievous insult in the ancient world (apart from inflicting serious physical harm), and in many cultures was listed alongside the "eye for an eye" laws. Both Jewish and Roman law permit prosecution for this offense.

32. See *Matthew Henry's Commentary* on Matt 5 at https://biblehub.com/commentaries/mhc/matthew/5.htm.

33. See *Barnes' Notes on the Bible* on Matt 5:41 at biblehub.com/commentaries/matthew/5-41.htm.

MacLaren's Exposition looks at Christ's command in the perspective of love. The Christian should still love in the face of insults, wrongs, and domineering tyranny. MacLaren argues that "if the cheek is turned, or the cloak yielded, or the second mile trudged with a lowering brow, and hate or anger boiling in the heart, the commandment is broken."[34] In northern Nigeria there are cases where people are pacifists because they can do nothing about the persecution—but rather than love, they harbor anger. For example, Ezra M. in an interview with me confessed that his pacifism was because he could do nothing. He was a pacifist with bitterness in his heart. In this case, these kinds of believers have already avenged in their hearts. MacLaren also argues that if yielding is going to make the evildoer more vicious, then resistance becomes a form of love for the sake of the wrongdoer and helpless persons who would be exposed to evil and a duty for the sake of the society.[35]

Comparing the firm responses of Jesus and Paul to injustices against them (John 18:23–23; Acts 23:2–5), and their responses in other circumstances (John 8:40–44; Acts 16:37; 22:25; 25:11; 26:25) in which they did not retaliate in their own interest, demonstrates that Matt 5:38–42 does not rule out all forms of resistance. "Persecuted Christians should respond with love and kindness. . . . We must resist injustice and refuse to comply with demands that compromise justice; but we must do so in kindness and love, not with violence or retribution."[36]

The discussion above establishes that Christ was not condemning the law as given by Moses but was trying to cut the excesses of leaders of the Jews for introducing personal vengeance to the law of retribution. The Pauline letters reinforce this. Paul in 1 Cor 6:1–11 admonished believers not to take fellow believers to court; instead, cases that had to do with fellow believers should be settled within the church. Paul assumed that church elders would always be truthful and unbiased in the settlement of conflicts involving believers. What about cases that involve believers and nonbelievers? From the analysis of this passage, I hold the following opinion. First, if the offense is life threatening or if left untreated would bring further harm to other people and society, it should be settled in a court of law, as the government is responsible for the protection of the lives of citizens involved in the case. Second, if it is a personal matter, Paul advised, "Why do you not rather

---

34. See *MacLaren's Expositions* on Matt 5:43 at https://biblehub.com/commentaries/matthew/5-43.htm.

35. See *MacLaren's Expositions* on Matt 5:43 at https://biblehub.com/commentaries/matthew/5-43.htm.

36. See IVP New Testament Commentary on Matt 5:41 at https://www.biblegateway.com/resources/ivp-nt/Love-Even-Your-Oppressors.

accept wrong? Why do you not rather let yourselves be cheated?" (v. 7) This by implication agrees with Christ's command not to resist the evil person. Christians in northern Nigeria should continue to turn the other cheek in matters of interpersonal relationships, but where rape, torture, murder, and genocide are involved, they should stand with the weak and vulnerable to resist the evil person as much as they can.

Matthew 5:43–45b

> You have heard that it was said, "Love your neighbor and hate your enemy." But I tell you, love your enemies and pray for those who persecute you, that you may be children of your Father in heaven.

Loving or hating the enemy in this passage is important when dealing with responses to persecution, particularly in cases like those of northern Nigeria. In some cases, a Christian may know the person in the attack who killed his friend or close relation or may know those who pursued him so that he narrowly escaped death. Also, sometimes a woman may know the man who raped her or the old man who directed the youths to come and burn down their house. After the crisis, they come back to live as neighbors on the same street. It takes the grace of God to forgive and love such a person. That is why this passage is important for Christians in northern Nigeria. The passage above and its parallel in Luke 6:27–28 enjoin believers to love not only their neighbors but also their enemies, to pray for them, and to do good to them. The law of Moses in Lev 19:18 emphasized the love of neighbors, but the clause "and hate thine enemy" is not found in the Scripture.[37] This rabbinic addition is what Jesus was dealing with and not the law as such.[38]

Commenting on this passage, the *Pulpit Commentary* commentators do not see anything wrong with the additional clause as far as the nation of Israel is concerned. The clause is seen from one point of view as a "legitimate deduction" from the law and represents the summary of the sense of the law.[39] It further states, "The primary sense . . . of the whole precept is love to an Israelite, hatred to a non-Israelite (cf. Deuteronomy 25:17–19). As such, the precept was of value in cementing the unity of the nation and preventing greater exposure to the evils, moral and religious, found

---

37. See *MacLaren's Expositions* on Matt 5:43–48 at https://biblehub.com/commentaries/matthew/5-43.htm.

38. See *Elliott's Commentary for English Readers* at biblehub.com/commentaries/matthew/5-43.

39. See *Pulpit Commentary* on Matt 5:43–48 at https://biblehub.com/commentaries/matthew/5-43.htm.

outside it."⁴⁰ The writers argue rather that the clause of hating the enemy created an exclusive nation that was unwilling to extend the love of God to gentile nations. Jesus sought to correct such anomalies with the parable of the Good Samaritan wherein the enemy becomes the good neighbor that loved (Luke 10:29–37).

Love from the perspective of a believer comprises two kinds. The first is when you love someone and approve of their conduct, and the second is to wish a person well, though you do not approve of their conduct.⁴¹ In loving the enemy, responsibility is placed upon the believer to discern between the enemy to be loved and the conduct to be hated. The enemy to be loved in this passage includes those who curse and persecutors who "despitefully use you." Enemies are to be prayed for and blessed. The experiences many Christians are having in northern Nigeria are painful. Jesus, with teaching to love the enemy, had similar experiences. He forgave and loved his enemies. Christians in northern Nigeria should learn from Christ and walk the path of forgiveness and love the enemy.

Romans 12:14, 17–21

> *Bless those who persecute you; bless and do not curse. . . . Do not repay anyone evil for evil. Be careful to do what is right in the eyes of everyone. If it is possible, as far as it depends on you, live at peace with everyone. Do not take revenge, my dear friends, but leave room for God's wrath, for it is written: "It is mine to avenge; I will repay," says the Lord. On the contrary: "If your enemy is hungry, feed him; if he is thirsty, give him something to drink. In doing this, you will heap burning coals on his head." Do not be overcome by evil but overcome evil with good.*

The background of this passage may relate to Jesus' teaching about not repaying evil for evil in Matt 5:39. Paul's elaboration of Christ's teaching on the treatment of the enemy provides lessons for Christians in northern Nigeria on how to respond to persecutors. By the time of Paul's writing, the teachings of Jesus were already circulating orally. According to Keener, some teachers of the Jews had already recommended non-retaliation, and among Greco-Roman politicians and some Jews, this was a virtue. He adds, "Stoic philosophers opposed seeking revenge; they believed that fate was

---

40. See *Pulpit Commentary* on Matt 5:43–48 at https://biblehub.com/commentaries/matthew/5-43.htm.

41. See *Barnes' Notes on the Bible* on Matt 5:44 at https://biblehub.com/commentaries/matthew/5-44.htm.

sovereign, and one's best resistance to fate was to cooperate with it and refuse to allow one to be manipulated by circumstances."[42]

When Paul wrote to the Romans to "bless those who persecute you," the church was not yet experiencing persecution by Roman authorities, although the Neronian persecution was soon to break out. That does not mean that there was no persecution at all. It was happening on a private scale.[43] The four "do not" commands in this Rom 12 passage show there was something serious happening that believers needed to respond appropriately. Paul instructed: "Do not curse," "do not repay evil with evil," "do not take revenge," and "do not be overcome by evil." Believers are not only to show kindness to fellow believers and friends, but they must not harbor anger against enemies.[44]

This is the most critical statement in this passage that needs explanation: "If it is possible, as far as it depends on you, live at peace with everyone." When you look at the statement on the surface, it seems to suggest that when you are overstretched, you can fight back, or it is left to you to choose whether to live at peace. MacLaren in his *Expositions* contends that the meaning goes deeper. He states, "Be you at peace with all men whether they are at peace with you or not. Don't you quarrel with them even if they will quarrel with you. That seems to me to be plainly the meaning of the words."[45] Reconciliation and peace in a quarrel has two parts, your part and that of your opponent. This passage seems to insist that on your part you must try to live in peace, even if your opponent continues to harass you.

MacLaren further observes in this instruction: "It does not follow that there is never to be opposition. It may be necessary for the good of the opponent himself, and for the good of the society, that he should be hindered in his actions of hostility, but there is never to be bitterness; and we must take care that none of the devil's leaven mingles with our zeal against the evil."[46] MacLaren here tries to guide against blind pacifism and sees wisdom in attempting to defend the defenseless in the face of aggression, injury, and threat to life. Believers should be able to fight injustice without harboring bitterness.

---

42. Keener, *New Testament*, 449–50.

43. See *Cambridge Bible for Schools and Colleges* at biblehub.com/commentaries/romans/12-14.htm.

44. See *Matthew Henry's Commentary* on Rom 12:17–18 at biblehub.com/commentaries/mhc/romans/12.htm.

45. See *MacLaren's Expositions* on Rom 12:17–18 at https://biblehub.com/commentaries/romans/12-17.htm.

46. See *MacLaren's Expositions* on Rom 12:17–18 at https://biblehub.com/commentaries/romans/12-17.htm.

Matthew Henry's comment on "do not be overcome by evil" beautifully concludes this discussion as he writes, "The last verse suggests what is not easily understood by the world; that in all strife and contention, those that revenge are conquered, and those that forgive are conquerors."[47] Jesus conquered not by destroying his enemies but by dying on the cross and being the greatest conqueror of all ages. Christians in northern Nigeria, by implication of the passage interpreted above, should be proactive in the treatment of the enemy and design programs and projects that will show the Muslims that the Christians they maltreat still love them. In this way, the light of Christ will shine brightly and attract some to the kingdom.

Matthew 10:23

> When you are persecuted in one place, flee to another. Truly I tell you, you will not finish going through the towns of Israel before the Son of Man comes.

The persecution of Christians in northern Nigeria has caused the movement of many Christians across the country and to neighboring countries for safety, including Chad, Niger, and Cameroon. Christ permitted the apostles to flee, and by implication, Christians in northern Nigeria can flee for safety but should remember the primary motivation for the flight is mission. In the passage above, MacArthur is of the opinion that it has "eschatological significance that goes beyond the disciples' immediate mission. The persecutions he describes seems to belong to the tribulation period that precedes Christ's second coming, alluded to in v. 23."[48] Keener reinforces the idea of the eschatological dimension of this command: "A Jewish tradition that may have been in circulation in Jesus' day warns that in the time of final tribulation, Jewish people persecuted for their faith would have to flee from one city to another. The disciples may have understood Jesus' words in these terms."[49]

The instruction to flee when persecuted had a purpose. John Gill posits, "Flee ye into another; not so much for their own safety, though this, according to the circumstances of things, is lawful, but for further spreading of the Gospel."[50] If Jesus was encouraging his disciples to run for fear, he would have contradicted his instruction when he told the disciples

---

47. See *Matthew Henry's Commentary* on Rom 12:17-21 at biblehub.com/commentaries/mhc/romans/12.htm.

48. MacArthur, *MacArthur Study Bible NKJV*, 1410.

49. Keener, *New Testament*, 72.

50. See *Gill's Exposition of the Entire Bible* at https://biblehub.com/commentaries/matthew/10-23.htm.

not to fear those who can kill the body and cannot do anything with the soul (Matt 10:28). The scattering of the disciples during the early persecution of the church that resulted in the planting of the church in Antioch exemplifies this type of response to persecution (Acts 11:19–21). Paul's ministry was also characterized by these missionary movements because of his response to persecution. He fled when persecuted, which resulted in the planting of new churches.

If the disciples followed this method of spreading the gospel, they would not have gone through all the cities of Israel before the coming of the Son of Man. The coming of the Son of Man is argued to be the destruction of Jerusalem in AD 70. Thus, "the passage in Luke 21, which is to a great extent parallel to this, treats the destruction of Jerusalem; and no one who carefully weighs our Lord's words can fail to see that in real sense he came in the destruction of Jerusalem."[51] The command to preach the gospel to all nations has made the command of flight for the sake of spreading the gospel relevant to contemporary believers. By implication, Christians in northern Nigeria who flee to places of safety should be mindful of their mission to the new places that they have found themselves—in parts of Nigeria and in other countries of the world.

HISTORICAL RESPONSES TO PERSECUTION IN THE EARLY CHURCH

Having examined Jesus and his teaching about responding to persecution, this section examines how the early church responded to persecution. There are divergent opinions about the validity of persecution in the early church that are not within the scope of this argument.[52] For the purposes of this discussion, I accept the historical records of the early church as depicting accurate descriptions of persecution that occurred and the response of the early church. This section of the research features a brief historical discussion on persecution in the early church as an overview of the historical narrative of events. This leads to types of persecution and the reason why early Christians were persecuted. Together, this overview and examination of types and reasons provide a solid background to enable fruitful discussion of the responses to persecution in line with Penner's theoretical framework of fight, flight, and fortitude. Finally, the positive and negative impacts of early Christian responses to evangelism and discipleship are discussed.

---

51. See *Cambridge Bible for Schools and Colleges*, commentary on Matt 10:23, at https://biblehub.com/commentaries/matthew/10-23.htm.

52. See appendix L for the arguments.

PERSECUTION IN THE EARLY CHURCH

The importance of history is to reflect on the past. This reflection helps a person live a better life today and prepare for the finest tomorrow through incorporating aspects of history that are positive and avoiding those that are negative. The history of persecution and responses of early Christians herein is intended to help Christians in northern Nigeria in their personal experience of persecution, to learn lessons from the past and avoid pitfalls in their responses to persecution. The periods of the persecution of the church in the Roman Empire are traditionally accepted to be under ten Roman emperors: Nero (c. 64–68), Domitian (81–86), Trajan (112–17), Marcus Aurelius (161–80), Septimius Severus (202–10), Maximus the Thracian (235–38), Decius (250–51), Valerian (257–59), Aurelian (270–75), and the culmination occurring with Diocletian and Galerius (303–24). Constantine made Christianity a legal religion, which ended the persecutions. The first phase is Jewish persecution of Christians, the second phase is Nero's persecution of AD 64, the third Trajan's, and the fourth Decius's to the Great Persecution of Diocletian and Galerius. The justification for these phases is that each is a unique stage in the development of persecution of Christians in the Roman Empire, up until the time when Christianity was fully legalized. These phases also illustrate the various degrees of Roman authority involvement in the persecution of Christians.

First Phase: Jewish Persecution from Birth of the Church to AD 64

The uniqueness of this phase is that persecution was mostly by Jews who still considered Christians a Jewish sect. Roman authorities protected Christians in the bid to restore law and order in the Jewish communities, whether at home or in the diaspora. At this stage, there was no persecution of Christians by the Roman authorities.

Jesus came into the world within the context of Judaism and the church was birthed in the same context. When it emerged, both the Jews and the Christians thought of it as a sect within Judaism, hence the reference to Christianity as "the way" (Acts 22:4). Until around AD 135, when the clear line of distinction between the two religions was drawn, Judaism and Christianity were still considered to be the same religion.

The persecution of early Christians began with the apostles and Christians of the apostolic period and was by the Jews. Peter and John were arrested for healing a cripple and they were beaten and warned not to preach in the name of Christ again. They rejoiced for being "counted worthy to suffer persecution for the sake of Christ" (Acts 5:40–41). Stephen was stoned to death (Acts 7:57–58). Saul of Tarsus persecuted Christians even in foreign lands (Acts 9:1, 2). Herod killed James (Acts 12:1, 2) and arrested and imprisoned Peter with the intention to kill him, but God intervened. The ministry of Paul and his associates was replete with persecution. Paul and Barnabas were persecuted in Iconium (Acts 14:1–6) and fled to Lystra and Derbe where they performed a miracle of healing on a cripple. Paul and Barnabas were beaten, and Paul was left half-dead (Acts 14:19). Paul and Silas were again beaten publicly and imprisoned in Philippi (Acts 16:22–23). Paul experienced serious opposition in Ephesus (Acts 19:24, 28–30). His final arrest in Jerusalem and subsequent trial and movement to Rome attest to the difficult experiences of the apostolic church by Jews and unbelieving gentiles.

Persecution in the first three decades after the death and resurrection of Christ was largely a fratricidal clash between rival Jewish groups, and Christianity was considered one of them. W. H. C. Frend emphasizes that "this element continued to be represented strongly until at least the end of the second century."[53] Buttressing this point, Adolf Harnack affirms that "the Synagogues, together with individual Jews, carried on the struggle against Christianity by acts of hostility and by inciting hostility."[54] By inciting hostility, it meant that even during persecutions that involved the Roman state, Jewish leaders continued to incite hostility by providing false information to the Roman authorities against Christians.[55]

Christianity, even after the fall of Jerusalem, continued to be seen by both Jews and Roman authorities as a Jewish sect. The influence of Christianity in Palestine was dealt a deadly blow that shifted its influence beyond Palestine. Frend remarks, "From scattered evidence of the Rabbinic sources, we can trace how, in the thirty or forty years after the fall of Jerusalem, the Christians in Palestine faded into a despised and dwindling heretical sect of Nazoreans."[56] With the loss of Palestine as Christianity's base and the shift to gentile nations, it was now straightforward for Judaism to define a clear distinction between the two religions. The first step was to reconstruct the canon of Jewish Scripture to exclude the Gospels. To further confirm that the Jews and Christians were no more linked together, Rabbi Samuel the Lesser added the following phrases to the traditional Jewish malediction:

53. Frend, *Martyrdom and Persecution*, 116.
54. Harnack, *Expansion of Christianity*, 2:115.
55. See appendix L for the arguments. With the fall of Jerusalem in AD 70, the Jews could not continue direct attacks against the Christians, but their influence continued throughout the empire in the form of malicious charges against the Christians.
56. Frend, *Martyrdom and Persecution*, 134.

"Let the Christian (*notzrim*) and the heretics (*minim*) perish as in a moment. Let them be wiped out of the book of life and with the righteous let them not be written."[57] This benediction was ordered by Gamaliel to be recited by the Jews three times a day. In Frend's view, the separation between the religions of the Jews and the Christians was now complete.[58]

It should be noted, according to Frend, that "not until 64, when the conflagration at Rome forced Nero to find his scapegoat among those whom popular opinion associated with the fiery extinction of the world, does the Empire take cognizance of the new religion that had arisen in Palestine."[59] The clear distinction between Judaism and Christianity, with its distinguishing features as noted by the Roman authorities, designated it for persecution. Harnack comments, "Once Christianity presented itself in the eyes of the law and the authorities as a religion distinct from Judaism, its character as a *religio illicita* was assured."[60] The Romans respected ancient established religions, as the Jewish religion was considered, which was why the Jews were not experiencing persecution. The Christians were seen as a group that had deserted their ancient religion and, as such, should not continue to enjoy the favor they had when considered a Jewish sect.[61] This understanding of Christianity and what it represents directs the discussion to the second phase of the persecution of Christians: the Neronian Persecution.

Second Phase: The Neronian Persecution

The Neronian phase is unique in that it was the first encounter of persecution with the Roman government that involved the emperor. There was no official edict proscribing Christianity or the Christians as illegal. It was the sheer cruelty of Nero using the persecution of Christians to cover his atrocities.

Most accessible accounts begin the history of Roman persecution of early Christians with Emperor Nero, who wanted to rebuild the imperial city of Rome and decided to burn a significant part of the city on July 19, AD 64. Nero, finding a scapegoat in the Christians who were already hated for their faith, blamed them for the fire.[62] The people of Rome vented their anger on the Christians by killing many of them. Though this was not an empire-wide persecution, it was the first to involve the state in the

57. Frend, *Martyrdom and Persecution*, 134.
58. Frend, *Martyrdom and Persecution*, 134.
59. Frend, *Martyrdom and Persecution*, 116.
60. Harnack, *Expansion of Christianity*, 2:116.
61. Ste. Croix, *Christian Persecution, Martyrdom*, 8.
62. Workman, *Persecution in Early Church*, 21.

persecution of Christians. Peter and Paul were most likely martyred during the Neronian persecution.[63]

Publius Cornelius Tacitus (52–120), the Roman historian and governor of the province of Asia at the time of the writing of his annals, stated that the conflagration in Rome was a result of an order from Nero the Emperor. "Consequently, to get rid of the report, Nero fastened the guilt and inflicted the most exquisite tortures on a class hated for their abominations, called Christians by the populace."[64] Tacitus further described the level of inhuman treatment of Christians. "Mockery of every sort was added to their death. Covered with the skins of beasts, they were torn by dogs and perished, or were nailed to the crosses, or were doomed to the flames and burnt, to serve as a nightly illumination, when daylight had expired."[65]

Tacitus described Nero as a very cruel man who killed his mother and brother and destroyed his guardian and tutor.[66] Tacitus was not a Christian historian, but in his writings he expressed sympathy for the sufferings of the Christians: "Hence, even for criminals who deserved extreme and exemplary punishment, there arose a feeling of compassion; for it was not, as it seemed, for the public good, but to glut one man's cruelty, they were being destroyed."[67]

Leon Hardy Canfield argues for the reliability of the Tacitus account of the persecution: "We are confronted then with the fact that Tacitus alone gives the fire as the cause of the persecution. Not only that, but every other available source on the persecution gives an explanation of the cause, which if not actually inconsistent with Tacitus, must be reconciled by most ingenious theories."[68] Canfield is not denying the Neronian persecution of Christians. His main argument is that Tacitus links the cause of the persecution to the fire in Rome of 64. He advocates that the content of Tacitus's *Annals* that connects the Neronian persecution with the fire should be discarded.[69] He believes that the Tacitus historical record is a valuable resource that should not be cast off but be used with utmost care.[70]

---

63. Foxe, *Foxe's Book of Martyrs*, 13. The martyrdom of Peter and Paul during the persecution is confirmed by Eusebius (*Hist. eccl.* 3.1).
64. Tacitus, *Complete Works*, 380.
65. Tacitus, *Complete Works*, 381.
66. Tacitus, *Complete Works*, 392.
67. Tacitus, *Complete Works*, 381.
68. Canfield, *Early Persecutions of Christians*, 56–57.
69. Canfield, *Early Persecutions of Christians*, 68.
70. Canfield, *Early Persecutions of Christians*, 69.

Canfield's argument about earlier, contemporary, and later writers not connecting the cause of the Neronian persecution to the fire is valid for scholarship, but it should be noted that given the time Tacitus was born, he must have been old enough to hear and understand stories about the fire in Rome. Tacitus trained as a lawyer, and his preparation assuredly exposed him to credible materials that would have properly informed him about the fire in Rome in 64. Another valid point is that Tacitus served as a senator and was governor at the time he wrote his annals. As a member of the inner circle of the Roman government in his time, he probably knew the official position of the Roman government with respect to the fire in connection with the Christians. To further solidify this argument, Tacitus was not a Christian writer. He even called the Christians criminals; therefore, he could not have linked the cause of the fire to Nero to favor the Christians. Considering the arguments above, I believe that the Tacitus account should be considered credible. It should be remembered that Christian persecution was not a continuous event throughout the first three hundred years of Christianity. Each of the phases identified in this section denote a unique era in the historical narrative. The next phase is the persecution that took place in the reign of Emperor Trajan.

Third Phase: Persecution during the Reign of Emperor Trajan

The third phase of the persecution of the early Christians occurred during the reign of Trajan as emperor of Rome from AD 98 to 112. It is a distinguishing persecution phase because it was the first time an emperor issued a rescript that affirmed Christianity as an illegal religion, though the rescript was not a binding law.[71] Canfield says that the rescript "is the first legal authorization of persecution or at least the first that we know anything about."[72] Pliny the Younger was made governor of Bithynia by Trajan in 110, when he had already commenced the persecution of Christians in his province. Pliny probably thought there was a law against the Christians which he did not know about. Therefore, he wanted to understand if he was doing the right thing. Mason Hammond summarizes the Pliny-Trajan correspondence:

> In one exchange, Pliny asked Trajan how he should handle the rapidly spreading sect of Christians, who, refusing to conform to normal religious practices suffered from great unpopularity but were, as far as Pliny could see, harmless. In his reply, a

---

71. Liftin, *Early Christian Martyr Stories*, 4.
72. Canfield, *Early Persecutions of Christians*, 96.

model of judiciousness, Trajan advised Pliny not to ferret out Christians nor accept unsupported charges and to punish only those whose behavior was ostentatiously recalcitrant. Clearly in Trajan's time the Roman government did not yet have (indeed, was not to have for another century) any policy of persecution of the Christians. Official action was based on the need to maintain good order, not on religious hostility.[73]

It is clear in this correspondence that Christians were not being punished for criminal offenses but for their faith. "They were no longer punished for ritual crimes of which they were supposed to be guilty; they were punished for the crime of Christianity."[74] When Christians were brought to the tribunal, Pliny would ask them—with the threat of death—whether they were Christians. When they persisted that they were still Christians, he "ordered their execution, considering that, whatever their confession of Christianity involved, their obstinacy and invincible disobedience at any rate deserved punishment."[75]

As to whether Trajan's rescript could be considered an imperial edict proscribing Christianity, Hardy is of the opinion that "to speak of Trajan's letter, therefore, as an edict either of proscription or toleration is a complete misconception of the facts. Undoubtedly, however, though a recommendation given under particular circumstances, it may safely be regarded as an index of imperial policy."[76]

Though the persecution of Christians during the reign of Trajan was not an imperial policy yet, the persecution was probably not localized to Bithynia. As Hardy writes, "In all probability, indeed, Pliny was not the only governor who consulted Trajan on the subject: the collection and publication of Pliny's letters has preserved this particular rescript, which may well have been only one among many, just as the persecution in Bithynia almost certainly, had its counterpart in other provinces."[77] Hardy's statement does not claim an empire-wide persecution but assumes that a couple of the provinces in their local context were involved in the persecution of Christians. Though Trajan's rescript has been accepted by many scholars as not an imperial law against the Christians, certainly it provided a basis for future persecutors of Christians to have a reference point.

---

73. Hammond, "Trajan," para. 9.
74. Canfield, *Early Persecutions of Christians*, 97.
75. Hardy, *Christianity and Roman Government*, 82.
76. Hardy, *Christianity and Roman Government*, 93–94.
77. Hardy, *Christianity and Roman Government*, 93.

Fourth Phase: Decius to the Great Persecution

The uniqueness of the Decius to Great Persecution phase is that there were official edicts enforcing sacrifice to the Roman gods. Christians were severely persecuted when they refused. Therefore, the persecution of Christians was made official and merely having the name "Christian" became a criminal offense. Emperor Philip had just died in battle in 249. The senate ratified Decius to succeed him, but he became emperor amid serious challenges. He had to secure the loyalty of the military in the face of an approaching, invading army making inroads along the European frontiers, a major challenge confronting the empire. Decius was also faced with economic challenges as "the economy was falling apart. Trade had collapsed and prices of basic commodities were high and rising rapidly. Taxes were soaring."[78] The question of what went wrong and how to get it fixed led Decius to the conclusion that the problem must be from the neglect of the Roman gods resulting from the influx of other religions. To solve this problem, he opted for a revival of sacrifice to the Roman gods to secure their favor to make Rome great again.

The methodology employed by Decius was to enforce paganism in the empire by requiring sacrifice to the gods throughout the empire. It should be noted that this enforcement was limited not only to Christians, but the authorities surely knew that the Christians were averse to sacrifice and worship to idols. Decius enacted an imperial edict that required "all inhabitants of the Empire to sacrifice to the gods, taste the sacrificial meat, and swear that they had always sacrificed."[79] This imperial policy distinguished this phase from the former phase in which Trajan rescript was not a binding law.

Decius wanted to be certain that sacrifices were made to the gods. Decius, according to A. D. Lee, produced certificates of compliance called *libelli* when it was discovered after some months that Christians were not performing sacrifices.[80] Following is an example of a *libellus* that survived from Egypt:

> To those appointed to oversee the sacrifices, from Aurelius Sakis, from the village of Theoxenis, with his children Aion and Heras, staying in the village of Theadelphis. We have always sacrificed to the gods and now too in your presence in accordance with the decree we have offered sacrifice and have poured a libation and we have eaten of the sacrificial offering, and we ask you to undersign. May you continue to prosper.

78. Stark, *Triumph of Christianity*, 141.
79. Stark, *Triumph of Christianity*, 142.
80. Lee, *Pagans and Christians*, 50.

{2nd hand} We, Aurelius Serenus and Aurelius Hermas, saw you sacrificing.

{1st hand} The Year 1 of the Emperor Caesar Gaius Messius Quintus Trajan Decius, devout, blessed, Augustus, Pauni 23 {17 June 250}[81]

From the empire-wide edict that involved people of all religions, it could be deduced that Decius was not primarily intending to persecute Christians. Like Trajan, he could not understand why these Christian refused a simple request to sacrifice to the gods in addition to their own religion. This "stubbornness" of Christians offended the emperor. Leaders were targeted in this persecution. Rodney Stark reports:

> The bishops of Rome and Antioch were tortured and executed almost at once. The bishops of Jerusalem and of Antioch died in prison. Efforts to arrest Dionysius in Alexandria and Cyprian in Carthage failed when both went underground. But some ordinary Christians also were seized, including harmless elderly women such as Apolonia of Alexandria, who had all of her remaining teeth smashed out before being burned alive.[82]

The persecution did not last long because Decius soon died in battle. His son Valerian, who continued the persecution, was captured in battle by the Persians and died from great torture. His grandson Gallienus in 260 became the emperor and was favorable to the Christians, repealing all the anti-Christian policies. Stark pointed out the probability of the influence of Salonia, wife of Gallienus, on his favorable disposition to the Christians. Christians enjoyed freedom, honor, and prosperity for a couple years.[83]

The hornet of persecution was to be stirred once again in 303 when Emperor Diocletian and others in his government initiated the Great Persecution. In this persecution, Christians were brutally tortured and killed. This empire-wide persecution went on for a few years in some provinces, while continuing for a decade in others.[84] Stark argues that it is unwarranted to persist in blaming Diocletian for initiating the Great Persecution. He states that the following facts back up his claim: "Both Diocletian's wife and daughter were Christians. In addition, Diocletian had allowed Christians to build a large new church directly facing his palace (Diocletian resided in Nicomedia). Finally, he did nothing to upset the 'peace of

---

81. Lee, *Pagans and Christians*, 51.
82. Stark, *Triumph of Christianity*, 143.
83. Stark, *Triumph of Christianity*, 144.
84. Liftin, *Early Christian Martyr Stories*, 6.

Gallienus' during his first twenty years on the throne."[85] Instead of blaming Diocletian, Stark prefers that Galerius, who was a "fanatical pagan," should be blamed for initiating the Great Persecution. Diocletian did succumb to pressure and presided over some tortures.[86] When Diocletian was incapacitated, Galerius acted on his behalf and probably signed the edict against the Christians on the behalf of Diocletian.

The Diocletian edicts revealed four phases of the Great Persecution. First, churches should be ruined and Scriptures burned. The church directly opposite the Diocletian palace in Nicomedia was looted and destroyed. Christians in positions of honor were to be degraded. Second, presbyters should be imprisoned. Third, presbyters should by torture be compelled to sacrifice. The fourth edict required all Roman citizens, including clergy and laity, to worship Roman gods; those who did not were tortured and killed.[87]

Galerius succeeded Diocletian in 305 and continued the persecutions, but in 311 while on his deathbed, he revoked all the decrees he promulgated against the Christians and asked them to pray for his recovery. In 313, the fires of the persecution were ended with Constantine's Edict of Milan.[88]

TYPES OF PERSECUTION IN THE EARLY CHURCH

Persecution of Christians from the inception of Christianity in the Roman Empire can be categorized into three types. Mob violence primarily was used internally in Judaism when Christianity was still being perceived as a sect within the Jewish religion. There was government initiated and sponsored persecution where Roman authorities were directly involved in the persecution of Christians. Finally, there was Christian persecution within Christianity itself when perceived heretics were persecuted by Christians.

Mob Violence

Mob violence is one of the strategies used in the persecution of Christians in northern Nigeria, as it was in early Christian persecution. Muslim youths are mobilized to go and fight for God, which typically results in the killing of many Christians and the destruction of churches and houses belonging to Christians. The mob violence is frequently planned and executed. Mark J., an ecumenical Christian leader in Borno State in northern

---

85. Stark, *Triumph of Christianity*, 145.
86. Stark, *Triumph of Christianity*, 146.
87. Eusebius, *Eusebius' Ecclesiastical History*, 307–8.
88. Liftin, *Early Christian Martyr Stories*, 6.

Nigeria, confirmed such coordination in an interview with me. During the Danish cartoon crisis in 2006 in Maiduguri, the capital of Borno, fifty-six churches were burned within forty-five minutes. This establishes evidence of a well-coordinated mob attack.

It is incomplete when authors limit the study of persecution of early Christians to martyrdom or imperial action against Christians by Roman authorities. Jewish persecution of Christians predates Roman persecution of Christians and was generally carried out by mobs who were often mobilized by envious Jewish leaders. Some persecutions of Christians by local gentile communities in the Roman Empire were carried out by mobs.[89] By reading about mob violence, the reader will understand that this approach to persecution is not new. Muslims use it to persecute Christians in northern Nigeria today.

There are several examples of mob violence in the Acts of the Apostles where such an approach was used to persecute Christians. In the case of Stephen, Jews could not tolerate hearing his argument and they agitated "the people and elders and teachers of the law" (Acts 6:12). The mob seized Stephen, brought him to the Sanhedrin, and lied by using false witnesses who said, "For we heard him say that this Jesus of Nazareth will destroy this place and change the customs Moses handed down to us" (Acts 6:14). In defense of the false charge laid against him, Stephen preached a sermon. When he finished, the mob was enraged and dragged Stephen out of the city where they stoned him to death (Acts 7:57). How were the Jews able to kill Stephen since they did not possess the power for capital punishment? Canfield is of the opinion that sometimes the Roman authorities deliberately refused to interfere in the Jewish-Christian sectarian differences,[90] which I also recognize.

Paul and his companions had several experiences of persecution using mob violence. In Iconium, they escaped a mob that was already gathering to stone them (Acts 14:5–6). They fled to Lystra, but the Jews from Antioch and Iconium followed them, stirred a mob, and "stoned Paul and dragged him out of the city, thinking he was dead" (Acts 14:19). In Ephesus, some gentiles with economic interests saw Paul's preaching and the conversion of the Ephesians as a threat to their business of producing idols (Acts 19:27–41). The Ephesians stirred up a riot against him, and the uproar of the multitude was so loud that it filled the theatre and attracted the attention of the city clerk. The clerk's address is important in understanding mob violence:

---

89. Stark, *Triumph of Christianity*, 140.
90. Canfield, *Early Persecutions of Christians*, 43.

> You have brought these men here, though they have neither robbed temples nor blasphemed our goddess. If then, Demetrius and his fellow craftsmen have a grievance against anybody, the courts are open and there are proconsuls. They can press charges. If there is anything further you want to bring up, it must be settled in a legal assembly. As it is, we are in danger of being charged with rioting because of what happened today. In that case we would not be able to account for this commotion since there is no reason for it. (Acts 19:37–40)

In mob violence, instigators often have an agenda that may be hidden or unclear to the participants. In the riot instigated by Demetrius and his colleagues, the mob caused the participants to see themselves engaged in a religious cause. Meanwhile, the instigators were protecting their personal economic interests. There have been cases in northern Nigeria where religious violence had economic roots. For instance, the Zango Kataf violence of 1992 concerned the relocation of the market. Its location in Zango Kataf was favorable to the Hausa Muslims but the indigenous Kataf townspeople, who were Christians, wanted the market relocated outside of town to benefit themselves economically.[91]

When Paul came to Jerusalem, he was persuaded by the apostles and elders to perform a Jewish ritual to absolve him of the allegation that he taught people doctrines contrary to the law. He was persuaded and entered to perform the ritual of purification. In the temple he was sighted by Jews from the province of Asia, who stirred up the people shouting, "Fellow Israelites, help us! This is the man who teaches everyone everywhere against our people and our law and this place. And besides, he has brought Greeks into the temple and defiled this holy place" (Acts 21:28). The Jews seized Paul and were about to kill him, but due to the timely intervention of the military commander and his troops, they were unable to do so.

Tertullian said, "If the Tiber floods the city, or the Nile refuses to rise, or the sky withholds its rain, or disasters occur in the shape of earthquake or famine or pestilence, the cry is raised at once '*Christianos ad leones*'" (The Christians to the lions).[92] This type of complaint, I argue, implies violent mob attack on Christians. Mob violence has been used and is still being used as an instrument of persecution of Christians.

---

91. Ukanah, *In God's Name*, 145–46.
92. Hardy, *Christianity and Roman Government*, 92.

Government-Sponsored Persecution

When it comes to government persecution, northern Nigeria differs from the Roman Empire. Nigeria is a secular state, and the Constitution of the Federal Republic of Nigeria in section 38, subsection 1, provides for freedom of religion.[93] Therefore, there is no official government persecution. However, Muslim leaders, especially in Muslim-dominated areas like northern Nigeria, use government institutions and the power vested in them to persecute Christians. Persecution of early Christians by Roman authorities is the most common type of persecution known by contemporary Christians. Discussions of these persecutions have been exaggerated to the extent that some Christians believe that Christians who lived during the first three centuries were constantly persecuted until the reign of Constantine.[94] This theory has been debunked because persecutions by the Roman government in most cases were not empire wide but local and sporadic. There were emperors who did not persecute Christians and, as such, Christians enjoyed periods of peace and prosperity, as in the reign of Gallienus previously mentioned.

Roman officials persecuted Christians not because they initially hated the religion. From their perspective, they were using persecution for the welfare and prosperity of the state. Bryan Liftin calls this a clash of worldviews. Roman authorities are simply punishing criminals they called Christians while Christians are complaining of being persecuted by Roman authorities.[95] To buttress the point of the Roman view on persecution, Canfield shares the following insight: "Persecution, viewed from the standpoint of the dominant group of society, is the preservation of ancient belief and cult from the attack of sacrilege; it is part of the august process of maintenance of the moral order."[96] It is the victim who suffers the pain that complains of persecution.

When the Roman authorities commanded sacrifices to be made to the gods, it was not only Christians under the edict but other groups as well, including Manicheans and gnostics. When Christians, because of their faith, refused to sacrifice, they were punished. There was an exception for the Jews for they did not sacrifice and were not punished, because the Jewish religion was considered an ancient religion and Romans had respect for ancient religions.

---

93. See http://www.nigeria-law.org/ConstitutionOfTheFederalRepublicOfNigeria.htm, §38.1.
94. Moss, *Myth of Persecution*, 18.
95. Liftin, *Early Christian Martyr Stories*, 7.
96. Canfield, *Early Persecutions of Christians*, 17.

In summary, according to Tacitus's historical account of the Neronian persecution, only Christians were targeted. Both government machinery and mob violence were used to attack and kill Christians. In Trajan's rescript, Christians were not to be sought out, but governors were to use their discretion to deal with each case. Christians would be executed only if they proved stubborn and refused to sacrifice. Trajan also prohibited anonymous accusations. Marcus Aurelius imperial rescripts were primarily designed "to safeguard the administration of justice and the police against the encroachments of anti-Christian mob as well as against the excesses of local councils who desire to evince their loyalty in a cheap fashion by taking measures against the Christians."[97] This appears in some extent to favor the Christians. Hadrian had rejected the popular petition "to move governor to severe measures against the Christians."[98] Pius, in some of his rescripts, prevented officials from going beyond Trajan's recommendation of not seeking out Christians. Anyone who renounced the faith was to be set free with no action against them.[99]

On the attitudes of some governors and officials, Harnack says, "Most governors or magistrates recognized that there was no occasion for them to interfere with Christians; convinced of their real harmlessness, they let go their own way."[100] He further writes, "Apart from the keen anti-Christian temper of a few proconsuls and the stricter surveillance of the city-prefects, this continued to be the prevailing attitude of the state down to the days of Decius."[101] This long period of accommodation and peace for the Christians was, however, interjected with three attempts at making some stringent policies against Christians. Marcus Aurelius "impressed upon magistrates and governors the duty of looking more strictly after extravagances in religion including those of Christianity. The results of this rescript appear in the persecution of 176–180."[102] The next attempt was that of Septimius Severus who in 202 forbade conversion to Christianity. By this, a stricter watch was kept on Christians.[103] The third attempt was by Maximinus Thrax "who ordered the clergy to be executed, which implied the duty of hunting them

---

97. Harnack, *Expansion of Christianity*, 2:117.
98. Harnack, *Expansion of Christianity*, 2:117.
99. Harnack, *Expansion of Christianity*, 2:118.
100. Harnack, *Expansion of Christianity*, 2:118.
101. Harnack, *Expansion of Christianity*, 2:118–19.
102. Harnack, *Expansion of Christianity*, 2:119.
103. Harnack, *Expansion of Christianity*, 2:119.

out—in itself a fundamental innovation in the imperial policy."[104] These three strict policy attempts were each of short duration.

Harnack also points this out: "But the comparative favour shown to Christianity, upon the other hand, by Commodus, Alexander Severus, and Philip the Arabian, led to a steady improvement in the prospect of Christianity with the passage of every decade, all the more so as the fanaticism of the mob and the repugnance shown by society towards Christians gradually declined after the opening of the third century."[105] The Roman government persecutions ended with the fiercest under Diocletian and Galerius from 303. On his deathbed, Galerius revoked the edicts against the Christians and then Constantine ended the persecutions in 315.

Persecution of Christians by Christians

There have been minor clashes, disagreements, and bickering among Christians in northern Nigeria but Nigerian Christians have not taken up arms against each other. Persecution has compelled Christians in Nigeria to unite under the umbrella of CAN, the voice of the Christians in Nigeria. Studying the Catholic-Donatist schism will help the Christian appreciate the unity and fellowship under CAN and recognize the danger of allowing internal strife within Christianity.

The Christian faith has faced fierce internal battles, probably more than external enemies. Beginning early in Christianity, differences arose from varying interpretation of Scripture, contrasting essences in liturgy and practice, power tussles, economic interests, and many other factors. It is important for the reader to understand that Christian persecution does not only come in from outside the church but also from within. Believers should be able to appropriately respond to external attacks as well as internal persecution. In early Christianity, dissident groups that were persecuted by Orthodox Christianity included Donatists, Montanists, Manichaeans, Arians, Valentinians, Marcionites, and gnostics.

REASONS FOR THE PERSECUTION OF CHRISTIANS

Having discussed types of persecution of Christians in the early church, this discussion now considers reasons why Christians were persecuted to help understand the thinking of the persecutors. At times from their own perspectives, persecutors had good reasons for their actions. However, the people groups who were suffering persecution perceived such actions as

---

104. Harnack, *Expansion of Christianity*, 2:119.
105. Harnack, *Expansion of Christianity*, 2:119–20.

injustices. Compared to northern Nigeria, there were religious, political, ethnic, and economic reasons for the persecution of Christians. Appendix D, table 3, and appendix E, table 3, reveal that the reasons for persecuting Christians in northern Nigeria are like those of the Roman Empire. They differ in that the Roman persecution did not have ethnic reasons and the Nigerian persecution does not have legal reasons, since it is not an official government persecution. This section, therefore, examines the religious, political, social, and legal reasons for the Roman persecution of early Christians.

Religious Reasons

Religion was a very important element of Roman society and government. The religious reasons for persecution in the Roman Empire compared to northern Nigeria are similar. In Islam, religion and politics are not separated. In Roman society, religion and politics were so intertwined that it was not possible to separate them, unlike the modern separation of church and state in many Western countries today. Persecution in this context will always naturally assume religious connotation. Hardy in *Christianity and the Roman Government* points out the interrelationship between the Roman government and Christianity. Thus, "the Roman religion was essentially and before all things a national religion; its object was primarily, not the honour of the gods, but the safety of the state, of which the goodwill of the gods was supposed to be the necessary condition."[106] Candida Moss in *The Myth of Persecution* adds, "It is simply anachronistic to divide ancient motivations into religious and political. They were tangled up together." She understands, "for ancient Romans, the state was both political and religious."[107] I find it contradictory for Moss to accept the fact of the intertwining of state and politics in the Roman state and still raise objection to the religious background of the persecution of early Christians by the Roman state. She writes, "It is claimed that Christians were persecuted for their religious beliefs, as if the treatment of Christians was a clean-cut case of religious persecution."[108] After agreeing that religion and politics are inseparable in the Roman society, I may ask whether Moss is trying now to introduce the separation. If religion and the state are inseparable in Roman society, then it is more logical to conclude that Christians, whose sufferings were connected to their faith, experienced religious persecution.

Arguing for the religious nature of Roman persecution of early Christians, Geoffrey de Ste. Croix's study of the early Christian persecution places

---

106. Hardy, *Christianity and Roman Government*, 3.
107. Moss, *Myth of Persecution*, 174.
108. Moss, *Myth of Persecution*, 174.

religion at the center of the persecutions. He does emphasize the importance attached to maintaining proper relationship with the gods by the inhabitants of the Greco-Roman world.[109] Based on the evidence above, I argue that one of the major reasons for the persecution of early Christians by the Roman government was religion.

Jewish persecution of early Christians also has religious reasons. When Christianity emerged, it was considered a sect within Judaism and persecution of the sect was corrective in intention.[110] The leaders of the Jews were simply punishing erring members and trying to prevent the contagious new teaching from infecting the rest of the Jews. In the same vein, the orthodox Catholic church persecuted dissenting groups as heretics to preserve the unity of the church and the purity of her doctrines.[111] Religion by its nature encompasses different leanings and aspects, then adds different interpretations of Scriptures and rituals. These divergences easily attract internal conflicts, resulting in persecution. With outsiders, it is misunderstanding that easily brings about conflicts. That is why there is need for understanding in interfaith relationships.

Political Reason

Another reason for the persecution of Christians in the Roman Empire was political. In northern Nigeria also, there are political reasons for the persecution of Christians. The political space in Nigeria is highly contested. This was the reason for the violence in 2011, popularly known by Nigerians as "postelection violence," which erupted because a Christian won the election. Christians are highly persecuted in the workplace so that they will not compete favorably in the public space with Muslims in northern Nigeria.

The persecution that had a political undertone in the Roman Empire was the Neronian persecution. Nero wanted to rebuild sections of the city of Rome and decided to set that part on fire. To escape the anger of the people, he used a dishonest political game of passing the blame to Christians, who were already hated for their perceived evils. The people of Rome vented their anger on the Christians and Nero, in a show of excessive cruelty, destroyed many Christians.[112]

Another emperor involved in the persecution of Christians was Marcus Aurelius, who ruled the Roman Empire from 161 to 180. Confronted with the plague that swept through the empire, he came to agree with the

---

109. Ste. Croix, *Christian Persecution, Martyrdom*, 15.
110. Moss. *Myth of Persecution*, 133.
111. Stark, *Triumph of Christianity*, 177.
112. Stark, *Triumph of Christianity*, 137.

explanation that the plague was a result of the neglect of the gods. The culprit blamed was a notorious group called Christians, who refused to sacrifice to the gods.[113] The motive of the persecution here is political because Marcus Aurelius was looking for a solution that would bring healing and restore prosperity to the empire.

In a similar situation in 249, Decius became emperor and came to power during a very critical period of the Roman Empire. Confronted with impending war, the European invaders were making inroads against the empire. The dwindling loyalty of the army and failing economy were a source of worry to him. Seeking for an explanation, he concluded that the gods that made Rome great were affronted and neglected. The solution was to embark on a religious revival throughout the empire, "requiring all inhabitants of the Empire to sacrifice to the gods, taste the meat and swear that they had already sacrificed."[114] To ensure compliance, *libelli* were produced and used as proof that one had sacrificed. It should be noted that it was not only Christians who were required to sacrifice, but Christians were averse to these sacrifices. Many Christians refused and suffered martyrdom though many also compromised their faith and performed sacrifices. The last case to be considered is the Great Persecution of Diocletian and Galerius, continuing the Decian persecution with the same goal of restoring a ruined empire. The same method of requiring sacrifice was adopted and different forms of severe persecutions were unleashed on the Christians who refused to sacrifice. This time, the persecution included the destruction of church buildings, burning of Scriptures, torture, and murder.[115] With Constantine, the political climate changed to favor Christians and the church.

Social Reasons

There do not appear to be social reasons for persecuting Christians in Nigeria. Christians and Muslims have always mixed in sports, marriage ceremonies, and other activities. In Nigeria, soccer is a binding force that easily brings Christians and Muslims together. After some violent religious crisis, the first place you will find Christians and Muslims mixing easily is where they gather to watch soccer. Social reasons for persecution, if there are any, are negligible.

On the contrary, there were social reasons that caused Christians to be the hated group in the Roman Empire, attracting persecution both from authorities and the people. Four issues caused the disaffection that attracted

113. Frend, *Martyrdom and Persecution*, 198–99.
114. Stark, *Triumph of Christianity*, 142.
115. Stark, *Triumph of Christianity*, 146–47.

this persecution: false allegation of incest, cannibalism, and superstition; the Christian lifestyle that contradicted a pagan lifestyle; Christian refusal to sacrifice to idols, which was perceived to bring disaster; and Christian loyalty to Christ as king instead of Caesar.

One of the issues that caused disaffection between the Christians and the Romans was the false accusation of incestuous immorality labeled on Christians. The secret Holy Communion meetings were interpreted as cannibalism because Christians were eating "the flesh and blood of Christ." In addition to the false accusation, it was difficult for pagans to interpret Christianity as a religion since they did not have gods and did not sacrifice. This misunderstanding led to the accusation of superstition and atheism, which the Romans detested as evil and criminal, and as such, the Christians were severely persecuted.[116] However, Pliny in his letter to Trajan exonerated the Christians by concluding that the accusation was baseless.[117]

Continuing the discussion on social reasons for persecution, Christian refusal to sacrifice to Roman gods resulted in friction not only with the Roman authorities but also with the masses. Christian nonparticipation in a social life that revolved around the worship of the gods portrayed them as anti-social. When there was a plague or disaster, Christians became objects of attack because they were suspected to be the cause since they refused to offer sacrifice to the gods. Stark reports such an uprising in Alexandria in 248 when pagan mobs "rampaged through the streets looting, burning, and destroying property belonging to Christians."[118] This violence against Christians happened at times without Roman authorities doing anything. The authorities were directly or indirectly supportive of the destructive violence against Christians.

Another contributing factor to social friction was the Christian worldview which influenced their lifestyle. The Christians saw themselves as strangers and pilgrims on this earth, who eagerly awaited their permanent home in heaven. They lived a new life that was a contradiction to the old life of sin, which the pagans continued to live. The writer of First Peter clearly stated the social conflict of this new life as it is lived among the pagans: "For you have spent enough time in the past doing what pagans choose to do—living in debauchery, lust, drunkenness, orgies, carousing, and detestable idolatry. They are surprised that you do not join them in their reckless, wild living, and they heap abuse on you" (1 Pet 4:3–4). First Peter was written to

---

116. Moss, *Myth of Persecution*, 181.
117. Frend, *Rise of Christianity*, 150.
118. Stark, *Triumph of Christianity*, 140.

Christians scattered all over the empire who were either facing persecution or awaiting impending persecution (1 Pet 4:12).

Legal Reasons

The persecution of Christians in northern Nigeria differs from persecution of the early Christian church in that Nigeria persecution is not government-sponsored, as it was at times in Roman society. Therefore, the Muslims cannot claim legal reasons for persecuting Christians. There were legal reasons for the persecution of Christians in the Roman Empire because the government continually became involved in the persecution of Christians. In the Roman Empire, there were already policies dealing with other religions before Christianity. Hardy writes, "Christianity was not the only foreign cult with which the government had to deal; it was not the only foreign cult with which it had to interfere."[119] Examples of cults crushed by the Roman authorities include the cult of Bacchus, the Druids, and the cult of Cybele and Isis.[120] Canfield adds that "Christianity by no means presented a new problem in the Roman state. Long before this sect was heard of, the state had developed a well-defined policy for dealing with foreign religions."[121] If the Roman government already had policies that dealt with new religions and Christianity as an emerging religion did not play by the rules, it was a crime, and Christians could legally be charged for criminal offenses. In this sense, Moss says that "Romans saw themselves not as persecutors, but prosecutors."[122]

However, there is evidence that Christians were singled out simply for being Christians. The first legal documents that became a reference point for persecution of Christians as a group by the authorities was Trajan's rescript. Though the rescript was not a binding law, subsequent Roman authorities would probably have used it as a legal basis for persecuting the Christians. The Pliny-Trajan communication established that the name "Christian" is enough crime that could be punished by death. This law existed until the time of Tertullian, when he argued in his apology: "Why do they call them unjust? Nay, if they punish a name, they are even irrational; but if they punish acts, why do this on the ground of a name alone, while in the case of others they insist that these acts be proven by evidence, not by a name" (*Apol.*

---

119. Hardy, *Christianity and Roman Government*, 2.
120. Stark, *Triumph of Christianity*, 23–27.
121. Canfield, *Early Persecutions of Christians*, 18.
122. Moss, *Myth of Persecution*, 163.

4:11).[123] Tertullian is pointing to the irrationality of punishing Christians based on a name and not on crimes committed by the Christians.

RESPONSES TO PERSECUTION

This section of the research on responses to persecution is very important to the reader because it is the core of the research. I strongly believe that proper Christian response to persecution can significantly minimize violence, improve community relationships, and aid in effective evangelization and discipleship in northern Nigeria. Responses of early Christians to persecution categorized as fight, flight, and fortitude are discussed with the aim of drawing implications for Christians in northern Nigeria.

Fight

In northern Nigeria there have been cases where young people who are Christians make reprisal attacks on Muslims who have attacked a community. This action is not acceptable and has been condemned by Christian leaders. The research data also shows that Christians from both the northeast and the Middle Belt have rejected the use of attack or vengeance as a response to persecution. (See appendices D and E, tables 4, for analysis.)

The response of fight, which is fighting the persecutor, is almost nonexistent among early Christians. Available sources on early Christian persecution accessible to me indicates that there was no effort by the Christians to fight the Roman authorities. They did not even fight the ordinary people who hated and persecuted them. Why were the early Christians not fighting back? I suggest the following possible reasons, beginning with early Christian obedience to the Scriptures. The pacifist teachings of Christ included turning the other cheek, loving the enemy, and not paying evil with evil. The teachings of the apostles expanded these teachings concerning treatment of the enemy, enduring persecution, rejoicing when persecuted, and following the footsteps of Christ in suffering (1 Pet 2:19–21). Obedience to Scriptures like these offer no place for vengeance or retaliation.

Another reason is the early Christian view on martyrdom. So many were ready to die rather than renounce their faith. Others volunteered to die to achieve the status of martyr. Frend writes, "Behind their action lies the whole theology of martyrdom in the early church. They were seeking by their death to attain to the closest possible imitation of Christ's passion

---

123. As cited in Canfield, *Early Persecutions of Christians*, 133.

and death."[124] This type of worldview that welcomes death instead of avoiding it has no room for attacks or vengeance.

A third possible reason could also be the size of the Christian population. There were not enough Christians to fight. However, this argument can be countered by the fact that there were times in some cities when Christians formed a very significant population. This is evidenced by Tertullian's boast of the growth of early Christianity, saying, "We are but of yesterday, and we have filled everything you have cities, tenements, forts, towns, exchanges, yes! And camps, tribes, palace, senate, forum."[125] Frend argues that Tertullian exaggerated the impact of Christianity in his time.[126] Yet if there was no visible growth, he would not have boasted of Christianity this way.

The only evidence of attack and vengeance I discovered in early Christianity was in the schism that involved the Catholic Church and the Donatists. The Donatist use of Circumcellion to fight their opponents proves that there were elements of attack and vengeance in early Christianity. The Circumcellion have been described as "the strange revolutionary fringe of Donatism" and portrayed as "the violent arm of the Donatist Church."[127] The way they were structured, and their deeds, might cause them today to be labeled terrorists. The Circumcellion are further described as "religious fanatics" or the "storm troopers of Donatism."[128] This group was used to attack or take vengeance against the opponents of the Donatists. On the other hand, as previously discussed, Augustine's use of Roman forces to crush the Donatists is additional evidence that attacks, and vengeance existed in some measures in the early church between different factions.

Flight

Flight, as described in this research, comprises all pacifistic responses to persecution, which can include literal flight, refusal to take revenge, or not defending oneself in the face of aggression. Christians in northern Nigeria are essentially pacifists with the largest population in the northeast. The interviews conducted by the author indicate that Christians in the northeast part of Nigeria have never used revenge or arms to defend themselves, which equates with the early Christians. There are pacifists in the Middle Belt, but in practice the majority subscribe to self-defense as a form of response to persecution. This section discusses early Christians who suffered torture and

124. Frend, *Martyrdom and Persecution*, 15.
125. Frend, "Persecution," 512.
126. Frend, *Origins to Constantine*, 512.
127. Shaw, *Sacred Violence*, 632.
128. Shaw, *Sacred Violence*, 632.

died without denying the faith. Another response discussed is those who literally fled during the persecution. Then there are those who responded with voluntary martyrdom, and finally those who responded by sacrificing and/or denying the faith. All these responses will be discussed.

The first category of pacifist responses is those who were tortured and died as martyrs of the faith. Ignatius, the bishop of Antioch, was arrested and taken to Rome for execution. What little is known of him comes from his letters to Polycarp and the churches in Ephesus, Magnesia, Tralles, Philadelphia, and Smyrna. He also sent a letter to Rome ahead of his arrival, requesting the believers in Rome not to interfere with his case in a bid to free him. He was set for martyrdom. He said, "May nothing at all, whether of this world or the invisible world above, fight against me from reaching Jesus Christ."[129] Though no written information about his end was accessible to me, it is believed Ignatius achieved his goal of becoming a martyr for Christ.

Another martyr is Polycarp, the bishop of Smyrna, a reputable leader and a godly, aged pastor who had gained respect from churches in the whole of Asia. Polycarp is said to have been a disciple of the apostle John. When the governor tried to persuade him to renounce Christ and be freed, Polycarp responded, "For eighty-six years I have been his servant, and he has done me no wrong. How could I now blaspheme my king who saved me?" He was martyred at the age of eighty-six in about 156.

The martyrdom of Christians from the village of Scilli near Carthage is probably the first experienced by North African Christians. Twelve Scillian martyrs, seven men and five women, were put to death on August 1, 180 by the governor of the African province, Vigellius Saturninus.[130] After some form of persuasion to recant their faith, these believers proved intransigent and were willing to die rather than sacrifice to idols. Liftin comments, "Their utter rejection of not only pagan worship but the very world in which they lived would become a distinctive of the North African church which was prone to fanaticism and dogmatism."[131] The Scillian martyrs became the first "seed of the church" sown on African soil.

On African soil again, one of the most celebrated martyrdoms in the early church was the aristocratic Vibia Perpetua and her slave, Christian sister, and friend, Felicitas. It is important to reference Perpetua's Montanist background that likely prepared her and her Christian sister for heroic martyrdom. Liftin writes about Perpetua's Montanist background:

129. Liftin, *Early Christian Martyr Stories*, 49.
130. Hastings, *World History of Christianity*, 25.
131. Liftin, *Early Christian Martyr Stories*, 88.

Although its beginnings under Montanus were somewhat cultish, the New Prophecy in Africa operated as a theologically orthodox and Spirit-led faction within the broader church. It claimed the material things of the world are passing away, God was speaking anew to his people, and no price—not even death—was too high to pay for the glory of Jesus's name. These are the ideals for which the smart and virtuous daughter of a pagan aristocrat found herself imprisoned in 203.[132]

Perpetua's heavenly visions and her readiness to part with earthly things, including family, children, and the comforts of life, are evidence of her Montanist faith as described above. These noble and heroic women were arrested and thrown to wild beasts in 203. The death of the two women proved that Christianity had broken the class distinction that existed between Perpetua and her slave. Perpetua's aged father's plea for her to sacrifice to idols and be free could not dissuade her, nor even the cries of her infant child. The two women were gored by a bull and later killed by gladiators.[133]

Persecution in the Roman Empire was typically sporadic. However, Christians in the cities of Lyons and Vienna in 177 experienced extreme persecution. As in some other locations in the empire, "the believers were suspected of practicing magic and committing moral atrocities, such as orgies and cannibalism."[134] Though the Christians rejected these allegations, they were severely persecuted. Liftin adds, "The vicious persecution killed Christians from the upper ranks of society all the way down to slaves. Lyon's first bishop, the elderly Pothinus, died in prison from the harsh conditions. Others died in the Amphitheater of the Three Gauls, which was part of the temple complex that hosted the annual Gallic congress."[135] The letter from believers in Lyons and Vienna to sister churches in Asia (Eusebius, *Hist. eccl.* 5.1.156–68) is the primary source of information for the persecution that took place in these Gallic cities.

A summary of the sufferings endured by believers includes Blandina, a physically weak and fragile woman. Her earthly Christian mistress was concerned that Blandina would not be able to make the bold confession of Christ. All were surprised that she not only confessed being a Christian, "Blandina was filled with such strength that her torturers, who worked in shifts from dawn to dusk tormenting Blandina with every possible method,

---

132. Liftin, *Early Christian Martyr Stories*, 92.
133. Kealy and Shenk, *Early Church and Africa*, 199–200.
134. Liftin, *Early Christian Martyr Stories*, 72.
135. Liftin, *Early Christian Martyr Stories*, 72.

were exhausted and finally gave up." All she kept confessing as she was tortured was: "I am a Christian! We don't do anything wrong."[136]

Biblis is another woman who was martyred in the persecution in Lyons and Vienna. In her case, she had denied the Lord. The Roman authorities wanted to use her to raise false allegation of cannibalism against the Christians, but she instead told the truth: "How could the Christians be guilty of eating human children, when they aren't even permitted to consume the blood of irrational animals?"[137] She then confessed to being a Christian and was killed.

Also among the martyrs of Lyons was Sanctus, who endured terrible sufferings from wicked persecutors. When the tribunal was examining Sanctus, he refused to disclose any information about himself. The answer he gave to any question he was asked was: "I am a Christian." Because he refused to say anything but his confession, his torturers were angry and applied all manner of torture that "Sanctus's frame was so mangled that he had lost any visible resemblance of a human being." He was able to endure to the end and was numbered among the martyrs. From the persecutions of Nero to the Great Persecution of Diocletian, Christians were attacked, tortured, and murdered without resistance.

The second category of pacifist responses are those who fled during the persecution. Cyprian, bishop of Carthage, fled during the Decian persecution. When he later came back, he took time to defend his action by saying that he weighed the responsibilities of his office against his personal desire for martyrdom.[138] He later came out to boldly confront death. Bishop Cyprian on September 14, 258, appeared before Galerius Maximus, who gave him the option of either denying Christ or facing death. Cyprian stood for Christ and chose the latter. Galerius ordered him to be beheaded.[139]

Frend adds a report about Gregory, who was having effective mission work in Asia Minor. He feared that his new converts might deny being a Christian if they faced the threat of persecution. He himself left the mission work and fled.[140] In addition to those who fled was Dionysius, whose flight resulted in church planting. He fled to "Cephro, an Oasis in Libya . . . he built a large Church that became the center of worship for Egyptian Christians."[141] Those who fled probably followed the instruction of the Lord

---

136. Liftin, *Early Christian Martyr Stories*, 75–76.
137. Liftin, *Early Christian Martyr Stories*, 77.
138. Gaddis, *There Is No Crime*, 38.
139. Sundkler and Steed, *History of the Church*, 23.
140. Frend, *Martyrdom and Persecution*, 305.
141. Frend, "Persecution," 516.

Jesus Christ who stated, "If they persecute you in this city, flee to another" (Matt 10: 23). Those who fled ended up spreading the gospel.

Commenting on Matt 10:23, Clement of Alexandria said it was clear in this passage that flight was advised, "though not in order that the Christian should seek to avoid death or that persecution was a bad thing, but that we should not be authors or abettors of evil, including evil to ourselves."[142] He said this to indicate his preference of flight to voluntary martyrdom. He further elaborated, "If he who kills a man of God sins against God, he who presents himself before the judgement seat becomes guilty of his death. The same was true of anyone who volunteered capture."[143] Clement's comment leads this discussion to the next category of pacifistic responses to persecution.

The third category of pacifistic responses is voluntary martyrs. Some early Christians were not afraid to die for their faith. Peter Leithart says, "They had been nurtured in the practice of courageous and often defiant witness . . . to expect to share the cross with Jesus."[144] Frend, quoting Eusebius, says that Christians suffered decapitation, punishment of fire, and more. He continues that there was a time when "the murderous axe was dulled, and worn out, and was broken into pieces while the executioners grew utterly weary. . . . Yet the volunteers of martyrdom never ceased and received 'the final sentence with gladness.'"[145] Moss in *The Myth of Persecution* cites an episode of voluntary martyrdom in Asia Minor that took place around 185 when "a mob of Christians marched to the home of C. Arrius Antoninus, the governor of Asia, and demanded to be executed. The governor sent the Christians away, telling them that if they wanted to die, they have cliffs to leap off and ropes with which to hang themselves."[146]

It is true that early Christians courted martyrdom. To them, being martyred was the means to demonstrate their supreme love for their Lord. In northern Nigeria, although there have been martyrs beheaded by Boko Haram for their faith, there is no record of voluntary martyrdom. Paul Middleton writes concerning voluntary martyrs: "To embrace death is a rush towards eternal life."[147] It is a fact that some demonstrated some form of extremism, and Cyprian condemned them for such an extreme position. It is good for one to lay down their life for the faith when the condition

---

142. Frend, *Martyrdom and Persecution*, 363–64.
143. Frend, *Martyrdom and Persecution*, 364.
144. Leithart, "Witness unto Death," 50.
145. Frend, "Persecution," 521.
146. Moss, *Myth of Persecution*, 144.
147. Middleton, "Early Christian Voluntary Martyrdom," 560.

warrants such response. I agree with Cyprian that it is not appropriate for one to go looking for death. The harvest is still plentiful, and the laborers are few. More believers should stay alive and evangelize lost souls and bring them to the kingdom rather than choosing voluntary martyrdom.

Fortitude

In this book, strength of mind and character in fortitude are considered self-defense and a response to persecution. In early Christianity, except for the Donatist Circumcellion, it is difficult to identify any case of Christians using dangerous weapons to defend themselves. Compared to northern Nigeria, there have been cases in the Middle Belt where Christians have used arms to defend themselves, such as the Shari'a violence in Kaduna in the year 2000. In some instances, as with *Kautikari* in the Chibok Local Government of Borno State, Christians organized a vigilante group that has been helpful to the community in repelling Boko Haram.

The major tools of self-defense in the early church were the writings and oral defense of the apologists. Chief among these apologists were Justin and Tertullian. Philosopher Justin Martyr argued for reason in defense of the Christians: "We demand that the charges against the Christians be investigated, and that, if these be substantiated, they be punished as they deserve. But if no one can convict us of anything, true reason forbids you, for the sake of a wicked rumor, to wrong guiltless men."[148] Justin saw injustice being done to Christians because they were not convicted but still punished for crimes against humanity, all due to a name that had been deliberately criminalized.

In the same line of argument, Tertullian argued as a professional lawyer that there should be no segregation in the treatment of Christians and other criminals if the Christians were truly criminals. He objected, "When others are accused as we are accused, they use both of their own and of hired lips to prove their innocence; they have full opportunity to answer and debate, since it is by no means permitted that they should be condemned undefended and without a hearing."[149] Christians were not given the opportunity to defend the accusations labeled against them in court. Confession of the name "Christian" was the only proof the authorities needed to punish them by torture and even death. Tertullian further commented, "You believe a Christian to be a man guilty of all crimes, an enemy of the gods, of the emperors, of the laws, of morality, and of all nature; still you compel him to deny that you may acquit him, which you could not do

148. Canfield, *Early Persecutions of Christians*, 124–25.
149. Canfield, *Early Persecutions of Christians*, 129.

had he not denied."[150] Tertullian was stating that if the name "Christian" is a criminal offense comparable to robbery or murder, you do not acquit someone you arrest for committing murder just because they turn around and confess to not being a murderer. If they do not acquit someone for mere confession of not being a murderer, then the name Christian is not a crime that warrants any punishment.

Tertullian concluded, "In our case alone you are ashamed or too conscious of error to pronounce sentence with precise designation of crimes. If the word Christian is not the name of any crime, it is indeed most absurd if there should be crime in the name alone."[151] As a legal luminary, Tertullian felt the authorities should be ashamed of such injustices they perform against the Christians. In further defense of Christians, Tertullian assured the authorities that "a Christian is an enemy to none, least of all to the Emperor of Rome, whom he knows to be appointed by God, and so cannot but love and honor."[152]

In addition, Athenagoras used philosophy to disprove the accusation of atheism against Christians by equating the monotheism of Christians with that taught by philosophers like Plato, Aristotle, and the Stoics. He wrote, "If Plato is not an atheist when he considers the one uncreated maker of the universe to be God, neither are we atheists when we recognize and affirm him to be God by whose Word all things were created, and by whose Spirit they are held together."[153] He argued that Christians were not atheists just because they do not worship visible objects, rather they worshipped the Father and creator of the universe who is invisible, immortal, and eternal. Another group that used apologetics to defend the faith were the Scillian martyrs who, when they appeared before the proconsul, defended the sound morals of the Christian faith and the submissive obedience of the Christians in all matters except sacrifice to idols. They were at the defense with the letters of Paul in case there arose a need to refer to them as evidence of what Christians believed and practiced.[154]

In conclusion, rather than violent resistance in the second and third centuries, Christians defended themselves by developing answers to their critiques using the rhetorical forms of their era. Apologists did not always agree on the methods that Christians should use. As Russell states:

---

150. Canfield, *Early Persecutions of Christians*, 131.
151. Canfield, *Early Persecutions of Christians*, 131.
152. Middleton, "Enemies," 168.
153. Frend, *Martyrdom and Persecution*, 214.
154. Hastings, *World History of Christianity*, 25.

In some cases, writers such as Justin Martyr and Clement of Alexandria sought to use the intellectual tools of their day to describe, defend, and advance early Christianity through philosophical and rhetorical concepts. Tertullian represented the opposite extreme by rejecting the use of philosophy and warning that the wisdom of the world was foolishness. He was convinced that society was corrupted by demonic powers. Irenaeus, on the other hand distanced himself from those who demonized the state. He had a more positive attitude toward the state and directed his writings toward heretics within the early communities of Christ followers. There was no consistent intellectual response by the post-Pauline communities to pagan society.[155]

This is like the present situation for the churches in northern Nigerian. There is no single response. There are some who believe in absolute pacifism, others who believe in self-defense with caution if it does not become vengeance, and still others who believe self-defense requires the use of arms, if necessary, to protect the vulnerable.

IMPACT OF RESPONSES TO PERSECUTION ON EVANGELISM AND DISCIPLESHIP

Having discussed how early Christians responded to persecution, it is important to recognize how these responses affected evangelism and discipleship in the early church. In turn, Christians in northern Nigeria have lessons to learn from early Christians to be applied to responses in this way to avoid negative responses. Responses are considered positive if they contribute to bringing souls to the kingdom; others are considered negative if they inhibit evangelism and discipleship. Positive responses to persecution include pacifistic attitudes of nonviolence in the face of aggression, endurances of torture and martyrdom, and flight that resulted in further missionary activity. Negative responses include schisms, voluntary martyrdom, and denial of the faith.

Positive Impact of Responses to Persecution

The positive responses to persecution of the early Christians can primarily be attributed to their pacifistic attitude towards persecution as they were led "as sheep to the slaughter," and that they did not resist their persecutors. Instead, there were those rejoicing to be counted among the martyrs.

---

155. Russell, *In the World*, 218.

Early Christian endurance of torture unto death resulted in the conversion of pagans and torturers to Christianity.[156]

This is comparable to the findings in interviews of Christians in northern Nigeria. Pacifism was the only response to persecution that was successful in reaching the Muslims. Recently, Reverend Lawan Andimi was captured by the Boko Haram. They wanted this well-known Christian leader to deny his faith on video. He instead preached the gospel and was subsequently beheaded. For Christians, this is a triumph of the gospel. For moderate Muslims, this is a shameful act by Boko Haram.

Concerning the pacifistic response to persecution, endurance of suffering, and the martyrdom impact on evangelism and discipleship, Stark comments:

> Accounts of martyrdom make frequent mention of pagans having gained respect for the faith from having observed, or having even taken part in, the torture of martyrs. The pagan onlookers knew full well that they would not endure such tribulations for their religion. Why could so many Christians do so? Were they missing something about the strange faith? These sorts of unease and wonderment often paved the way for new conversions.[157]

This observation of the conversion of pagans because of the way martyrs boldly confront death is reinforced by Frend. The sight of the torture of Blandina invoked thoughts that "proved to be the first stirring towards acceptance of the Christian faith." Martyr death is a reenactment of the crucifixion and death of the Savior, resulting in the salvation of mankind. Frend proves the evangelistic import of the suffering of the early Christians, as this led to the conversion of Tertullian. He writes that "the sight of men and women prepared to die rather than accept the conventional form of loyalty to the Severan age led him to Christianity."[158] Tertullian is an example of a pagan who came to Christ because of the faithful endurance of torture and martyrdom of the early Christians. His maxim was: "The blood of the martyrs is the seed of the church."

The other positive response of the early Christians is flight. The literal flight to safety, achieved with the motive of gospel expansion instead of avoiding persecution and death, is the type being discussed here. At times it is difficult to distinguish between the two motivations. It should be noted that it is possible for someone running away to avoid persecution to do exploits, to find themselves in fertile and fruitful soil doing missionary work.

156. Frend, *Martyrdom and Persecution*, 270.
157. Stark, *Triumph of Christianity*, 151–52.
158. Frend, *Martyrdom and Persecution*, 271.

A good example is Bishop Dionysius who refused to worship the Roman gods and was exiled to "Cephro, an oasis in Libya..., he built a large church that became the center of worship for Egyptian Christians."[159] This type of positive response connects to the response of the Christians in Acts 11 who were scattered because of persecution. These disciples spread the good news throughout Judea and even to gentile nations, resulting in the planting of the first gentile church in Antioch (Acts 11:19–25). Flight in the case of Dionysius resulted in a positive outcome for the gospel.

In northern Nigeria, flight has provided an opportunity for the witness of the gospel to Muslims who fled to the southern part of Nigeria. Boko Haram attacks not only Christians but also Muslims who do not adhere to their ideology. Muslims who leave the north have a greater openness to the gospel when they are no longer in a predominately Muslim territory. As fellow refugees from the north, Christians have a greater opportunity to reach Muslims who have also fled the north because of terrorists' activities.

Negative Impact of Responses to Persecution

One of the responses to persecution that negatively impacted evangelism and discipleship in early Christianity was compromise. The response of compromise was found to have similar results in northern Nigeria. Some Christians in northern Nigeria have returned to idolatry and fetishes to obtain power and protect themselves from persecution, which has had a negative impact on evangelism. Although not a response of early Christians, vengeance and reprisal attacks by Christians in northern Nigeria have also had a negative impact on evangelism and discipleship.

Those who denied the faith as their response to persecution also had a negative impact on evangelism and discipleship. "Thousands of Christians offered sacrifices to the gods rather than endure certain torture and death."[160] Pliny's letter to Trajan testified that some Christians denied ever becoming Christians and were made to recite prayer to the gods before they were released.[161] In accord, Frend specifically speaks about the apostates of the North African church: "At Carthage, there was mass apostasy. The crowd of would-be sacrificers was so great that the priest begged them to return the next

---

159. Frend, "Persecution," 516.
160. Kealy and Shenk, *Early Church and Africa*, 202.
161. Hyldahl, *History of Early Christianity*, 271.

day."[162] Kalu Ogbu adds that Bishop Cyprian said that Christians trampled each other to obtain *libelli* compliance certificates.[163]

Describing the level of compromise of certain Christians, Ste. Croix remarks, "Some Christians successfully deceived the authorities by inducing pagans to impersonate them at the ceremony of sacrificing, or by sending their own slaves (some of them Christians themselves) to sacrifice in their stead."[164] When Christians compromise or deny their faith in this way, it is difficult to reach unbelieving neighbors. If they do, there can scarcely be meaningful impact because these Christians have lost the message and integrity before the unsaved.

Another form of response to the persecution of early Christians that had a negative impact on evangelism and discipleship was the Catholic-Donatist schism over the position of lapsed priests and bishops. In attempting to address the problem, nomenclatures were used: Those who died for the faith attained the status of martyrs. Those who suffered and were eventually not put to death were named "confessors," while the lapsed were labeled *traditores*. A schism started between "the Catholics, who were prepared not to provoke the authorities, and their opponents, for whom martyrdom was the highest Christian good."[165] There were also the rigorists who insisted that "anyone who had been guilty of cooperating with the persecution could not hold office, anyone ordained by them had dubious orders."[166] This tension gave birth to the Donatist movement, which claimed that the church should be pure. "Donatus claimed that his Church was the Catholic Church in Africa, 'sanctified by the martyrs and purified from its errors by their leader Donatus.'"[167] Augustine later stamped out Donatism as a heresy.[168]

It was almost impossible to have meaningful evangelism and discipleship during the schism, as the Donatists used "terrorists" in the name of Circumcellion to attack the Catholics, and Augustine used Roman forces to crush the Donatists. The response of confessors concerning the lapse in Gaul differed from the Donatists in that the confessors "did not boast over the fallen but shed tears in their behalf to the Father, praying for life, and he

---

162. Frend, "Persecution," 514. There were bishops who apostatized. Examples of such are Repostus of Abitina, Paul of Cirta, and Mensurius of Carthage.

163. Kalu, *African Christianity*, 53. *Libelli* was a certificate given to apostates to prove that they sacrificed to idols.

164. Ste. Croix, *Christian Persecution, Martyrdom*, 63.

165. Frend, *Martyrdom and Persecution*, 521.

166. Middleton, "Enemies," 179.

167. Sundkler and Steed, *History of the Church*, 27.

168. Sundkler and Steed, *History of the Church*, 26.

gave it to them" (Eusebius, *Hist. eccl.* 5.2). This should be the right disposition of a Christian to a fallen sister or brother.

Voluntary martyrdom also presented a response that had negative impact on evangelism and discipleship. Some early Christians voluntarily offered themselves to be killed even when they were not sought out and arrested. Some went to the authorities and presented themselves as Christians so that they could be killed to be listed among the martyrs. Ste. Croix says that Clement condemned the practice of voluntary martyrdom in the "most vigorous terms." Clement further "rebukes volunteers with most ingenious argument: they become accomplices in the crime of those who put them to death."[169] The voluntary martyr response negatively affected evangelism and discipleship, according to Jesus saying, "The harvest is truly plentiful, but the laborers are few" (Matt 9:37). These bold disciples of Christ who could volunteer to die, in my opinion, could have been effective frontier missionaries if they had continued to live.

IMPLICATIONS FOR CHRISTIANS IN NORTHERN NIGERIA

The chapter concludes by drawing implications from the foregoing discussion on fight, flight, and fortitude. What implications should Christians in northern Nigeria draw from biblical, historical, and theological responses to persecution?

First, fight involves a Christian carrying out vengeful attacks against their enemies. Typically, those who claim that the Bible encourages violence use the Old Testament for support. Note that in the Old Testament, the nation of Israel was not dealing with personal enemies, dispelling Old Testament personal vengeance justification. The gentile nations were essentially enemies of God due to their abominable and evil practices. God was using Israel to deal with his enemies. In the section on biblical response, I focused on the New Testament, which encourages loving the enemy and doing good to them. There is no passage in the New Testament that encourages vengeance or an attack. The early Christians in their responses never attacked persecutors. The example in the Catholic-Donatist case shows how vengeance brought about divisions in the church which in turn had negative impact on the credibility of the church.

This implies that Christians in northern Nigeria should never get involved in attacking their enemies or carrying out reprisal attacks on Muslims. Some of the Muslims are innocent of the evils perpetrated against the

---

169. Ste. Croix, *Christian Persecution, Martyrdom*, 158.

Christians in northern Nigeria. Attacks and revenge will never encourage evangelism and discipleship, but rather discourage them. Loving the enemy and doing good to them are essential in winning enemies to Christ.

The second implication is pacifism. The pacifistic enemy-treatment passages in the New Testament, including "turning the other cheek," "going the extra mile," and "releasing the other piece of cloth," have popularized pacifism as the only valid response of Christians to persecution. The pacifist actions of early Christians to persecution—how they endured without resisting their enemies and how some fled instead of putting up some resistance—all contributed to pacifism being the solitary way to respond to persecution. The discussions above show that in the New Testament, the Bible is in full support of Christian pacifism as an approach to confronting the enemy. Historically, early Christians were absolute pacifists who either endured torture and martyrdom or fled. An exception was Augustine, who advocated the just war theory.

Dietrich Bonhoeffer was a pacifist. Though he later changed to resistance, he did so against the Nazi government and not against personal enemies. In relation to personal enemies, in my opinion, Bonhoeffer must have remained a pacifist. This is evident in a prison letter to Eberhard Bethge where Bonhoeffer expresses, "It is only when God's wrath and vengeance are hanging as grim realities over the heads of one's enemies that something of it means to love and forgive can touch our heart."[170] In addition, Christiane Tietz argues that "Bonhoeffer does not reach the conclusion that there are situations in which it is permissible to kill, that is, act in disobedience to the Fifth Commandment."[171] Bonhoeffer saw his action against Adolf Hitler as an extraordinary situation because of the millions of people targeted for massacre. Bonhoeffer could still advocate love and forgiveness for the enemy while in prison, and also saw his involvement in the attempt to assassinate Hitler as an extraordinary case. It was only in this case that he took such a radical decision, because of the millions of lives involved. He did not write anything later that contradicted his earlier *Cost of Discipleship*, where he taught pacifism based on the Sermon on the Mount in Matt 5.

Christians in northern Nigeria who were pacifists in the 1970s and 80s should go back and embrace the pacifist Christian virtue. It would be helpful in carrying out evangelism and discipleship in the region. As biblical, historical, and theological as pacifism is, it still leaves Christians in northern Nigeria with unanswered questions. What about the mass murder going on in Christian villages in the Middle Belt of Nigeria? Should the Christians

---

170. Bethge, *Friendship and Resistance*, 157.
171. Tietz, *Theologian of Resistance*, 86.

flee? To where will they flee? Presently, churches and Christian families are overstretched trying to cope with the care of the Christians who have already fled and are in refugee camps by the thousands. Can Christians defend themselves when they have a sizeable population to put up some resistance against persecutors? This leads to the last implication.

The third implication for Christians in northern Nigeria is self-defense. Unlike pacifism, which has been studied and, in some Christian denominations, incorporated into church doctrine, self-defense may be called "a child of necessity." In the face of extreme violence, mass murder, and wanton destruction that characterize contemporary Christian persecution, Christians are forced to consider defending themselves in the face of apparent genocide. If we reexamine previous discussions, we will find that there are no direct passages in the New Testament instructing Christians to defend themselves. However, most commentators on the passages of "turning the other cheek" and "not resisting the enemy" interpret these as addressing interpersonal relationships and not war or genocide. Historically, early Christians were involved in self-defense apologetically, as they defended the faith and argued logically against injustices done to them.

The case study of Bonhoeffer provides an example of one committed to a pacifist response to persecution but finding under certain circumstances that Christians must resist. His case is a valuable contribution to the ongoing discussion in the northern Nigerian church as to whether self-defense is a legitimate response to persecution.

In a conference in Denmark in 1934, Bonhoeffer was asked what he would do if war came. "I shall pray to Christ to give me the power not to take up arms."[172] This statement underscores his earlier beliefs in pacifism. The pacifistic ideas of Bonhoeffer are articulated in *The Cost of Discipleship*, Bonhoeffer's book on Christ's Sermon on the Mount. His commentary on Matt 5:5 states, "'This community of strangers' referring to the meek, 'possess no inherent right of its own renounce every right of their own and live for the sake of Christ.'"[173] Disciples of Christ endure all manner of maltreatment and injustice and do not defend their legal rights.

Bonhoeffer continues with interesting thoughts on pacifism. "The right way to requite evil, according to Jesus, is not to resist it." He adds, "The only way to overcome evil is to let it run itself to a standstill because it does not find the resistance it is looking for."[174] Jesus taught that the believer should not resist evil at all. The believer should be able to turn the other cheek to the aggressor. On loving the enemy, Jesus said, "Christian love draws no distinction between one enemy and another, except that

---

172. Bonhoeffer, *Cost of Discipleship*, 17.
173. Bonhoeffer, *Cost of Discipleship*, 17.
174. Bonhoeffer, *Cost of Discipleship*, 141.

the more bitter our enemy's hatred, the greater need for love."[175] This love, he further argues, includes love for political and religious enemies. This pacifism of his is truly absolute pacifism.

Having discussed Bonhoeffer's absolute pacifism, one now may tend to ask why he shifted his position from pacifism to resistance. This question may be answered in his ecumenical involvement as a youth secretary of the World Alliance for Promoting Friendship. The group emphasis on practical and social issues clearly influenced him. These discussions resonated with his core belief that "one cannot be a Christian just for oneself, but always only in the community of the faithful, in *the communion sanctorum*, the community of the saints."[176] The exposure to these practical and social issues caused him to question: "How should this worldwide proclamation be conceived? What should be the nature of church statements on current political, social, and ethical questions, and how should they be reached? How in particular should the church speak to the question of peace?"[177] These questions and his exposure on practical social and political issues became a watershed for young Bonhoeffer.

As noted above, Bonhoeffer experienced genuine conflict between killing Adolf Hitler and the fifth commandment, "You shall not kill." Bonhoeffer devised the theory of "extraordinary necessity," which interprets the tension between disobeying the law, which leaves you guilty, and obeying it, which equally leaves you guilty. This was in context of the Hitler-era realities in Germany.[178] The reality was either to obey the law to not kill (and spare Hitler's life as millions of people are massacred) or to disobey the law and kill one person—Hitler (and save millions). It was because of the millions of souls he envisioned perishing, and preserving the church against Nazi infiltration, that Bonhoeffer felt compelled to change his position from pacifism to resistance.

In the discussions above, there are compelling reasons to conclude that Christians in northern Nigeria can defend themselves, as it is a right accorded to them in the Constitution of the Federal Republic of Nigeria. In the face of mass murder and genocide in northern Nigeria, Christian self-defense should be considered a responsibility on behalf of the weak and vulnerable. The main issue with self-defense in this context is the separation line between vengeance and self-defense. Church leaders and scholars should work on the self-defense response and provide a guide for Christians in northern Nigeria.

---

175. Bonhoeffer, *Cost of Discipleship*, 148.
176. Tietz, *Theologian of Resistance*, 19.
177. Tietz, *Theologian of Resistance*, 87.
178. Tietz, *Theologian of Resistance*, 87.

5

Towards a Proper Response to Persecution

INTRODUCTION

As THE RESEARCH CONCLUDES, it is important to summarize and call attention to the findings. Since the 1980s, Christian persecution in northern Nigeria has been a source of concern to all Christians and Muslims who desire peace and progress in the region. The violence that is being experienced is so devastating that it has negatively affected the social, economic, religious, and political life of the nation and impedes development in the nation, especially northern Nigeria. Religious persecution of Christians has shifted from casual insults to marginalization and discrimination to mob violence. Targeted attacks on Christians by Muslim groups have resulted in massive loss of lives and property. Responses to persecution by Christians have changed from pacifism to self-defense, and occasional vengeance. The motivation for this research and cause of concern for me is the future of Christianity and the church in Nigeria.

This chapter summarizes the research findings and conclusions with recommendations for responses to persecution by the church in northern Nigeria.

SUMMARY OF FINDINGS

The purpose of this research was to investigate the experiences of persecution of Christians in northern Nigeria, their responses to persecution, and the effect responses to persecution had on evangelism and discipleship. Also investigated was the response of the early church to persecution, assisting in making recommendations for responses to persecution that would have a positive impact on evangelism and discipleship. To effectively compare responses to persecution by Christians in northern Nigeria and the early church, Penner's framework of responses to persecution of fight, flight, and fortitude was used. I believe that the proper response to persecution could significantly minimize the violence experienced in the region, restore good community relations, and enhance evangelism and discipleship so that the church in northern Nigeria will continue to experience growth, even while experiencing extreme persecution.

To compare responses to persecution of Christians in northern Nigeria with the responses of early Christians, a study of the background of conflicts in the region was important. Findings indicate that legacies of Islamic colonization and its continuation under British rule empowered Hausa-Fulani Muslims over non-Muslims in northern Nigeria. This has been a major source of conflict in northern Nigeria. The struggle to break free from this oppression by non-Muslims and the effort of Hausa-Fulani Muslims to maintain the status quo remain a source of conflict in northern Nigeria. Another major source of conflict is the incompatibility of Shari'a ideology with democracy. Christians in northern Nigeria resisted the implementation of Shari'a and it has affected Christian-Muslim relations, especially in Kaduna State, as in the bloody violence in the year 2000.[1] Another conflict factor is the emergence of Islamic fundamentalist and terrorist groups that have their roots in the ideology of eighteenth-century Uthman Dan Fodio jihad. These conflicts have resulted in persecution of Christians in northern Nigeria. The most active groups in current persecution of Christians are Boko Haram and Fulani herdsmen.

Data obtained from the field research discussed experiences of persecuted Christians in northern Nigeria, ranging from mild to extreme persecution. Mild forms of persecution included discrimination in places of work, denial of government services, denial of rights, and oppression of ethnic Christian minorities in northern Nigeria. The findings of the data also revealed that many forms of mistreatment and suffering experienced by Christians in northern Nigeria go unreported. Extreme persecution, including mass murder by Boko Haram and Fulani herdsmen, is ongoing while the government ignores it. The widespread destruction of church buildings, houses belonging to Christians, and businesses of Christians has not been quantified. Many Christian villages have been attacked on night raids that have resulted in the deaths of hundreds of Christians in a single attack.

---

1. Ukanah, *In God's Name*, 204–5.

In this research, efforts were made to uncover the reasons why Christians in northern Nigeria are being persecuted. Reasons include some or all of the following: Christian faith, political, economic, and ethnic. Respondents from Borno State are of the opinion that the reason for the persecution is because of their Christian faith.[2] In Kaduna State, however, the Christian faith and all other reasons are perceived as reasons for persecution.[3] The reasons for persecution are complex because Islam, the source of the persecution of Christians in northern Nigeria, does not practice the separation of "mosque" and state. Therefore, political, economic, or ethnic reasons can have religious undertones. This compares to early Christians in which Roman society was religious and every sphere of life was connected to religion.

There has been discussion as to whether the persecution is the result of ethnic conflict or religious conflict, but northern Nigerian Christians who were interviewed clearly state that they are suffering persecution because of their faith.[4] This was the experience of early Christians who were also persecuted just for being Christian, as noted in the Trajan rescript reply to Pliny's letter.[5]

The research also presented different forms of responses to persecution by Christians in northern Nigeria, with differences by region. Some Christians are pacifists and most of the Christians in northeast Nigeria align to pacifism. There are also pacifists in the Middle Belt but a sizeable number in this region stated that self-defense is the best response to persecution. The Christians in northern Nigeria totally reject the idea of Christians initiating attacks on the Muslims or carrying out vengeful attacks.[6] Christians in both Borno and Kaduna States do not approve of attacks. This is like the response of early Christians who did not fight or attack their persecutors.

One of the major contributions of this study examined how responses to persecution impact evangelism and discipleship, so that the church can continue to grow during persecution. In interviews of Christians in northern Nigeria, research shows that there are responses that have a positive impact and there are responses that have a negative impact. Christians in northern Nigeria overwhelmingly agree that the pacifistic approach as a response to persecution aids in the continuation of evangelism and discipleship. Pacifistic responses were noted as having a positive impact while attacks and vengeance were noted as having a negative impact. Negative

2. See appendix E, table 3.
3. See appendix D, table 3.
4. See appendices D and E, tables 1.
5. Stark, *Triumph of Christianity*, 138.
6. See appendices D and E, tables 4.

Christian responses to persecution have brought about enmity, suspicion, and broken relationships to the extent that in some quarters, Christians and Muslims live in separate communities.[7] In Borno State, the responses show that the people of the northeast still live in peace with their Muslim neighbors, though a good number of the respondents indicated that there are broken relationships.[8]

Self-defense is a growing response to persecution, especially the defense of the weak and vulnerable, which is seen as a Christian duty. There is an emerging discussion among Christians as to whether defense can be an option for Christians experiencing extreme persecution that results in mass murder or genocide. Christian leaders from the Middle Belt who have seen the horrors of mass murder from Fulani herdsmen have advocated self-defense.

After reporting the experiences in northern Nigeria, I examined Bible passages in the New Testament to establish the biblical basis for responses to persecution and how they were practiced by the early church. New Testament Scripture passages all support pacifism. Some Scripture is interpreted to encourage flight in times of persecution, but flight motivated by mission, not by fear. Other passages advocate loving the enemy, doing good to enemies, praying for enemies, and not resisting the evil person.

However, it is argued by Christians in northern Nigeria that such treatment of the enemy, if well interpreted, is limited to interpersonal relationships which are a different context than war and genocide. Brown O. in an interview argues that what Jesus was addressing were quarrels, not war, so Brown O. advocates self-defense because the killings in northern Nigeria are more like war than a quarrel.

Early church responses to persecution were also examined as an example to Christians in northern Nigeria, and to identify downsides to their responses to evangelism and discipleship that should be avoided. The study discovered that most early Christians were pacifists, which is the response of Christians in northeast Nigeria. Self-defense in the early church was mainly apologetic. There was never a fight response against the aggressor except in the case of the Catholic-Donatist schism, which was a Christianity internal crisis. Christians in northern Nigeria can learn from the patient endurance of early Christians in times of persecution. In early Christian experiences, the patient endurance through suffering and even death had a positive impact on evangelism, while those who denied the faith, the schismatics, and voluntary martyrs all had negative impacts on evangelism and discipleship.

---

7. See appendix D, table 7.
8. See appendix E, table 7.

Self-defense was also evident in the early church through the defense of the faith by apologetics, which presented a case for Christianity. Today, advocates support self-defense through ethics. Bonhoeffer calls this type of action "extraordinary necessity." Ethically, the believer is left with the choice of either resisting a few criminals, even if it means killing them, or allowing hundreds or thousands of innocent people to perish at the hands of those criminals. If nothing is done, according to interviewee Kenneth C., this type of inaction is irresponsibility.

Another aspect of self-defense is caring for the vulnerable, which was one of the hallmarks of the early Christians. Stark notes that invasions and disasters often created populations in cities that were impoverished and homeless, like vulnerable Christians in northern Nigeria.[9] Like the early Christians, churches in northern Nigeria can reach out to help and provide community and hope.

However, not all was well with the early Christians in their responses to persecution. As such, there are some pitfalls to avoid, including Christians who feared torture and death in the hands of Roman authorities and sacrificed to Roman gods to avoid suffering and death. When proof of sacrificing to the gods was required from citizens of the empire, some Christians lied, and some gave bribes to evade the sacrifice. These are not good examples to be emulated by Christians in northern Nigeria. Another negative response to persecution that contemporary Christians should avoid is voluntary martyrdom, condemned by some of the early Christian leaders. Death for the cause of Christ should be accepted but not sought after.

IMPLICATIONS AND RECOMMENDATIONS

Evangelism and discipleship are ingrained in the life, ministry, and theological understanding of John Wesley. It is important to establish a background before recommending to the church appropriate responses to persecution that can positively impact evangelism and discipleship. This is an important connection with the vision of Asbury Seminary and my understanding of "The Bible for the Whole World" vision. In every context, evangelism and discipleship are what sustains the growth and development of the church.

James C. Logan makes this remarkable comment about John Wesley and evangelism: "Wesley's evangelism was marked by a vision of the wholeness of authority, motive, and goal. He proclaimed Christ in his fullness: the Christ of Bethlehem (incarnation), the Christ of Galilee (ministry), the Christ of Calvary (atonement)."[10] Logan emphasizes, "A theology of evange-

---

9. Stark, *Triumph of Christianity*, 161.
10. Logan, "Evangelistic Imperative," 25.

lism would do well to check itself constantly with this criterion of the fullness of Christ."[11] What is interesting in this quote is that in evangelism, Christ should be presented wholly to the world. This is the type of evangelism and discipleship ministry that will make an impact, a perspective providing an important motivation for recommending responses to persecution that have a positive impact on discipleship and evangelism.

Response to Persecution in Northern Nigeria through Evangelism

Proclamation of the gospel through word and deed is important during persecution, though difficult in the context of persecution. Paul declares that "faith comes by hearing the word of God" (Rom 10:17). This underscores the need to proclaim the word of God. Larai U., a woman from Chibok, has not stopped speaking about Jesus despite the persecution from Boko Haram. She recommended that Christians use the Bible to respond to persecution.

Scot McKnight also supports proclamation: "The gospel, I am arguing, is declaring the story of Israel as resolved in the story of Jesus."[12] In McKnight's use of declaring, proclamation is implied.

Proclamation in the context of persecution can involve the use of mass media wherever the media is accessible for evangelism. In the early church, mass media was primarily in written form. Writings included apologetics as defense of the gospel, testimonies both of what Jesus did and how his followers lived as well as instructions for missional living. Writings also recorded messages of hope, courage, and perseverance in the biographies of the saints.[13] The gospel was also presented in a visual way through signs, symbols, and decorations in the home and church.[14] The goal of the message was to always explain Jesus and salvation.[15]

Digital media in the modern world have a vast reach and are, as Jones notes, "inescapable tools for communicating the gospel."[16] Digital media are particularly important where physical contact is impossible, which is often the situation in northern Nigeria. For effective communication, the correct media must be chosen. Among the Hausa-Fulani Muslims in northern Nigeria, radio is the most effective media for evangelism. In northern Nigeria,

11. Logan, "Evangelistic Imperative," 25.
12. McKnight, *King Jesus Gospel*, loc. 1148.
13. Green, *Evangelism in Early Church*, 349, 386; Smither, *Mission in Early Church*, 77.
14. Smither, *Mission in Early Church*, 125.
15. Green, *Evangelism in Early Church*, 346.
16. Jones, *Evangelistic Love of God*, 187.

the radio is one of the primary means for people to receive information about political events, religious teaching, and social events. Many times, I witnessed Hausa-Fulani Muslims in their fields and homes listening to radio. Due to its effectiveness for reaching this group of people, I participated in a radio program broadcast in the Hausa language from 2010 to 2013.

The program was a feature of the Kaduna State Broadcasting Corporation titled *Filin a Tambayi Fasto*—meaning, "a forum to ask pastors some questions." During the thirty-minute weekly program, I designed themes for discussion that attempted to answer Muslim questions about the Christian faith, such as "Is Jesus the Son of God?" The questions were answered in a dialogue format in which pastors parsed the question and answered them in a dialogue. Listeners were given a number to text and ask questions. Each program generated several questions and comments, not always positive. These questions often formed the dialogue for future programs. There were testimonies of conversions to Christianity through the radio program. Although I am in the United States for a season, I have been informed that the recorded programs are still being played.

One-way proclamation, however, is not enough, whether personal or mass media. People are more responsive to two-way conversations.[17] George Hunter notes that evangelism through conversation is not new. The majority of converts in the early church were through conversations across social networks.[18] Many of these social networks were in the family itself—husband converting wives, wives husbands, and so on.[19] Other conversations took place through hospitality, chance encounters in daily life, and visiting.[20] Through these conversations, people were able to see a new quality of life in the early Christians.[21] Hospitality in a community or home was a "central witness to the truth of the gospel and its transforming power."[22] Hunter also notes the powerful role hospitality played in Celtic evangelism.[23]

In northern Nigeria, networks with Muslim neighbors are an important means of evangelism. Like the early church, many Christians and Muslims are related to one another. These natural kin relationships provide Christians with opportunities to have conversations about the gospel with their Muslim relatives. Hospitality also provides opportunities to welcome Muslims.

---

17. Hunter, *Apostolic Congregation*, 85.
18. Hunter, *Apostolic Congregation*, 87.
19. Green, *Evangelism in Early Church*, 318–22.
20. Green, *Evangelism in Early Church*, 286–341.
21. Green, *Evangelism in Early Church*, 381.
22. Pohl, *Living into Community*, 162.
23. Hunter, *Celtic Way of Evangelism*, 41.

Invitations to meals, festivals, and religious celebrations allow people to connect on a deeper level. Christine Pohl notes, "We see fresh expressions of welcome when congregations make a place for unchurched children, international students, and isolated older people."[24]

There are also natural places where people connect in northern Nigeria such as work and at the market, which are shared by both Muslims and Christians. Conversations also happen in places where people gather. For northern Nigerians, this is the soccer field to either play together or watch a game.[25] Several churches have sports ministries and use soccer as a means for evangelism. One church, Mountain of Fire and Miracle, sponsors a national soccer team that plays at the national level in Nigeria.

Doing good is also a form of evangelism. Proclamation, as mentioned earlier, is difficult in the context of extreme persecution. However, strategic use of good works is important as a means of reaching out with the gospel to communities during persecution. From the very beginning of the church in Acts, charity had a role in the life of the church.[26] The early church was committed to loving God and loving people, which was evidenced in supporting the poor and needy.[27] Good works, especially reaching out to the poor, was the hallmark of the early church and an effective witness.[28] As Myers notes,

> Therefore, in dealing with the gospel message, we cannot separate word, deed, and sign without truncating our message. Words clarify the meaning of deeds. Deeds verify the meaning of words. Most crucially signs announce the presence and power of the One who is radically other and who is both the true sources of all good deeds and the author of the only words that bring life in the fullest.[29]

Christians in northern Nigeria should plan and sponsor social ministry outreaches in Muslim communities to demonstrate the love of Christ to the "enemy." Where Christians are able, they can build development projects in the name of the church for Muslim communities to demonstrate the love of Jesus. Christ's ministry was primarily taking the gospel to the poor (Luke 4:18–19), hence his involvement with the poor and the marginalized of society. In the footsteps of Jesus, John Wesley was involved in ministry to the

---

24. Pohl, *Living into Community*, 164,

25. Hollinghurst, *Mission Shaped Evangelism*, 225–29; see also Aldrich, *Life-Style Evangelism*, 201–17.

26. Rhee, *Loving the Poor*, 39.

27. Rhee, *Loving the Poor*, 107.

28. Stark, *Triumph of Christianity*, 87.

29. Myers, *Walking with the Poor*, 10.

poor and marginalized.[30] In Nigeria, where the government has failed to provide social services to the citizens, it would be good news to have a Christian organization or church provide a well for water in a Muslim community or build a bridge that links two or three Muslim communities.

Another way to witness through social concern is to rally around victims of violent attacks. When Christians are attacked, those who survive have often lost almost everything. It is recommended through these research findings that Christian churches in northern Nigeria form support groups to raise support to help those in need. The support could be food, medical care, trauma counseling, or prayer. Bonhoeffer's community motif resonates with the support that persecuted Christians need. He is "convinced that one cannot be a Christian just for oneself, but always only in the community of the faithful."[31] In community, persecuted Christians would be able to receive necessary encouragement and support.

Proclamation can also be done through flight in times of persecution. This type of response can be facilitated through intentional and strategic movement of bi-vocational missionaries to areas of extreme persecution. Rundle and Steffen note: "Using business as a vehicle for missions and ministry is not new."[32] Businessmen, merchants, colonialists, and soldiers in the early church played a significant role in the spread of the gospel.[33]

When Christian professionals flee persecution, they find themselves in new places where their professions are needed. They are accepted in a community where they can brightly shine the light of Christ in the dark corners of the earth by showing the light and love of Christ. When convenient, they proclaim the gospel. In the early church, the Nestorian Christians who fled persecution from their homelands provided an example of this kind of response to persecution. Edward Smither writes about them: "The Nestorians were distinct in history because of their ability to do business well in the central Asia marketplace. As they worked with excellence, they also apparently had a robust verbal witness." The Nestorian Christians were the first to reach China with the gospel.[34] Christian professionals from northern Nigeria should be proactive by moving into Muslim communities with their professions and living the life of Christ among them. This will prompt the community to ask who they are and why they behave differently, thus providing a door for witness.

30. Carder, "Proclaiming Gospel of Grace," 91.
31. Tietz, *Theologian of Resistance*, 10.
32. Rundle and Steffen, *Great Commission Companies*, 18.
33. Smither, *Mission in Early Church*, 43.
34. Neill, *History of Christian Missions*, 82.

The introduction of bi-vocational ministry to the Nigerian Baptist Convention by the immediate past general secretary Dr. Ademola Ishola is an example. Professionals who feel they have the call of God are encouraged to seek theological training and enter the ministry while continuing their professions. The motif is strategic church planting—where these professionals can open doors and break new ground not possible with traditionally trained pastors and missionaries. They go to areas where their professions are needed and will not be solely dependent on the salary from the church.

A practical example is the ministry of Rev. Gibson Tal, the general overseer of Back to God Bible Church in Kano Nigeria. Tal answered the call of God as a trader and maintains his profession. He has used his profession for his family income and as a primary ministry contact to the unsaved. The success in ministry that Tal has recorded demonstrates that integral ministry is doable in northern Nigeria. I have been a mentor to Gibson Tal for over ten years.

Another response to persecution that has evangelistic implications is interfaith dialogue. S. Wesley Ariarajah defines dialogue as "an attempt to help people to understand and accept the other in their "otherness."[35] Christians in northern Nigeria can initiate interfaith programs where both Christians and Muslims would be at the table as equal partners in search of peace. In such interfaith meetings, each religious tradition should be respected. I prefer to use respect for the other rather than tolerance. Interfaith meetings can promote understanding and provide contacts for further evangelistic discourses. I also recommend interfaith sports, feasts, celebration, and potlucks initiated by Christians to promote understanding. Christians should also accept reciprocal invitations if such gestures are extended to them by Muslims. There are Christians already doing great work of dialoguing with Muslims in northern Nigeria.[36] Churches and Christian organizations can build upon what is already happening.

Response to Persecution in Northern Nigeria through Discipleship

The need for discipleship in northern Nigeria cannot be overemphasized and is one of the greatest needs in the church in Nigeria. When the gospel is presented and converts are left without discipleship, the converts soon return to their old ways. Jay Moon echoes the need for discipleship in the church: "Several leaders have openly decried the lack of discipleship

---

35. Ariarajah, *Not without My Neighbour*, 14.

36. See Akinade, *Fractured Spectrum*; Iwuchukwu, *Christian-Muslim Dialogue*; Ashimi, "Significance of Interreligious."

in the church to transform individuals and communities. While many 'decisions for Christ' are made, few of these decisions results in further discipleship."[37] To buttress this point, Dallas Willard calls the neglect of discipleship by the church the "great omission."[38]

The need for discipleship in the church in northern Nigeria is evident in the way some Christians respond to persecution negatively, going to witch doctors or to idols to obtain powers to protect themselves and the church. Why should people who profess faith in Christ return to their traditional beliefs? Moon answers by saying that the life of discipleship, when properly done, "forms mature followers of Christ who overcome the extremes of syncretism (in which culture is not critiqued, thereby blending two faith systems) and split-level Christianity (in which culture is ignored, thereby pushing people to find solutions to intimate issues elsewhere)."[39] Northern Nigerian Christians who fall back into traditional religious practices are in the category of split-level Christianity. The lack of trust in the Lord demonstrated by these Christians underscores the need for discipleship among Christians in northern Nigeria. Pastors and church leaders should design discipleship programs and strongly emphasize them for their members. Discipled Christians trust the power of God to protect them—rather than seeking power from the spirits.

Christian leaders in northern Nigeria have a responsibility to design discipleship programs for three categories of Christians, subject to their responses to persecution. First are secret believers. Second, unfaithful Christians. Third, faithful Christians. The goal of discipleship is to prepare Christians to remain faithful to the Lord, even while undergoing persecution.

Secret Christians in the context of northern Nigeria are new believers from the background of Islam whose lives are under threat, should the Islamic community or their family know that they have been converted to Christianity. For such new Christians, a model of "secret discipleship" should be designed to help them grow in the faith. In northern Nigeria, new believers were lost back to Islam because they were exposed to persecution too soon by the open and flamboyant advertisement by Christians of new believers from Islam. The persecution becomes too severe, and they return to Islam. The concept of secret discipleship has its biblical basis in the parable of the sower, where seed that fell on rocky ground germinated and had rapid growth but

---

37. Moon, *Intercultural Discipleship*, loc. 2.
38. Willard, *Great Omission*, loc. 156.
39. Moon, *Intercultural Discipleship*, loc. 53.

dried up when the heat of the sun descended on it (Matt 13:1–13). The Lord Jesus said that the scorching sun is persecution.

I hereby propose a dimension of discipleship that will enable Muslim converts to stand in the Lord. That is secret discipleship. The new believer keeps secret his profession of faith and is provided a small group of Christians as a community for fellowship and spiritual nourishment. This is until the new believer feels strong enough to damn the possible consequences of proclaiming his new faith. In this period of liminality, he may occasionally appear in the mosque and pray to Jesus in his heart while continuing with the secret small group, growing as a disciple. Don Little in *Effective Discipling in Muslim Communities* envisions "discipling new believers and planting of churches that express uncompromisingly bold and culturally appropriate witness for Christ by believers and churches that remain inside Muslim communities."[40] I believe that the model of secret discipleship will make this vision possible.

The method currently practiced by many Christians in northern Nigeria is to take a new believer to a place of safety and disciple the individual there. This has created more enmity between the family of the new believer and the Christians. The new believer is not given the opportunity of witnessing to his family and community with a new lifestyle. It is important to note that the effective discipleship of a new believer from the background of Islam is best done in community, because in Islam, they were in community. Jay Moon reinforces this fact by saying, "Holistic discipleship recognizes that individuals do not exist in isolation; rather, they are part of larger systems. Healthy, maturing disciples often arise from healthy, maturing communities."[41] The small group, and subsequently the larger church fellowship, should provide such community.

The second category of Christians is those who were unfaithful when they experienced persecution. In northern Nigeria, it has been noted that some Christians in their self-defense have returned to African traditional religion and fetishes to seek diabolical power to protect themselves or the church. This evidence indicates that either the person is not yet converted or lacks discipleship. These are two types of unfaithful Christians which need to be approached differently for discipleship.

The first type of unfaithful Christian is the casual Christian. Casual Christians are those people who do not have a deep commitment to follow Jesus and abandon their faith during persecution, in some cases converting to Islam. These are people whom Rodney Stark refers to as "free riders," people

---

40. Little, *Effective Discipling*, 125.
41. Moon, *Intercultural Discipleship*, 218.

who want to enjoy benefits of the faith community without commitment.[42] A biblical example of free riders is Ananias and Sapphira in Acts 5, who wanted to be known as great givers without the commitment. For these people, they should be taught about salvation with the goal that they will become committed followers of Jesus. For them, the ritual of baptism marks their decision of leaving their old life with incorporation into the church as followers of Jesus. Brenda Colijn writes about the experience: "The new birth makes possible a new way of living, but it also calls believers to cooperate with the Word and Spirit to make that new life an experiential reality."[43] The new believer will continue in discipleship in the form of church programs of teaching and prayer that can guide them to maturity. New believers can also benefit from a close relationship with mature believers in the church.

The second type of unfaithful Christian is the backslider—those who have been baptized but were unfaithful in persecution. For these, there is a need to rededicate their lives to the Lord. Those in this category are to be placed under church discipline for a period. Within this liminal period, they should be placed under a mature Christian family for discipleship. When there is evidence of repentance, the persons should be brought to the front of the church and accepted back into fellowship in a ritual of reincorporation. This acceptance gives them a sense of a new beginning. Then further discipleship can continue until they become fully mature. As part of discipleship, Bonhoeffer believes in the discipline of erring believers: "When punishment is meted out to the stubborn and refractory, it must be administered in the Spirit of meekness and patience."[44] The church should aim at the recovery of the erring member back into fellowship rather than mere punishment.

The third category of Christians is those who remained faithful during persecution. The response to persecution demonstrated by people who have been discipled is patient endurance during discrimination, torture, and even martyrdom. There are Christians in northern Nigeria who have endured suffering for Christ unto death. There is a case of eleven Christians in northern Nigeria beheaded by Boko Haram on Christmas Day in 2019.[45] On January 20, 2020, a Christian leader, Rev. Lawan Andimi, was beheaded by the same Islamic terrorists in northern Nigeria.[46] This faithful endurance

---

42. Stark, *Triumph of Christianity*, 174.

43. Colijn, *Images of Salvation*, 111.

44. Bonhoeffer, *Cost of Discipleship*, 290.

45. Morely, "IS Militants Behead."

46. "Nigerian Pastor Lawan Andimi Executed by Terrorist Group," *Christian Century*, Feb. 26, 2020 (christiancentury.org/article/people/Nigerian-pastor-lawan-andimi-executed-terrorist-group).

to the end is comparable to the early Christians who endured martyrdom for their faith. It was this endurance that some pagans saw and by which they were consequently converted to Christianity.[47] Christians in northern Nigeria are encouraged to persevere to the end.

The need for pastors and Christian leaders to design discipleship programs and emphasize their importance to members in northern Nigeria has been noted. Most of the programs for discipleship have the traditional training model adopted from the West. In the Nigerian Baptist Convention, for example, a member seeking to be discipled has a wide range of discipleship materials they need to undergo training, including: (1) Believer's Handbook, (2) Six Lessons, (3) Follow the Master, (4) Serve the Master, (5) Master Life, (6) In God's Presence, (7) Experiencing God, and (8) The Mind of Christ. These trainings finish with an award of certificates upon completion. The impact of such westernized discipleship model is minor because it does not touch the core of the culture of the people being discipled. Smart sinners can enroll in the program and pass with distinction and be certified as disciples. This might account for the split-level Christianity of those who still go back to African traditional religion to seek protection against persecution.

This book encourages pastors and church leaders to seek discipleship resources from the culture and in context for the disciple. Such resources might include songs, proverbs, stories, rituals, and symbols, which are already in the culture. In northern Nigeria, Church Women Fellowship choirs have been so creative in composing songs that are being dramatized during presentation, resources that can impact both the literate and oral learners. There is also Hausa traditional music contextualized into gospel songs. There are rich proverbs and idiomatic expressions that can be used in discipling Hausa-Fulani Muslim-background believers. The moonlight storytelling model is where children gather around an elderly man or woman in the night to listen to or share stories. Through this medium, moral lessons and family history are passed to a younger generation. This model can be used for discipleship in the rural areas among oral learners.

With the numerous tribes and ethnic groups existing in northern Nigeria and the cultural diversity they represent, it is advisable for pastors and church leaders to look for discipleship resources within the culture of each people group around naming ceremonies, traditional weddings, cultural festivals, burial ceremonies, initiation ceremonies, and rites of passage. These are rich resources more useful in discipling Christians in northern Nigeria than the resources adopted from the West.

---

47. Stark, *Triumph of Christianity*, 151–52.

CONCLUSION

I feel highly blessed and enriched by this research on responses to persecution. Interaction with the literature and human subjects on the field has been awesome. I am hereby concluding with the following final notes regarding the threefold response to persecution.

Fight: In view of the abundant data and literature evidence, attack and vengeance should be rejected as a Christian response to persecution. The Bible does not encourage them, and early Christians did not practice vengeance and attacks in their response to persecution. This research, therefore, concludes that vengeance should not be practiced by Christians in northern Nigeria.

Flight: Pacifism as an age-old Christian response to persecution has been studied again and remains a valid form of Christian response to persecution. Abundant data supports pacifism, the literature reviewed supports it, and most early Christians studied were pacifists. Thus, this research concludes that pacifism should be practiced by Christians in northern Nigeria. Within the context of persecution, it has been shown to aid evangelism and discipleship and further improve interfaith and community relationships in northern Nigeria.

Fortitude: As used in this research, this is self-defense and is a new conversation on the theme of Christian response to persecution. The research data indicates that some respondents agree that self-defense can be a valid option for Christian response to persecution, which came primarily from the Middle Belt region. Others who reject it are mainly from the northeast. I believe self-defense can be a valid option for Christians on the grounds that self-defense is not limited to armed conflict. There are other means of self-defense. Armed conflict must be the last alternative and used only when other options are exhausted.

Self-defense is also important to maintain a Christian witness in northern Nigeria, especially for the weak and vulnerable who need to be defended. In the case of violence in northern Nigeria where women and children are raped and killed, it is a Christian duty to defend them when the government is not providing any defense. Self-defense is also important for maintaining a Christian witness in northern Nigeria so that the church can thrive. Recent attacks are based on an ideology that seeks to make Nigeria an Islamic state. Self-defense is needed to allow churches to remain and continue our rich Christian heritage.

This research has made three major contributions to knowledge. First, there are abundant resources on Christian persecution, but very few focus attention on responses to persecution. The particular attention given to the effect of responses to persecution on evangelism and discipleship is a unique contribution of this research to the field of Christian persecution. This dimension of understanding about persecution will help promote kingdom values and the growth of the church through evangelism and discipleship even within the context of persecution. Second, most Christians facing persecution in different parts of the world have not been prepared for it. Jesus prepared his disciples for persecution. This research will be an additional resource for the preparation of Christians on how to face and respond to persecution. Third, self-defense has not had extensive discussion by scholars to determine whether it could be a valid response to persecution. The attempt of this research to address self-defense is to provide a contribution to the ongoing conversation.

I do not claim to have exhausted the theme on Christian responses to persecution. There needs to be further research on the subject, specifically on self-defense as a response to persecution. There needs to be further research on self-defense and its effect on evangelism and discipleship and how it could benefit the persecuted church worldwide.

Appendix A

Methodology

INTRODUCTION

CHRISTIANS IN NORTHERN NIGERIA and their counterparts in places such as Sudan, Somalia, Iraq, Afghanistan, North Korea, Syria, and Kenya share similar experiences of persecution as the early Christians in the first three centuries of the Christian era. Of the persecution of Christians, Paul Marshall wrote in 1998, "In the last five years, the persecution of Christians has taken place in approximately forty countries, and legal repression and discrimination in an additional thirty countries."[1] The change in the response of Christians in northern Nigeria from pacifism to occasional vengeance and how it affects evangelism and discipleship is of great concern to me.

My desire for peace, the continual growth of the church, and the hope that Christians live and serve their communities as salt and light in the world despite the persecutions are the motivations for conducting this research, subtitled *Early Christian Responses to Persecution and Implications for Christians in Northern Nigeria*. I believe that the study of early Christian responses to persecution and how they impacted evangelism and discipleship can provide guidance for Christians in northern Nigeria in their response to persecution.

RESEARCH BACKGROUND

I, Yakubu Tanko Jakada, was born to the family of Ishaya Jakada in Wuroko, Lere local government, in Kaduna State in northern Nigeria. I teach missions and evangelism at the Baptist Theological Seminary in Kaduna, Nigeria. I am married to Yagana and our marriage is blessed with four

---

1. Marshall, "Persecution of Christians," 4.

children: Gamaliel, Comfort, Irene, and Karen. My location for work, ministry, and personal life contributes to this research the unique experiences of an insider who has experienced ethno-religious violence.

My first encounter with ethno-religious violence was in 1975 when Muslims of Kayarda village came to Yalwa, my village, with weapons of war to fight during the planting season of that year. The result was the destruction of some farmlands, and the incident is known as *Kubaje*, which is the name of the slogan chanted by the Muslims of Kayarda. *Kubaje* means "scatter." The Christians of Yalwa refrained from any negative reactions due to their Christian values. Siman, one of the leaders of the community, went to the local government (county) headquarters and reported the incident. The police made several arrests, and the perpetrators were prosecuted. The violence was religious because it involved Kayarda, a Muslim community, and Yalwa, a Christian community. It was ethnic because Kayarda is a Hausa community while Yalwa is a Kurama community. A land dispute was the main basis for the squabble.

I grew up with stories and experiences of marginalization and oppression of non-Muslims, which characterized the relationships between the non-Muslims of the Middle Belt of Nigeria and the Hausa-Fulani Muslims and rulers of northern Nigeria. I and my siblings were told stories of slave-raiding and slavery of ethnic minorities by the Hausa-Fulani Muslims. Similar stories are passed down to children in different contexts among diverse communities in the Middle Belt of Nigeria. Our forefathers were levied heavy taxes, and those who could not pay were sent to prison or sold as slaves. When Muslim rulers visited non-Muslim communities, they often rode on horses and insisted that their horses not eat straw. Therefore, non-Muslims had to feed them with their grain from their food stores. During the visit, Muslims chose the women to sleep with, even if the women were married. Early in life, I grew up being referred to as an infidel by Muslims. I began experiencing discrimination based on religion in primary school in the form of posting of grades and class position. In most instances, at the end of school term I realized that I would have topped the class if not for my religion or ethnicity.

I experienced religious persecution while attending the College of Education Kafanchan shortly after the 1987 crisis, when tension was still in the air. I was a student of Kaduna Polytechnic on the Tudun Wada campus in 1992 during the Zangon Kataf violence that spilled over to Kaduna. The Tudun Wada community experienced the deadliest massacre of Christians. In 2001, there was a reprisal attack in Kano on Yoruba people, who are mostly Christians. A crisis occurred between Hausa-Fulani and the Yoruba of Shagamu in the southwest. An evangelist, a close friend, was killed in that violent attack. During this crisis, I returned from a trip to discover that my house had been vandalized. I needed to take refuge in the church for a couple of weeks with others who lost houses and properties.

In 2004, I was in the city of Kano where there was a massacre of Christians, which was masterminded by the governor of Kano State to revenge the killings of Hausa-Fulani Muslims in Yelwa Shendam in Plateau State. There were several crises and threats in Kano against Christians, which I experienced. In those days, Christians were attacked when there was a lunar eclipse, a fight between Israel and the Palestinians, a United States attack on Afghanistan, and so on.

I answered the call to ministry on August 2, 1996, in Kano, Nigeria, where believers in Christ experience extreme persecution, as noted above. My primary assignment was to reach the Maguzawa people in the rural areas with the gospel by training indigenous workers and planting churches from 1996 to 2010. Among others, three rural churches planted through my ministry in Hatsai, Banaka, and Tsoro were demolished by Muslim fanatics. We went to court as part of our response to persecution. The injustices mirrored in the courts were reflections of this ongoing persecution experience. Other forms of persecution that I have experienced and witnessed in northern Nigeria include the refusal to sell land to Christians to build churches; confiscation of inherited land of Christian converts; abduction and forceful marriage of Christian girls to Muslims; destruction of church buildings, houses, and business areas belonging to Christians; severe persecution of Muslim converts to Christianity, including death threats against each of them; denial of admission to schools, scholarships to children who are Christians; denial of jobs and promotions to Christian graduates and workers; and outright humiliation of workers who are Christians, even those who are employed in the federal service in Muslim areas.

I moved to Kaduna in 2010 to teach at the Baptist Theological Seminary. The seminary was completely burned down by Muslims in the Shari'a crisis of 2000. I was in the city of Kaduna when the postelection violence took place in 2011. I witnessed the mayhem against Christians because Dr. Goodluck Jonathan, a Christian, won the presidential election. In the summer of 2013, there was a bomb blast two hundred meters from the classroom where I was teaching and a few meters from my home. The blast left our young daughter struggling with the trauma for months.

My desire for peaceful coexistence in Nigeria and the need for the salvation of Muslims inspired my involvement in ministry to Muslims, which includes Christian-Muslim dialogue. I was involved with the "Truth Seekers" Muslim group in Kano. In 2013–2014, I studied Christian-Muslim relationships in the International Peacemakers' Program at Hartford Seminary in

Hartford, Connecticut. With the training, I am hopeful that this book on Christian response to persecution has further equipped me to effectively mediate Christian-Muslim conflicts in Nigeria. As a teacher, leader, and minister of the gospel in northern Nigeria where there is ongoing persecution, this research benefited me as I gained deeper insights on how responses to persecution impacts evangelism and discipleship.

PROCEDURE FOR DATA GATHERING

I traveled to Nigeria to conduct my field research, arriving in Kaduna State on September 11, 2018. I took some time to connect with family members and friends. I also attended meetings as a participant-observer to listen informally to ongoing discussions by Christians and even non-Christians about Christian persecution in northern Nigeria. Even non-Christians referred to the current violence as religious violence.

To gather data through the participation-observation method, I joined Christian clergy on September 27, 2018, at an Inter-Religious Harmony committee meeting, which was organized and chaired by the executive governor of Kaduna State, Malam Nasir El-Rufa'i. I was privileged to listen to the discussions on incessant killings and kidnappings in Kaduna State and possible solutions. On September 28, I had a meeting and orientation with the research assistants for Kaduna State. The research assistants were duly informed on how to perform their duties and their responsibility to keep all research information confidential.

As part of participant observation, I attended the Northern Baptist Pastors' Conference on October 8–13, 2018, hosted by the Baptist Theological Seminary, Kaduna. The conference attracted Baptist pastors from different areas of northern Nigeria and beyond. I was able to listen to informal discussions from Baptist pastors on the ongoing Christian persecution. The conference also gave me the opportunity to connect with many pastors who supported me in different ways during the research process.

I commenced interviews in the city of Kaduna on October 23 (see fig. 1 for map of locations). I moved to Maiduguri to begin the interviews in Borno State on October 26 and continued until October 29. I had a meeting and orientation with the research assistants that helped me in Borno State on October 27. The research assistants were briefed on how to perform their duties and responsibilities regarding confidentiality. They were given the questionnaires to begin distribution.

I then moved from Maiduguri to Kafanchan in Southern Kaduna on October 29 and stayed until November 3. Kafanchan is a major town in Kaduna State that has suffered many bloody and violent religious crises since

1987. I conducted some interviews and questionnaires were distributed in Kafanchan, Gwantu, and Godgodo. I stayed in Kaduna November 4–11. Within this period, I conducted some interviews and renewed my visa at the US embassy in Abuja, Nigeria. November 12, I returned to Southern Kaduna and particularly Gwantu for interviews and follow-ups in Kafanchan. I returned to Kaduna November 15, 2018.

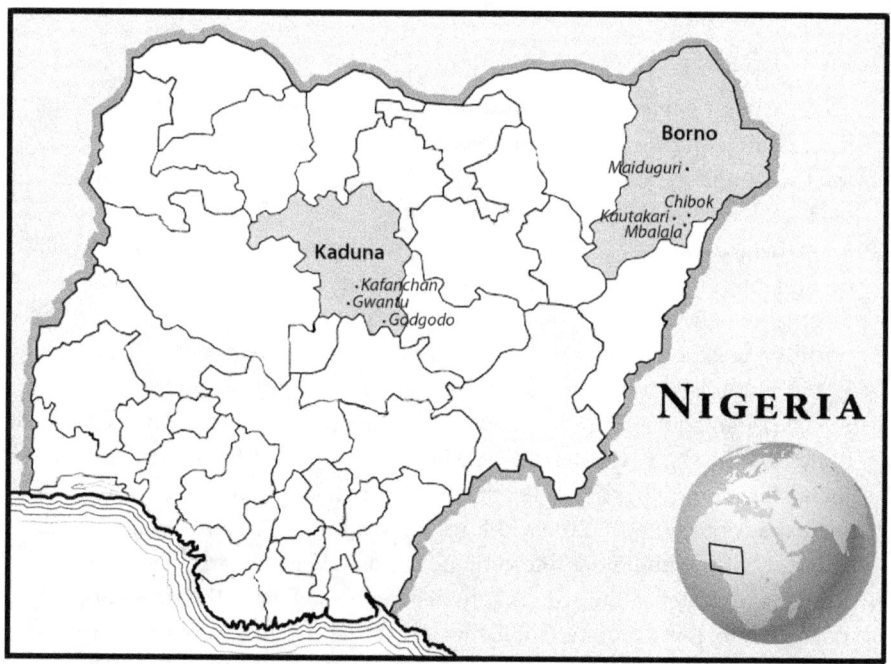

Figure 1. Map of Research Locations

On November 19, 2018, I set out again for the northeast and headed to the Chibok area. This was the most dangerous and strenuous trip I had during the research, and involved going around the Sambisa Forest, which is the stronghold of Boko Haram. I was in Chibok November 20–22, 2018, where I interviewed Christian leaders in Chibok town, Mbalala, and Kautikari villages, and collected the completed questionnaires. This trip was interesting because I had a meeting with thirty-two parents of the abducted Chibok girls. I had the privilege of encouraging, praying with, and sharing in the pain of the parents. I went back to Maiduguri from November 23 to 27 to continue with the interviews in the city and collect completed questionnaires.

After the trip to Chibok and Maiduguri, I took ill, probably due to stress. Therefore, I took time to rest and take some medications between November 28 and December 8. I continued interviews in Kaduna from December 9 to 16. I moved to Godogodo village and from December 17 to 19, I conducted interviews and collected questionnaires. From December 20 to 26, I followed up on the remaining questionnaires in Kaduna and prepared for my return to the United States.

PARTICIPANTS

To represent the view of Christians in Nigeria on responses to persecution, this research on "Early Christian Responses to Persecution and Implications for Christians in Northern Nigeria" drew participants from two states in northern Nigeria: Kaduna and Borno States.

Kaduna was selected from the northwest geopolitical zone of Nigeria because of its place as the former capital of the northern region during the colonial era and because it still retains its position as the political center of northern Nigeria. It has been a flash point of religious persecution since the 1980s. Kaduna State is divided along religious lines—the Muslim north and the Christian south. Religious crises and violence have further divided Kaduna city, the state capital, into the Muslim north and Christian south, and there are communities in the north where Christians do not live. Conversely, there are communities in the south where Muslims do not live, which made the study of Kaduna more interesting. Borno State is the birthplace of Boko Haram and center of the group's activities. Sambisa Forest, the stronghold of Boko Haram, is in the state. Chibok, where the Christian schoolgirls were abducted, is also in Borno State. About 80 percent of the attacks of Boko Haram in Nigeria are in Borno State, hence Borno is significant in this study.

I also selected Kaduna State because of my existing network of relationships. I was born, raised, and received all my early education in Kaduna State. This has given me the advantage of networks of kinship relationships and friends throughout the state and provided participants. My teaching ministry at Baptist Seminary Kaduna provided a network of former students and their friends across many church denominations in the state, who became informants as well as volunteers. The general secretary of the Kaduna State chapter of the Christian Association of Nigeria, Rev. Sunday Ibrahim, is a friend. With my connection to Ibrahim, I had access to leaders across denominations that are affiliated with the ecumenical body.

As a student, I was the president of the Fellowship of Christian Students (FCS), the largest Christian student movement in northern Nigeria, in Kaduna Polytechnic, and the coordinator of the postsecondary FCS groups in Kaduna State (1993–1994). Most of the Christian students I led are now leaders. These networks of relationships afforded me access to participants that I believe provided credible information.

In Borno State, I have family relationships. My wife is from Borno State, and I used the kinship relationships of my wife, her friends, and ministry and church relationships to obtain credible data. The immediate past chairman of the Christian Association of Nigeria Borno chapter, Rev. Titus Pona, and the current chairman, Bishop Mohammed Naga, were my schoolmates and remain friends. I used these connections to access leaders across church denominations that are affiliated with the Christian Association of Nigeria. Rev. Pona was particularly helpful in the research process. As an indigene of Chibok, he went with me to Chibok, used his connections to obtain interviews, and provided free accommodation and meals for the period of our stay in Chibok. As a faculty member of the Baptist Seminary Kaduna, I also had connections with my former students that extended into Borno State. The Baptist Seminary Kaduna is the major training institution for the Nigerian Baptist Convention in northern Nigeria. These connections provided participants that I believe gave me credible information for data.

Another reason for selecting Kaduna and Borno was based on opposing responses to persecution. In the northeast where Borno is located, the Christians seem to be pacifists. In Kaduna, which is in the northwest, the Christians are defensive with occasional vengeance. This sharp difference was of particular interest to me for the purpose of comparison and contrast.

I interviewed and administered questionnaires to Christian leaders. These leaders included elders/deacons, pastors, evangelists, missionaries, and denominational and ecumenical Christian leaders. Also, the leaders of non-church-based Christian ministries were included as participants. These leaders were aged twenty-five years and above. Elderly men, young men, and women leaders were also interviewed.

I had several criteria for the selection of people who were interviewed. First, they were people of influence in their communities, churches, or Christian organizations. This criterion includes Christians who were leaders in their local churches or ecumenical bodies, or Christians involved in community leadership. I also selected Christian leaders who were involved in issues of social justice, those advocating for the oppressed.

The choice of these leaders as participants was twofold. First was the fact that leaders are often targeted for persecution, and second to help ensure proper engagement with participants due to their level of awareness on the subject matter, with the hope of procuring optimum results. I carried out research in two cities, two towns, and four villages across the two selected states: in Kaduna State—Kaduna, Kafanchan, Gwantu, and

Godgodo, in Borno State—Maiduguri, Chibok, Mbalala, and Kautikari. Two hundred questionnaires were administered, one hundred in each state. I am confident that the information gathered in the selected areas represents the opinions of Christians in northern Nigeria.

RESEARCH METHODOLOGY

I reviewed literary resources on responses to persecution to examine what other writers have written on the subject, which enabled me to discover something unique that adds to existing knowledge about Christian persecution.

Since persecution in northern Nigeria is ongoing, it was necessary to carry out field research. I used both qualitative and quantitative approaches to research. Questionnaires and interview questions were designed and used for gathering data for the research. Quantitative research enabled me to reach a wider audience within a short period of time. Qualitative research helped me to explore more deeply the issues of persecution in northern Nigeria and to obtain more information. Since the research involved some rural communities, qualitative research was more effective in gathering data from nonliterate or semiliterate participants, since most of the clergy in the rural areas have very little education.

Other resources I used to gather information for the research included the following: documents, reports, documentaries, publications, photographs, and maps that were made accessible on the field. CAN is the voice of Christians in Nigeria. Most documents that contain reports, complaints, rejoinders, and other resources about the persecution of Christians are sent to the CAN office. My connection with the leadership of CAN in the two states afforded me access to these resources. The resources from the field and the library sources, together with the results of the data collected, were analyzed to form the conclusions of this book.

Research methodology included the process of obtaining both quantitative and qualitative data. The design of the questionnaire and interview questions was presented to my mentor for approval before production and administration. Relevant introductory letters and cover letters were collected before the trip to the field. The most important document that was obtained before proceeding for field research was the "Signed Statement of Informed Consent," protecting participants in the research from undue risk, and approved by the Institutional Review Board. Research assistants were trained and required to sign a confidentiality agreement. I used three types of ethnographic data gathering methods: open-ended interviews, questionnaires, and participant observation.

Open-Ended Interviews

Open-ended interviews were designed to be subject driven and allow the person being interviewed to tell their personal observations and experiences with persecution. Interviews were conducted, which gave me more in-depth engagement with the participants. I personally interviewed thirty Christian leaders across the two selected states within a period of four months of field research from September 2018 through December 2018. I was able to visit some of the participants two or three times to gather more information about responses to persecution in northern Nigeria. New facts forthcoming from interviews formed the basis for revisiting participants for further discussion. In some cases, when traveling was dangerous because of security issues, I used telephone calls to follow up on conversations with participants, such as those in Chibok. I recorded interviews and from January 2019 to April 2019 and transcribed the data gathered.

Examples of question prompts used for these interviews are as follows. Also see appendix F, "Interview Protocol."

1. Tell me about your experience with Christian persecution.
2. How have you personally responded to persecution?
3. How have you observed other Christians respond to persecution in northern Nigeria?
4. How have you seen responses to persecution impact your witness to your non-Christian neighbors?
5. What do you think is the best response to persecution that will impact evangelism and discipleship positively?
6. What do you consider the worst responses to persecution you have observed by Christians in northern Nigeria that will impact negatively on evangelism and discipleship?
7. Tell me some theological issues you struggle with when it comes to response to persecution as a Christian in northern Nigeria.
8. Is there any specific response to persecution required of Christians?

Questionnaire

The second methodology that I used was a questionnaire that helped me understand a broader range of responses to persecution and their impact on evangelism and discipleship. Two hundred questionnaires were produced and distributed to participants in selected areas using volunteer workers who received tokens of appreciation at the end of the exercise. These volunteer workers were Baptist pastors who work in these states and were also my former students. Based on previous relationships with them, I appreciated their commitment and sacrifice, which helped me accomplish my field research goal from October to December 2018. In both Borno and Kaduna States, I gathered the volunteers and provided training on how to distribute and collect the questionnaires. Most importantly, they were trained on confidentiality and its importance to the participants. Before commencing work, they were required to sign the "Research Assistant Confidentiality Form" (see appendix J). Participants were given two weeks to complete the questionnaires and then the completed copies were collected. Challenges encountered included participants who delayed beyond the two weeks and needed follow-up reminders as well as those who did not return the questionnaires, despite reminders.

Participant Observation

Participant observation was the third method, which was used to supplement and validate responses from interviews and questionnaires. Participant observation in public places was included as a means of obtaining data. For instance, I attended informal discussions at the northern Nigerian Baptist Pastor's Conference, Inter-Religious Harmony committee meeting at the statehouse in Kaduna, peer group meetings, and village council meetings. I focused on the places above where discussions of the problems of violence against Christians and possible solutions were taking place.

DATA ANALYSIS

The data from questionnaires, interviews, and participant observation were collated and compiled. The number of questionnaires produced was 200, 100 from each state. In Borno State, 78 were filled and returned, representing 78 percent; one questionnaire was returned unfilled, representing 1 percent; and 21 were not returned, representing 21 percent. In Kaduna State, 85 were filled and returned, representing 85 percent; one questionnaire was returned unfilled, representing 1 percent; and 14 were not returned, representing 14 percent

Of all 200 questionnaires distributed, the number returned was 163, representing 81.5 percent. Two were returned unfilled, representing 1 percent, and 35 were not returned, representing 17.5 percent. Recorded data from interviews was transcribed and used as evidence on how Christians in northern Nigeria respond to persecution.

Qualitative Data Analysis

This method of data analysis involves examining, categorizing, tabulating, and combining the data obtained. Coding (open, axial, and selective) and categorizing were used to make sense and meaning of the phenomenon. Open coding is the organization of data for analysis, axial coding is the interconnecting of data categories, and selective coding is the building of the story that connects the categories.[2]

In summary, qualitative data analysis is "the process in which we move from the raw data that have been collected as part of the research study and use it to provide explanations, understanding and interpretation of the phenomena, people and situations which we are studying."[3] The raw data in recorded form were transcribed and categorized and used to explain why Christians in northern Nigeria choose to respond to persecution in specific ways. In coding, the researcher looked for patterns within the data. Interviews about persecution were coded as mild to extreme, based on the level of violence that occurred. Responses to persecution were coded based on the framework of fight, flight, and fortitude. Responses were also coded based on the positive or negative impact they had on evangelism and discipleship.

Quantitative Data Analysis

Quantitative data analysis involves data preparation, descriptive statistics, and inferential statistics. Data preparation includes checking data for accuracy, transforming data, and developing a database structure that integrates the various measures. To describe the basic features of the data in the study, descriptive statistics are used. Descriptive statistics, together with simple graphic analysis, form the basis of virtually every quantitative data analysis.[4] Inferential statistics are used to investigate questions, models, and hypotheses, as well as infer from the data what the population thinks and make judgments on observations. Inferential statistics are also used to describe the results of the data.[5] In this research, a large sample of 200 questionnaires was administered. The data collected were summarized in tabular form and percentages calculated for each category based on the number of

---

2. Vickers and Offredy, "Developing Healthcare Research Proposal," para. 1 (under "Analysis"); para. 3 (under "The Constant Comparative Method").

3. Vickers and Offredy, "Developing Healthcare Research Proposal," para. 1 (under "Summary").

4. Trochim, "Analysis," para. 4.

5. Trochim, "Analysis," para. 5.

respondents in each category. The results were taken as representative of the opinions of Christians in northern Nigeria.

One purpose of the research was to hear firsthand from people experiencing persecution and learn their responses. The interviews and participant observations allowed me to listen to what people had experienced and what they thought was the appropriate response. I was also able to listen to how their response to persecution was affected by their relationships with their Muslim neighbors and other Christians. The geographical areas were specifically chosen for research because of the different responses Christians living there have had to persecution. Participant observation allowed me to hear the debates and conversations that were occurring about response to persecution. The data provided a broad cross section of Christians experiencing different forms of persecution with different responses and different results.

Appendix B

Questionnaires

Early Christian Responses to Persecution and
Implications for Christians in Northern Nigeria

INTRODUCTION

The researcher on the above-mentioned topic is a student of Asbury Theological Seminary, Wilmore, Kentucky, USA, on his PhD dissertation research. He is requesting you to kindly fill this questionnaire for him. The information filled will be used purely for the purpose of this research and he promises to maintain confidentiality on them.

Name (optional): _____

Age: 25–35 ( ), 36–45 ( ), 46–55 ( ), 56–65 ( ), 66 and above

City/Town/Village _____

Local Government _____

State _____

Leadership Position: Church Elder/Deacon ( ); Pastor ( ); Missionary ( ); Evangelist ( ); Denominational Leader ( ); Ecumenical Leader ( ); Others (specify) _____

QUESTIONS

1. What do you understand by the term "Christian persecution"? Christians in northern Nigeria are being persecuted for their faith in Christ: a) strongly agree (b) agree (c) disagree (d) strongly disagree (e) neutral

2. If Christians in northern Nigeria are being persecuted, it is (a) a mild persecution (b) extreme persecution (c) both mild and extreme (d) no persecution

3. What do you think are the reasons for the persecution of Christians in northern Nigeria? (a) Christian faith (b) political reasons (c) ethnic problems (d) economic reasons (e) all of the above

Briefly explain the reason for your choice above.

4. In their responses to persecution, you consider Christians in your state as: (a) pacifists (no revenge and no defense) (b) defensive (c) avengers (d) attackers

5. What do you consider to be a biblical Christian response to persecution? (a) pacifism (b) defense (c) revenge (d) all of the above

6. What impact have the responses to persecution of Christians in northern Nigeria had on evangelism and discipleship? Why?

7. What do you consider to be the future of Christianity in northern Nigeria should the persecution continue? (a) Christianity will survive the storm. (b) Christianity will grow stronger. (c) Christianity will be wiped out. (d) Christianity will be weakened and will remain weak.

8. What do you think has been the result of Christian responses to persecution in terms of relationship with their religious neighbors in northern Nigeria? (a) peaceful coexistence (b) enmity and suspicion (c) broken relationships

9. Describe in your opinion how proper Christian response to persecution can be a necessary bridge to peaceful coexistence between Christians and people of other faiths in northern Nigeria.

Thank you very much for taking your time to respond to these questions.

God bless you.

Yakubu Jakada

Appendix C

Interviews and Questionnaire Responses

INTERVIEWS WITH THE AUTHOR

B., Desmond. Maiduguri, Metro local gov., Borno State. Nov. 25, 2018.

B., Suleiman. Maiduguri, Metro local gov., Borno State. Oct. 24, 2018.

C., Kenneth. Kaduna, Kaduna South local gov., Kaduna State. Nov. 28, 2018.

C., Mike. Kaduna, Kaduna South local gov., Kaduna State. Nov. 5, 2018.

D., Raymond. Godogodo, Jema'a local gov., Kaduna State. Dec. 18, 2018.

F., Adamu. Kaduna, Kaduna North local gov., Kaduna State. Dec. 12, 2018.

F., Saleh. Maiduguri, Metro local gov., Borno State. Oct. 23, 2018.

G., Abraham. Gwantu, Sanga local gov., Kaduna State. Dec. 14, 2018.

J., Gregory. Mbalala, Chibok local gov., Borno State. Nov. 21, 2018.

J., Mark. Maiduguri, Metro local gov., Borno State. Nov. 26, 2018.

K., Caleb. Kaduna, Kaduna North local gov., Kaduna State. Dec. 16, 2018.

L., Bishara. Kautikari, Chibok local gov., Borno State. Nov. 21, 2018.

M., Darrell. Kafanchan, Jema'a local gov., Kaduna State. Oct. 31, 2018.

M., Ezra. Kafanchan, Jema'a local gov., Kaduna State. Oct. 31, 2018.

M., Judith. Maiduguri, Metro local gov., Borno State. Oct. 24, 2018.

O., Brown. Kaduna, Kaduna South local gov., Kaduna State. Nov. 4, 2018.

O., Elisha. Kautikari, Chibok local gov., Borno State. Nov. 21, 2018.

R., David. Bakin Kogi, Kafanchan, Jema'a local gov., Kaduna State. Nov. 1, 2018.

T., Balarabe. Chibok, Chibok local gov., Borno State. Nov. 21, 2018

Appendix C: Interviews and Questionnaire Responses

T., Collins. Interview with the Author. Personal Interview. Maiduguri, Metro local gov., Borno State, on November 26, 2018

U., Larai. Interview with Author. Personal Interview. Chibok, Chibok local gov., Borno State. Nov. 21, 2018

W., Charles. Interview with Author. Personal Interview. Kafanchan, Jema'a local gov., Kaduna State. Nov. 1, 2018

W., Jeremy. Interview with Author. Personal Interview. Kaduna, Kaduna North local gov., Kaduna State. Nov. 6, 2018

Y., Benjamin. Interview with the Author. Personal Interview. Godogodo, Jema'a local gov., Kaduna State, December 18, 2018

Y., Michael. Interview with Author. Personal Interview. Chibok, Chibok local gov., Borno State. Nov. 22, 2018

Z., Nuhu. Interview with the Author. Personal Interview. Kaduna, Kaduna North local gov., Kaduna State. Nov. 6, 2018

Z., Saratu. Interview with Author. Personal Interview. Mbalala, Chibok local gov., Borno State. Nov. 21, 2018.

QUESTIONNAIRE RESPONSES

A., Lawrence. Nov. 17, 2018.

A., Tanimu. Dec. 12, 2018.

B., John. Nov. 15, 2018.

H., Dora. Dec. 13, 2018.

K., Audu. Nov. 13, 2018.

L., Patrick. Nov. 12, 2018.

P., Thomas. Sept. 9, 2018.

R., Ruth. Oct. 29, 2018.

Appendix D

Analysis of Questionnaires: Kaduna State

Item 1. Christians in northern Nigeria are being persecuted for their faith in Christ.

Table 1.

Responses	No. of Respondents	Percentage Score
a. Strongly Agree	69	80%
b. Agree	16	20%
c. Disagree	0	0%
d. Strongly Disagree	0	0%
e. Neutral	0	0%
Total	**85**	**100%**

Item 1 above tried to find out whether Christians in northern Nigeria perceive that the persecution they are going through is because of their faith in Christ. Out of eighty-five respondents, sixty-nine strongly agree that Christians in northern Nigeria are persecuted for their faith in Christ, which represents 80 percent. Sixteen agree, which represents 20 percent. There were no responses for disagree, strongly disagree, and neutral. The responses above show that Christians in northern Nigeria perceive the persecution they are experiencing is because of their faith in Christ.

Item 2. If Christians in northern Nigeria are being persecuted, it is:

Table 2.

Responses	No. of Respondents	Percentage Score
a. A mild persecution	2	2.4%
b. Extreme persecution	33	39.8%
c. Both mild and extreme	48	57.8%
d. No persecution	0	0%
Total	**83**	**100%**

Item 2 tried to find out the degree of persecution of Christians in northern Nigeria, whether it is mild or extreme persecution. Out of the eighty-three respondents to this item, two responded that the persecution in northern Nigeria is mild, which represents 2.4 percent; thirty-three feel it is extreme persecution, which represents 39.8 percent; and forty-eight responded that it is a mixture of both mild and extreme persecution, which represents 57.8 percent. There was no response for no persecution. The responses to item 2 in table 2 above show that Christians in northern Nigeria experience both mild and extreme persecution.

Item 3. What do you think are the reasons for the persecution of Christians in northern Nigeria?

Table 3.

Responses	No. of Respondents	Percentage Score
a. Christian faith	28	33.3%
b. Political reasons	4	4.8%
c. Ethnic reasons	0	0%
d. Economic reasons	0	0%
e. All of the above	52	61.9%
Total	84	100%

Item 3 attempted to discover the reasons for the persecution of Christians in northern Nigeria. Twenty-eight who responded are of the opinion that Christians in northern Nigeria are persecuted solely for their Christian faith, representing 33.3 percent of the eighty-four persons who responded to this item. Four respondents, representing 4.8 percent, say it is for political reasons. Fifty-two respondents, representing 61.9 percent, are of the opinion that the reasons are a mixture of politics, ethnic, economic, and religious. The responses above show the complex nature of the reasons for the persecution of Christians in northern Nigeria includes faith, politics, economics, and ethnic dimensions.

Appendix D: Analysis of Questionnaires: Kaduna State

Item 4. In their responses to persecution, you consider Christians in your state as:

Table 4.

Responses	No. of Respondents	Percentage Score
a. Pacifists	26	31.3%
b. Defensive	55	66.3%
c. Avengers	1	1.2%
d. Attackers	1	1.2%
Total	83	100%

Item 4 above sought to uncover the kind of responses of Christians to persecution in Kaduna State in northern Nigeria. Twenty-six respondents say Christians in Kaduna are pacifists, representing 31.3 percent. Fifty-five respondents are of the opinion that Christians in Kaduna State are defensive when they are attacked, representing 66.3 percent of the eighty-three respondents. One respondent said they take vengeance when attacked, representing 1.2 percent. There was also one response for attackers, which represents 1.2 percent. The responses above show that Christians in Kaduna State, Nigeria, employ the use of self-defense when attacked by persecutors.

Item 5. What do you consider to be a biblical Christian response to persecution?

Table 5.

Responses	No. of Respondents	Percentage Score
a. Pacifism	35	44.3%
b. Defense	34	43%
c. Revenge	2	2.6%
d. All of the above	8	10.1%
Total	79	100%

Item 5 above tried to discover what Christians in northern Nigeria consider the most biblical response to persecution. Thirty-five out of the seventy-nine respondents to this question consider pacifism to be the biblical response to persecution, representing 44.3 percent. Self-defense was responded to by thirty-four persons, representing 43 percent. Two responses were for revenge, which represented 2.6 percent of all those who responded. All of the above had eight respondents, representing 10.1 percent. The responses above show that pacifism is considered the most biblical form of response to persecution.

Item 6. What do you consider to be the future of Christianity in northern Nigeria should the persecution continue?

Table 6.

Responses	No. of Respondents	Percentage Score
a. Christianity will survive the storm.	19	22.9%
b. Christianity will grow stronger.	31	37.4%
c. Christianity will be wiped out.	4	4.8%
d. Christianity will be weakened and remain weak.	29	34.9%
Total	83	100%

Item 6 above sought to understand what Christians in northern Nigeria think of the future of Christianity in the region if the persecutions continue. Nineteen of the eighty-three who responded to the question believed the Christian faith will survive the storm of the persecution, and they represent 22.9 percent. Thirty-one were optimistic that Christianity will grow even stronger, which represents 37.4 percent. Four respondents believed Christianity will be wiped out, which represents 4.8 percent. Twenty-nine responded that Christianity will be weakened, and it will remain weak if the persecutions continue, which represents 34.9 percent. The responses for item 6, table 6, indicate that Christians in northern Nigeria are optimistic that the Christian faith will survive the storm and grow even stronger.

Item 7. What do you think has been the result of Christian responses to persecution in terms of relationships with religious neighbors in northern Nigeria?

Table 7.

Responses	No. of Respondents	Percentage Score
a. Peaceful coexistence	21	25.6%
b. Enmity and suspicion	42	51.2%
c. Broken relationships	19	23.2%
Total	82	100%

Item 7 above tried to find out what Christians in northern Nigeria think has been the result of their responses to persecution in terms of relationships with people of other faiths in the region. Twenty-one respondents are of the opinion that the responses have resulted in peaceful coexistence, which represents 25.6 percent of the eighty-two that responded. Forty-two replied that the responses to persecution have generated enmity and suspicion, which represented 51.2 percent. Nineteen respondents are of the view that the responses have brought broken relationships between Christians and their religious neighbors, which represents 23.2 percent of the responses. The responses above show that responses to persecution by Christians in northern Nigeria have brought enmity and suspicion in community relationship in some or most parts of northern Nigeria.

Appendix E

Analysis of Questionnaires: Borno State

Item 1. Christians in northern Nigeria are being persecuted for their faith in Christ.

Table 1.

Responses	No. of Respondents	Percentage Score
a. Strongly agree	63	80.2%
b. Agree	14	17.4%
c. Disagree	1	1.2%
d. Strongly disagree	1	1.2%
e. Neutral	0	0%
Total	**78**	**100%**

Item 1 above tried to find out whether Christians in northern Nigeria perceive that the persecution they are going through is because of their faith in Christ. Out of seventy-eight respondents, sixty-three strongly agree that Christians in northern Nigeria are persecuted for their faith in Christ, which represents 80.2 percent. Fourteen agree, which represents 17.4 percent. One response was for strongly disagree, representing 1.2 percent; disagree had one response also, representing 1.2 percent; and there was no response for neutral. The responses above show that Christians in northern Nigeria perceive the persecution they are experiencing is because of their faith in Christ.

Item 2. If Christians in northern Nigeria are being persecuted, it is:

Table 2.

Responses	No. of Respondents	Percentage Score
a. A mild persecution	4	5.2%
b. Extreme persecution	32	42.1%
c. Both mild and extreme	39	51.3%
d. No persecution	1	1.3%
Total	76	100%

Item 2 above tried to find out the degree of persecution of Christians in northern Nigeria—whether it is mild or extreme persecution. Out of the seventy-six respondents to this item, four responded that the persecution in northern Nigeria is mild, which represents 5.2 percent. Thirty-two feel it is extreme persecution, which represents 42.1 percent, and thirty-nine responded it is a mixture of both mild and extreme persecution, which represents 51.3 percent. There was one response for no persecution, which represents 1.3 percent. The responses to item 2 in table 2 above show that Christians in northern Nigeria experience both mild and extreme persecution.

Appendix E: Analysis of Questionnaires: Borno State

Item 3. What do you think are reasons for the persecution of Christians in northern Nigeria?

Table 3.

Responses	No. of Respondents	Percentage Score
a. Christian faith	53	66.7%
b. Political reasons	4	5.1%
c. Ethnic reasons	0	0%
d. Economic reasons	0	0%
e. All of the above	22	28.2%
Total	78	100%

Item 3 attempted to discover the reasons for the persecution of Christians in northern Nigeria. Fifty-three who responded are of the opinion that Christians in northern Nigeria are persecuted purely for their Christian faith, representing 66.7 percent of the seventy-eight persons who responded to this item. Four respondents, representing 5.1 percent, say it is for political reasons. Twenty-two respondents, representing 28.2 percent, are of the opinion that the reasons are a mixture of politics, ethnic, economic, and religious. The responses above show Christian faith is perceived as the reason for the persecutions in northern Nigeria.

Item 4. In their responses to persecution, you consider Christians in your state as:

Table 4.

Responses	No. of Respondents	Percentage Score
a. Pacifists	45	63.4%
b. Defensive	18	25.4%
c. Avengers	1	1.4%
d. Attackers	7	9.8%
Total	71	100%

Item 4 above sought to uncover the kind of responses to persecution of Christians in Borno State in northern Nigeria. Forty-five respondents say Christians in Borno are pacifists, representing 63.4 percent. Eighteen respondents are of the opinion that Christians in Borno State are defensive when they are attacked, representing 25.4 percent of the seventy-one respondents. One respondent said they take vengeance when attacked, representing 1.2, there were seven responses for Attackers, which represents 9.8 percent. The responses above show that Christians in Borno State Nigeria are pacifists when attacked by persecutors.

Item 5. What do you consider to be a biblical Christian response to persecution?

Table 5.

Responses	No. of Respondents	Percentage Score
a. Pacifism	49	67.2%
b. Defense	6	8.2%
c. Revenge	3	4.1%
d. All of the above	15	20.5%
Total	73	100%

Item 5 above tried to discover what Christians in northern Nigeria consider the most biblical response to persecution. Forty-nine out of the seventy-three respondents to this question consider pacifism to be the biblical response to persecution, representing 67.2 percent. Self-defense was responded to by six persons, representing 8.2 percent; and three responses were for revenge, which represented 4.1 percent of all those who responded. All of the above was indicated by fifteen respondents, representing 20.5 percent. The responses above show that pacifism is considered the most biblical form of response to persecution.

Item 6. What do you consider to be the future of Christianity in northern Nigeria should the persecution continue?

Table 6.

Responses	No. of Respondents	Percentage Score
a. Christianity will survive the storm.	34	44.8%
b. Christianity will grow stronger.	22	28.9%
c. Christianity will be wiped out.	7	9.2%
d. Christianity will be weakened and remain weak.	13	17.1%
Total	76	100%

Item 6 above sought to understand what Christians in northern Nigeria think of the future of Christianity in the region if the persecutions continue. Thirty-four of the seventy-six who responded to the question believed the Christian faith will survive the storm of the persecution, and they represent 44.8 percent. Twenty-two were optimistic that Christianity will grow even stronger, which represents 28.9 percent. Seven respondents believed Christianity will be wiped out, which represents 9.2 percent. Thirteen responded that Christianity will be weakened and will remain weak if the persecutions continue, which represents 17.1 percent. The responses on item 6 in table 6 indicate that Christians in northern Nigeria are optimistic that the Christian faith will survive the storm and even grow stronger.

Item 7. What do you think has been the result of Christian responses to persecution in terms of relationship with religious neighbors in northern Nigeria?

Table 7.

Responses	No. of Respondents	Percentage Score
a. Peaceful coexistence	34	45.4%
b. Enmity and suspicion	11	14.6%
c. Broken relationships	30	40%
Total	75	100%

Item 7 above tried to find out what Christians in northern Nigeria think has been the result of their responses to persecution in terms of relationships with people of other faiths in the region. Thirty-four respondents are of the opinion that the responses have result in peaceful coexistence, which represents 45.4 percent of the seventy-five persons who responded. Eleven replied that the responses to persecution have generated enmity and suspicion, which represents 14.6 percent. Thirty respondents are of the view that the responses have brought broken relationships between Christians and their religious neighbors, which represents 40 percent of the responses. The responses above show that responses to persecution by Christians in northern Nigeria have brought peaceful coexistence in community relationships in some or most parts of northern Nigeria.

Appendix F

Interview Protocol

INTRODUCTION

The researcher is a student of Asbury Theological Seminary, Wilmore, Kentucky, USA, doing his PhD dissertation research on "Early Christian Responses to Persecution and Implications for Christians in Northern Nigeria." He is requesting you to please grant him some time and audience for an interview. The information you give will be used purely for the purpose of this research, and he promises to maintain confidentiality with them.

Name (optional): _____

Age: 25–35 ( ), 36–45 ( ), 46–55 ( ), 56–65 ( ), 66 and above

City/Town/Village _____

Local Government _____

State _____

Leadership Position: Church Elder/Deacon ( ); Pastor ( ); Missionary ( ); Evangelist ( ); Denominational Leader ( ); Ecumenical Leader ( ); Others (specify) _____

QUESTIONS

1. Tell me about your experience with Christian persecution.
2. How have you personally responded to persecution?
3. How have you observed other Christians respond to persecution in northern Nigeria?

4. How have you seen responses to persecution impact your witness to your non-Christian neighbors?
5. What do you think is the best response to persecution that will impact evangelism and discipleship positively?
6. What do you consider the worst responses to persecution you have observed by Christians in northern Nigeria that will impact negatively on evangelism and discipleship?
7. Tell me some theological issues you struggle with when it comes to response to persecution as a Christian in northern Nigeria.
8. Is there any specific response to persecution required of Christians?

Thank you so much for giving me your valuable time for the interview.

Blessings,

Yakubu Jakada

Appendix G

Informed Consent Letter

Early Christian Responses to Persecution and Implications for Christians in Northern Nigeria

You are invited to be in a research study being done by Yakubu Jakada from Asbury Theological Seminary. You are invited because you are one of the Christian leaders in northern Nigeria who are the subjects of his study on "Early Christian Responses to Persecution and Implications for Christians in Northern Nigeria." This interview may last for about one hour.

If you agree to be in the study, you will be asked to answer questions by filling out a questionnaire or being directly interviewed by the researcher on how Christians in northern Nigeria respond to persecution, and your valuable opinion on how they should best respond in the way that will positively impact evangelism and discipleship will be appreciated.

Confidentiality is very important in this research. Understanding the possible risk that may be involved in research like this such as criticism at place of work or from fellow Christians who may misunderstand your view, the researcher has assigned a code to represent your name. For example, KD009 will represent a respondent from Kaduna State, while BO009 a respondent from Borno State. Your code is [—]. This promising research, which has as one of its key objectives to prepare Christians on how to respond to persecution, will be of immense benefit to Christians and the church in northern Nigeria and beyond. If something makes you feel bad while you are in the study, please tell Yakubu Jakada. If you decide at any time you do not want to finish the study, you may stop whenever you want. The researcher wishes to get as much as possible from this discussion; as such he wishes to record this interview with an audio recording device. If you do not want this discussion recorded, check the box below. If you do not check the box, it means you have permitted the discussion to be recorded.

/ / I do not want this discussion recorded with a recording device.

You can ask Yakubu Jakada questions any time about anything in this study. You can also ask leaders of the Christian Association of Nigeria (CAN) Kaduna/Borno Chapter (as applies to your location) any questions you might have about this study.

Signing this paper means that you have read this, or had it read to you, and that you want to be in the study and your responses can be published. If you do not want to be in the study, do not sign the paper. Being in the study is up to you, and no one will be mad if you do not sign this paper or even if you change your mind later. You agree that you have been told about this study and why it is being done and what to do.

_____   _____

Signature of Person Agreeing to Be in the Study   Date Signed

Yakubu Jakada
Contacts: [phone number; email address]

Appendix H

Research Permission Letter

Asbury Theological Seminary
204 N Lexington Avenue
Wilmore, KY 40390
5/20/18

The Chairman,
Christian Association of Nigeria (CAN)
Kaduna State Chapter
Kaduna, Kaduna State

Dear Sir,

Permission to Conduct Ethnographic Research among Christian Leaders in Kaduna State

I hereby write to request for permission to conduct research among Christian leaders who are affiliated with the Christian Association of Nigeria (CAN) in Kaduna State. CAN being the largest ecumenical body in Nigeria will give me opportunity to research among a wide variety of Christian denominations. I am currently studying at Asbury Theological Seminary for a PhD in Intercultural Studies. My dissertation topic is "Early Christian Responses to Persecution and Implications for Christians in Northern Nigeria." The aim of the study is to investigate responses to persecution among early Christians to learn from them and to provide recommendations for appropriate responses to persecution that will impact positively on evangelism and discipleship among Christians in northern Nigeria.

The participants in this research will be Christian leaders of different denominations who are aged twenty-five and above. These participants will include elderly men, young men, and women leaders who shall participate voluntarily. The research method will include one-on-one interviews, administration of questionnaires, and participant observation in public places. Confidentiality will be highly observed. I will destroy both raw data and digital files that will be encrypted with passwords twelve months after graduation.

I want to specially request for permission to study archival materials related to my study that may be found in the CAN Secretariat of Kaduna State Chapter. I would appreciate it if you would refer me to any church or Christian organization in Kaduna State that may have materials that will be useful to this study. The field research will cover the period of September to December 2018.

Sir, if my request is granted, I would love to receive a letter of approval to conduct the research among Christian leaders who are affiliated with the Christian Association of Nigeria, Kaduna State Chapter. You may contact me at [phone number] or [email address].

Thanks for your support,

Yakubu Jakada

Appendix I

Research Permission Letter

Asbury Theological Seminary
204 N Lexington Avenue
Wilmore, KY 40390
5/20/18

The Chairman
Christian Association of Nigeria (CAN)
Borno State Chapter
Maiduguri, Borno State

Dear Sir,

Permission to Conduct Ethnographic Research among Christian Leaders in Borno State

I hereby write to request for permission to conduct research among Christian leaders who are affiliated with the Christian Association of Nigeria (CAN) in Borno State. CAN being the largest ecumenical body in Nigeria will give me opportunity to research among a wide variety of Christian denominations. I am currently studying at Asbury Theological Seminary for a PhD in Intercultural Studies. My dissertation topic is "Early Christian Responses to Persecution and Implications for Christians in Northern Nigeria." The aim of the study is to investigate responses to persecution among early Christians to learn from them and to provide recommendations for appropriate responses to persecution that will impact positively on evangelism and discipleship among Christians in northern Nigeria.

The participants in this research will be Christian leaders of different denominations who are aged twenty-five and above. These participants will include elderly men, young men, and women leaders who shall participate voluntarily. The research method will include one-on-one interviews, administration of questionnaires, and participant observation in public places. Confidentiality will be highly observed. I will destroy both raw data and digital files that will be encrypted with passwords twelve months after graduation.

I want to specially request for permission to study archival materials related to my study that may be found in the CAN Secretariat of Borno State Chapter. I would appreciate it if you would refer me to any church or Christian organization in Borno State that may have materials that will be useful to this study. The field research will cover the period of September to December 2018.

Sir, if my request is granted, I would love to receive a letter of approval to conduct the research among Christian leaders who are affiliated with the Christian Association of Nigeria, Borno State Chapter. You may contact me at [phone number] or [email address].

Thanks for your support,

Yakubu Jakada

Appendix J

Research Assistant Confidentiality Agreement

I, _____, the research assistant working with Yakubu Jakada on "Early Christian Responses to Persecution and Implications for Christians in Northern Nigeria" understand that I will have access to data on surveys that are strictly confidential. The participants who will participate in this research project will reveal information in good faith, anticipating the information to remain strictly confidential. I hereby agree to:

1. Keep all the research information shared with me confidential by not discussing or sharing the research information in any form or format.

2. Keep all research information in any form or format secure while it is in my possession. By this, I will provide a cabinet in my house or office in which I will keep the documents and lock them, and only I will have access to the documents as long as they will be with me before submission to the researcher after my job is done.

3. Return all research information in any form or format to the researcher when I have completed the research tasks.

4. After consulting with the researcher, I will erase or destroy all research information in any form or format regarding this research project that is not returnable to the researcher (e.g., information stored on computer hard drive).

Any violation of this agreement would constitute a serious breach of ethical standards, and I pledge not to do so.

Research Assistant

_____ _____ _____

Printed Name   Signature   Date

Appendix K

IRB Approval

THE WHOLE BIBLE FOR THE WHOLE WORLD

Approval by Asbury Theological Seminary's Institutional Review Board (IRB) Committee: The signature below indicates that Yakubu Jakada's proposal has been reviewed by the IRB Committee, necessary changes have been made by the researcher(s) to protect the research subjects, as determined by the IRB Committee; and the proposal has received the final approval by the IRB Committee.

SIGNATURE _Alexandra Anderson_   DATE 10-22-18

NAME TYPED   Alexandra Anderson
             Chairperson of the IRB Committee

asburyseminary.edu   800.2ASBURY
204 North Lexington Avenue. Wilmore, Kentucky 40390 | 859.858.3581

Appendix L

Debate about the Myth of Persecution

CONTRARY TO POPULAR VIEWS on early Christian persecutions, Candida Moss in her book *The Myth of Persecution: How Early Christians Invented a Story of Martyrdom* raises objections on the authenticity of the persecution stories. Moss holds that it is a myth that "only Christians are martyred, that being a Christian means being persecuted, and that experience of being persecuted is a sign both that one is right and that one is good."[1] She asserts that "Christians are not the first to have martyrs" and that "the Greeks, Romans and the Jews"[2] had them. She blames Eusebius of Caesarea for distorting the stories of the martyrs and "using the history of the martyrs as a means of drawing battle lines for the established church's orthodoxy against heresy."[3] One of her conclusions of interest to this research paper is that "the Romans rarely persecute the Christians, and when they did, they had logical reasons that made sense to any ancient Roman."[4] She further argues that the martyrs were violent, aggressive, and suicidal, who sought to die violently.[5]

Niels Hyldahl in his book *The History of Early Christianity* agrees with Moss and writes, "With the exception of Nero's persecution of the Gentile Christians in Rome, which was probably limited to the capital itself, real mass persecutions are unlikely to have occurred during the post-apostolic era. Not even the dramatic representation in Revelation suggests this: only one martyr, Antipas, is mentioned by name (Rev. 2:13, 6:11 & 20:4)."[6]

---

1. Johnson, "Prosecuting the Persecuted," 28.
2. Johnson, "Prosecuting the Persecuted," 28.
3. Johnson, "Prosecuting the Persecuted," 28.
4. Johnson, "Prosecuting the Persecuted," 29.
5. Johnson, "Prosecuting the Persecuted," 29.
6. Hyldahl, *History of Early Christianity*, 273.

Moss raises some valid objections which are being supported by some scholars in this field. Many scholars agree that not all persecution and martyrdom stories we have today are all true stories. There are so many spurious and romantic stories developed over the years by those who want to promote the cult of martyrdom. Leon Hardy Canfield buttresses this point as he says that the stories of persecution and martyrdom have been exaggerated by historians and "emphasized and worked over in every history of the Church."[7] To support this point, Anders Bergquist writes, "It is popular misconception that early Christian communities lived a hidden 'catacomb' existence and were subject to constant persecution by the Roman State until the conversion of Constantine introduced . . . a period of prosperity, privilege and establishment."[8] It has been argued that the persecutions were mostly sporadic and local and sometimes there were emperors who did not persecute Christians. To reinforce this argument: of the fifty-four emperors who ruled between AD 30 and AD 311, "only about a dozen went out of their way to persecute Christians,"[9] and "Christians experienced 129 years of persecution and 120 years of toleration" between AD 64 and AD 313.[10] That means there were periods when the church had peace and the opportunity to flourish and grow.

Moss blames Eusebius for distorting the stories of martyrdoms to promote his personal agenda of drawing a battle line between orthodoxy and heresy. She seems to weaken her argument about Eusebius's alleged distortion of history when she admits, "If we take away Eusebius out of the equation, then our knowledge of the second and third centuries becomes very clouded."[11] It is true that every writer, including historians, has reasons why they write, and it is difficult not to blame a writer for a personal agenda, including Moss in her *Myth of Persecution*. Church historians of the second and third centuries depend on Eusebius as a primary source. Unless Moss has earlier or contemporary sources to Eusebius that disprove him, in my opinion, his stories should still be taken as authentic and valuable.

The claim by Moss that there are those who say that only Christians were persecuted and martyred—if there is such a claim at all—is not true. There have been an uncountable number of people who have died for what they believe is the truth, and these truths may or may not be religious truths. In Scripture, Naboth was killed by Jezebel, and we can consider him

---

7. Canfield, *Early Persecutions of Christians*, 18.
8. Bergquist, "Persecution," 914.
9. Kostka, "Persecution in Early Church," para. 7.
10. Kostka, "Persecution in Early Church," para. 8.
11. Moss, *Myth of Persecution*, 216.

a martyr for the truth (1 Kgs 21:11–14). Several prophets were killed by the same Jezebel. Jesus in Matt 23:35 rebuked the Jews for shedding the blood of the prophets and gave the example of the martyr Zechariah, the son of Berachiah, who was "murdered between the temple and the altar." Even during early Christian persecution, there were times when non-Christians were included in the persecution. Anders Bergquist supports this claim that non-Christians sometimes suffered martyrdom, saying, "The resulting riots in Lyons and Vienne forced authorities to act to re-impose order. Although this action is presented as persecution of Christians, it is clear that non-Christians were also arrested and tried."[12] The fact that non-Christians were also massacred in Lyons does not negate the fact that Christians were the primary target in the persecution.

Persecution of Christians in the early church is real. The fact that Moss herself after her criticism accepts the Martyrdom of Polycarp, Acts of Ptolemy and Lucius, Acts of Justin and Companions, Martyrs of Lyon, Acts of Schillitan Martyrs, and Passion of Perpetua and Felicity as authentic accounts, supports the reality of the persecution stories.[13] Hyldahl, quoted above, raised some objections in his book *The History of Early Christianity* but still accepts the fact that early Christians were persecuted.

---

12. Bergquist, "Persecution," 915.
13. Moss, *Myth of Persecution*, 92.

Bibliography

Adamu, Abdulbarkindo, et al. "Nigeria: Southern Kaduna and the Atrocities of Hausa-Fulani Muslim Herdsmen." *Open Doors International* 1 (May 2016–Sept. 2017) 2–36.
Adeyemi, Ibrahim. "Left to Ruin: Sokoto's Multi-Million–Naira Almajiri School of No Schooling." *Sahara Reporters Newspaper*, May 10, 2019. saharareporters.com/2019/05/10/left-to-ruin-sokotos-multi-million-naira-almajiri-school-no-schooling.
Agang, Sunday Bobai. *No More Cheeks to Turn?* Bukuru, Nigeria: ACTS, 2017.
Akinade, Akintunde E., ed. *Fractured Spectrum: Perspectives on Christian-Muslim Encounters in Nigeria*. New York: Lang, 2013.
———. "Sacred Rumblings: Reflection on Christian-Muslim Encounters in Nigeria." In *Fractured Spectrum: Perspectives on Christian-Muslim Encounters in Nigeria*, edited by Akintunde E. Akinade, 1–11. New York: Lang, 2013.
Akinyele, Akintunde, and Kingsley Igwe. "Villagers Bury Their Dead after Nigeria Clashes." *Reuters*, Mar. 8, 2010. Reuters.com/article/us-nigeria-clashes/villagers-bury-their-dead-after-nigeria-clashes-idUSTRE6275D20100308. Link discontinued.
Aldrich, Joseph C. *Life-Style Evangelism: Crossing Traditional Boundaries to Reach the Unbelieving World*. Portland: Multnomah, 1981.
Aquinas, Thomas. *The Summa Theologica of St. Thomas Aquinas*. Translated by Fathers of the English Dominican Province. Chicago: Benziger, 1922.
Ariarajah, S. Wesley. *Not without My Neighbour: Issues in Interfaith Relations*. Risk 85. Geneva: WCC, 1999.
Asemota, Solomon. "Jihad in Nigeria: Burying the Head in Sand." Christian Social Movement of Nigeria, Sept. 7, 2017. csmnigeria.org/blog/313-jihad-in-nigeria-burying-the-head-in-sand.
———. "Project Nigeria 2018." Christian Social Movement of Nigeria, May 15, 2018. csmnigeria.org/blog/347-project-nigeria-2018.
———. "Testimony of Hope in Democracy: 'The Secularized Residue of Church Doctrine of the People of God.'" Christian Social Movement of Nigeria, May 21, 2019. csmnigeria.org/blog/434-testimony-of-hope-in-democracy.

Bibliography

Ashimi, T. A. "The Significance of Interreligious Dialogue in Building Muslim Christian Relationships in Northern Nigeria." *Hamdard Islamicus* 37 (Jan.–Mar. 2014) 47–72.

Azumah, John Alembillah. *The Legacy of Arab-Islam in Africa: A Quest for Inter-Religious Dialogue*. Oxford: Oneworld, 2001

Bagobiri, Joseph Danlami. *Christians: Seed of Another Humanity*. Ikeja, Nigeria: Nilesorphem, 2017.

———. "A Press Statement on the Asso Village Massacre in Southern Kaduna." Christian Association of Nigeria, Apr. 18, 2017. https://canng.org/news-and-events/news/116-a-press-statement-on-the-asso-village-massacre-in-southern-kaduna.

Barron, James. "Artist Who Set Off Muslim Fury Visits City." *New York Times*, Sept. 29, 2009. Nytimes.com/2009/09/30/nyregion/30cartoon.html.

Beaman, Jay. *Pentecostal Pacifism: The Origin, Development, and Rejection of Pacific Belief among the Pentecostals*. Pentecostals, Peacemaking, and Social Justice. Eugene, OR: Wipf and Stock, 1989.

Benge, Geoff, and Janet Benge. *Rowland Bingham: Into Africa's Interior*. Edmonds, WA: YWAM, 2003.

Bergquist, Anders. "Persecution." In *Encyclopedia of Christianity*, edited by John Bowden, 914–17. New York: Oxford University Press, 2005.

Bethge, Eberhard. *Friendship and Resistance: Essays on Dietrich Bonhoeffer*. Geneva: WCC, 1995.

Bingham, Rowland V. *Seven Sevens of Years and a Jubilee: The Story of the Sudan Interior Mission*. Toronto: Evangelical, 1943.

Bitrus, Ibrahim. "The Persecution of the Church in Northern Nigeria: A Theological Response." *Word and World* 36 (Fall 2016) 380–89.

Boer, Jan H. *Christian: Why This Muslim Violence?* Belleville, Can.: Essence, 2004.

Bonhoeffer, Dietrich. *The Cost of Discipleship*. New York: Touchstone, 1995.

———. *Prisoner for God: Letters and Papers from Prison*. Edited by Eberhard Bethge. Translated by Reginald H. Fuller. New York: Macmillan, 1953.

Britannica, The Editors of Encyclopaedia. "Boko Haram: Nigerian Islamic Group." *Encyclopedia Britannica*, Mar. 6, 2014; last updated Sept. 13, 2023. https://britannica.com/topic/Boko-Haram.

———. "Donatist." *Encyclopedia Britannica*, July 20, 1998. https://www.britannica.com/topic/Donatists.

———. "Manichaeism: Ancient Religious Movement." *Encyclopedia Britannica*, July 20, 1998; last updated Aug. 11, 2023. https://www.britannica.com/topic/Manichaeism.

———. "Montanism." *Encyclopedia Britannica*, July 20, 1998; last updated Sept. 23, 2022. https://www.britannica.com/topic/Montanism.

———. "Nestorianism: Christian Sect." *Encyclopedia Britannica*, July 20, 1998; last updated Oct. 6, 2023. https://www.britannica.com/topic/Nestorianism/.

Bryant, Bob. "The Secret Believer in the Gospel of John." *Journal of Grace Evangelical Society* 27 (Autumn 2014) 61–75.

Buhari, Muhammadu. "Don't Politicise Religion in Nigeria." *Church Times*, Nov. 20, 2018. https://www.churchtimes.co.uk/articles/2018/30-november/comment/opinion/don-t-politicise-religion-in-nigeria.

Burrell, R. M. *Islamic Fundamentalism*. London: Royal Asiatic Society, 1989.

Canfield, Leon Hardy. *The Early Persecutions of the Christians.* New York: AMS, 1968.
Carder, Kenneth L. "Proclaiming the Gospel of Grace." In *Theology and Evangelism in the Wesleyan Heritage,* edited by James C. Logan, 81–94. Nashville: Abingdon, 1994.
Chinweizu. "Caliphate Colonialism—The Taproot of the Trouble in Nigeria." *Black Renaissance* 14 (Fall 2014) 174–97.
Christian Elders Forum. "Fulani Herdsmen Are Foot-Soldiers of Islamists." *Today's Challenge Magazine* 14 (Aug. 2018) 13–14.
Christian Association of Nigeria, Borno State Chapter. *Christianity in Crisis: Lessons from Borno State.* Maiduguri, Nigeria: Christian Association of Nigeria, 2006.
Colijn, Brenda B. *The Images of Salvation in the New Testament.* Downers Grove, IL: IVP Academic, 2010.
Corwin, Gary. "What Are We to Do? A Question of Self-Defense." *EMQ* 50 (Jan. 2014) 10–11.
Crampton, Edmund P. T. *Christianity in Northern Nigeria.* Kaduna, Nigeria: Baraka, 2004.
Cunningham, Scott. *Through Many Tribulations: The Theology of Persecution in Luke-Acts.* Library of New Testament Studies. Sheffield, UK: Sheffield, 1997.
Davidson, Lawrence. *Islamic Fundamentalism: An Introduction.* 3rd ed. Denver: Praeger, 2013.
Doi, Abdurrahman I. *Islam in Nigeria.* Zaria, Nigeria: Gaskiya, 1984.
Dombrowski, Daniel A. *Christian Pacifism.* Philadelphia: Temple University Press, 1991.
Dymond, Lurting, ed. *The Historical Writings of Quakers against War.* Farmington, ME: Quakers Heritage, n.d.
Eusebius. *Eusebius' Ecclesiastical History.* Translated by C. F. Cruse. N.p.: Merchant, 2011.
Falk, Peter. *The Growth of the Church in Africa.* Grand Rapids: Zondervan, 1979.
Falola, Toyin. *Colonialism and Violence in Northern Nigeria.* Bloomington: Indiana University Press, 2009.
———, and Matthew M. Heaton. *A History of Nigeria.* Cambridge: Cambridge University Press, 2008.
Faroye, Esther. "Old Age Is Disturbing You, Miyetti Allah Tells Ex-Head of State Yakubu Gowon." *Royal Times,* July 29, 2018. https://royaltimes.net/old-age-is-disturbing-you-miyetti-allah-tells-ex-head-of-state-yakubu-gowon/.
Fleck, Ian. *Bringing Christianity to Nigeria: The Origin and Work of Protestant Missions.* Jos: ACTS, 2013.
Foxe, John. *Foxe's Book of Martyrs.* Springdale, PA: Whitaker, 1981.
France-Presse, Agence. "Amnesty Calls on ICC to Fully Probe Boko Haram Conflict Atrocities." *VOA,* Dec. 10, 2018. https://www.voanews.com/a/boko-haram-icc-probe/4693811.html.
Fregosi, Paul. *Jihad in the West: Muslim Conquests from the 7th to the 21st Centuries.* New York: Prometheus, 1998.
Frend, W. H. C. *Martyrdom and Persecution in the Early Church.* New York: Anchor, 1967.
———. "Persecution: Genesis and Legacy." In *Origins to Constantine,* edited by Margaret M. Mitchell and Frances M. Young, 503–23. Vol. 1 of *The Cambridge History of Christianity.* New York: Cambridge University Press, 2006.

———. *The Rise of Christianity.* Philadelphia: Fortress, 1984.
Gaddis, Michael. *There Is No Crime for Those Who Have Christ: Religious Violence in the Christian Roman Empire.* Berkeley: University of California Press, 2005.
Gaiya, Musa A. B. "A History of Christian-Muslim Relationship in Nigeria." In *Creativity and Change in Nigerian Christianity,* edited by David O. Ogungbile and Akintunde E. Akinade, 289–302. Ibadan, Nigeria: Malthouse, 2010.
Gaiya, Philip Maigamu. *Religion and Justice: The Nigerian Predicament.* Kaduna, Nigeria: Espee, 2004.
Geisler, Norman, and Abdul Saleeb. *Answering Islam: The Crescent in the Light of the Cross.* Grand Rapids: Baker, 1993.
Global Christian Update. "Demands of ECWA on the Persecution of Christians in the North." *Global Christian Update* 6.4 (n.d.) 15–17.
———. "Exposing and Truncating the Agenda to Islamize Nigeria." *Global Christian Update* 6.2 (n.d.) 3–4.
———. "Update of the Bloody Jihad in Plateau State." *Global Christian Update* 8.3 (n.d.) 15–21.
Green, Michael. *Evangelism in the Early Church.* Grand Rapids: Eerdmans, 2003.
Gwamna, Dogara J. *Religion and Politics in Nigeria.* Bukuru, Nigeria: Africa Christian, 2014.
———. "The Turning Tides of Religious Intolerance in Nigeria: The External Connections." In *Creativity and Change in Nigerian Christianity,* edited by David O. Ogungbile and Akintunde E. Akinade, 271–88. Ibadan, Nigeria: Malthouse, 2010.
Hammond, Mason. "Trajan: Roman Emperor." *Encyclopaedia Britannica,* May 27, 1999; last updated Aug. 10, 2023. https://www.britannica.com/biography/Trajan.
Hardy, E. G. *Christianity and the Roman Government: A Study in Imperial Administration.* New York: Macmillan, 1894.
Harnack, Adolf. *Expansion of Christianity in the First Three Centuries.* 2 vols. Translated by James Moffat. New York: Books for Libraries, 1972.
Hashmi, Sohail H. "Jihad." In *Encyclopedia of Islam and the Muslim World,* edited by Richard C. Martin, 1:377–79. New York: Macmillan Reference, 2004. archive.org/details/EncyclopediaOfIslamAndTheMuslimWorld_411/page/n3.
Hastings, Adrian, ed. *A World History of Christianity.* Grand Rapids: Eerdmans, 1999.
Hildebrandt, Jonathan. *History of the Church in Africa.* Achimota, Ghana: Africa Christian, 1996.
Hirst, Margaret E. *The Quakers in War and Peace: An Account of their Peace Principles and Practices.* New York: Garland, 1972.
Hollinghurst, Steve. *Mission Shaped Evangelism: The Gospel in Contemporary Culture.* London: Canterbury, 2010.
Hunter, George. *The Apostolic Congregation: Church Growth Reconceived for a New Generation.* Nashville: Abingdon, 2009.
———. *The Celtic Way of Evangelism.* Nashville: Abingdon, 2010.
Hyldahl, Niels. *The History of Early Christianity.* Studies in the Religion and History of Early Christianity. Frankfurt: Lang, 1997.
Ibemere, Emeka. "Nigeria: Christian Group Vows to Fight Boko Haram." All Africa, Sept. 29, 2011. http://allafrica.com/stories/201109290623.html.
Ibrahim, Raymond. "Islam's Doctrines of Deception." Middle East Forum, Oct. 2008. https://www.meforum.org/2095/islams-doctrines-of-deception.

Igboyin, Benson O., and Babatunde Adedibu. "Power Must Change Hands: Militarization of Prayer and the Quest for Better life among Nigerian Pentecostals." *Cyberjournal for Pentecostal-Charismatic Research* 26 (Feb. 2019). http://www.pctii.org/cyberj/cyberj26/Igboin_Adedibu1.html.

Ishaku, Jonathan. *Boko Haram: How Religious Intolerance Threatens Nigeria*. Jos: Courier, 2009.

———. "Herdsmen's Violence: Politics of Security in a Failed State." *Today's Challenge Magazine* 14 (June 2018) 33–34.

Iwuchukwu, Marinus. *Christian-Muslim Dialogue in Postcolonial Northern Nigeria: The Challenges of Inclusive Cultural and Religious Pluralism*. Christianities of the World. New York: Palgrave Macmillan, 2013.

James, Ibrahim. *Studies in the History, Politics, and Cultures of Southern Kaduna Peoples Groups*. Jos: Ladsomas, 1997.

John, Ime A., et al. "Gun Violence in Nigeria: A Focus on Ethno-Religious Conflict in Kano." *Journal of Public Health Policy* 28 (2007) 420–31. https://www.jstor.org/stable/4498981.

Johnson, Luke Timothy. "Prosecuting the Persecuted: The Myth of Persecution." *Commonweal* 140 (Aug. 2013) 28–30.

Johnstone, Patrick. *Operation World: The Day-to-Day Guide to Praying for the World*. Grand Rapids: Zondervan, 1993.

Johnstone, Patrick, and Jason Mandryk. *Operation World*. 21st Century ed. Waynesboro, GA: Paternoster, 2001.

Jones, Scott. *The Evangelistic Love of God and Neighbor: A Theology of Witness and Discipleship*. Nashville: Abingdon, 2003. Kindle.

Kadala, Ephraim. *Turn the Other Cheek: A Christian Dilemma*. Jos: ACTS, 2009.

Kalu, Ogbu U., ed. *African Christianity: An African Story*. Asmara, Eritrea: African World, 2007.

Kane, Ousmane. *Muslim Modernity in Postcolonial Nigeria: A Study of the Society for the Removal of Innovation and Reinstatement of Tradition*. Islam in Africa 1. Boston: Brill, 2003.

Kateregga, Badru D., and David W. Shenk. *A Muslim and a Christian in Dialogue*. Scottdale, PA: Herald, 1997.

Kealy, John P., and David W. Shenk. *The Early Church and Africa: A School Certificate Course Based on the East African Syllabus for Christian Religious Education*. Nairobi: Oxford University Press, 1975.

Keener, Craig S. *New Testament*. IVP Bible Background Commentary Set. 2nd rev. ed. Downers Grove, IL: IVP Academic, 2014.

Kelhoffer, James A. "Withstanding Persecution as Corroboration of Legitimacy in the New Testament: Reflections on the Resulting Ethical and Hermeneutical Quandary." *Dialog: A Journal of Theology* 50 (Summer 2011) 120–32.

King, Martin Luther, Jr. *A Testament of Hope: The Essential Writings and Speeches of Martin Luther King Jr.* Edited by James M. Washington. New York: HarperOne, 1986.

———. *Why We Can't Wait*. New York: New American Library, 1964.

Kostka, Arun Oswin. "Persecution in the Early Church." All Saints & Martyrs, Apr. 2, 2014. https://saintscatholic.blogspot.com/2014/04/persecution-in-early-church.html.

Bibliography

Kukah, Matthew Hassan. *Religion, Politics and Power in Northern Nigeria.* Ibadan, Nigeria: Spectrum, 1993.

Kukah, Matthew Hassan, and Toyin Falola. *Religious Militancy and Self-Assertion: Islam and Politics in Nigeria.* Making of Modern Africa. Brookfield, VT: Ashgate, 1996.

Laah, Danjuma. "A Call for Christian Communities to Defend Themselves against Jihadi Fulani Herdsmen." *Global Christian Update* 7 (n.d.) 27–28.

Lapidus, Ira M. *A History of Islamic Societies.* New York: Cambridge University Press, 1988.

Laremont, Ricardo Rene. *Islamic Law and Politics in Northern Nigeria.* Ibadan, Nigeria: Africa World, 2011.

Lee, A. D. *Pagans and Christians in the Late Antiquity.* New York: Routledge, 2000.

Leithart, Peter J. "Witness unto Death." *First Things* 229 (Jan. 2013) 45–50.

Levy-Rubin, Milka. *Non-Muslims in the Early Islamic Empire: From Surrender to Coexistence.* Cambridge Studies in Islamic Civilization. New York: Cambridge University Press, 2011.

Lewis, C. S. *The Weight of Glory.* New York: HarperCollins, 2001.

Liftin, Bryan M. *Early Christian Martyr Stories: An Evangelical Introduction with New Translations.* Grand Rapids: Baker Academic, 2014.

Little, Don. *Effective Discipling in Muslim Communities: Scripture, History and Seasoned Practices.* Downers Grove, IL: IVP Academic, 2015.

Logan, James C. "The Evangelistic Imperative: A Wesleyan Perspective." In *Theology and Evangelism in the Wesleyan Heritage*, edited by James C. Logan, 15–33. Kingswood Series. Nashville: Abingdon, 1994.

MacArthur, John, ed. *The MacArthur Study Bible NKJV.* Nashville: Thomas Nelson, 1997.

Mailafiya, Obadiah. "The Fulanis: A Lesson in Hegemony." *Today's Challenge Magazine* 14 (June 2018) 14–16.

Mambula, Musa Adziba. *Nigeria: Ethno-Religious and Socio-Political Violence and Pacifism in Northern Nigeria.* New York: Page, 2016.

Marshall, Paul. "Persecution of Christians in the Contemporary World." *International Bulletin of Missionary Research* 22 (Jan. 1998) 2–7.

Mbachirin, Abraham Terembur. "The Responses of the Church in Nigeria to Socio-Economic, Political, and Religious Problems in Nigeria: A Case Study of the Christian Association of Nigeria (CAN)." PhD diss., Baylor University, 2006.

McKnight, Scot. *The King Jesus Gospel: The Original Good News Revisited.* Grand Rapids: Zondervan, 2011. Kindle.

Middleton, Paul. "Early Christian Voluntary Martyrdom: A Statement for the Defense." *Journal of Theological Studies* 64 (Oct. 2013) 556–73.

———. "Enemies of the (Church and) State: Martyrdom as a Problem for Early Christianity." *Annali di Storia dell'Esegesi* 29 (2012) 161–81.

Mohammed, Abdulkareem, and Mohammed Haruna. *The Paradox of Boko Haram.* Kaduna, Nigeria: Moving Image, 2010.

Moon, W. Jay. *Intercultural Discipleship: Learning from Global Approaches to Spiritual Formation.* Encountering Mission. Grand Rapids: Baker Academic, 2017. Kindle.

Morely, Nathan. "IS Militants Behead 11 Christians in Nigeria on Christmas Day." *Vatican News*, Dec. 27, 2019. https://www.vaticannews.va/en/world/news/2019-12/islamic-state-nigeria-christians-killed-on-christmas.html.

Moss, Candida. *The Myth of Persecution: How Early Christians Invented a Story of Martyrdom*. New York: HarperCollins, 2013.

Myers, Bryant. *Walking with the Poor: Principles and Practices of Transformational Development*. Rev. ed. Maryknoll, NY: Orbis, 2011.

Ndujihe, Clifford, and Sam Eyoboka. "Insecurity: Danjuma, Lekwot, Others Take Nigeria's Case to UK." *Vanguard*, June 6, 2019. vanguardngr.com/2019/06/insecurity-danjuma-lekwot-others-take-nigeria-case-to-uk/. Link discontinued.

Neill, Stephen. *A History of Christian Missions*. Penguin History of the Church 6. London: Penguin, 1984.

Niebuhr, Reinhold. *The Nature and Destiny of Man: A Christian Interpretation*. New York: Scribner's Sons, 1949.

Nwedo, Anthony. *The Church, Colonialism, and Islam in Nigeria*. Ibadan, Nigeria: Umbrella, n.d.

Oborji, Francis Anekwe. "Is Christianity on Trial in Nigeria?" *Today's Challenge Magazine* 14 (Aug. 2018) 6–10.

Oguntola, Sunday. "No Cheeks Left to Turn: Church Leaders Debate Self-Defense." *Christianity Today* 55 (Dec. 19, 2011) 14.

Ojo, Matthews A. "Pentecostal Movements, Islam and the Contest for Public Space in Northern Nigeria." *Islam-Christian Muslim Relations* 18 (2007) 175–88.

Onaiyekan, John O. *Seeking Common Grounds: Inter-Religious Dialogue in Africa*. Vol. 1 of *The Collected Writings 1978–2013*. Nairobi: Paulines Africa, 2013.

Parker, Samuel, trans. *Ecclesiastical Histories of Eusebius, Socrates, Sozomen and Theodorit*. London: Bible and Crown, 1729.

Penner, Glenn M. *In the Shadow of the Cross: A Biblical Theology of Persecution*. Bartlesville, OK: Living Sacrifice, 2004.

Philip, John R. "A Theology of Risk and Suffering in the Gospels." In *Risk and Suffering in Church and Mission*, edited by John Stinger, 3–24. Groningen, Neth.: Grassroots Mission, 2011.

Philpott, Daniel, and Timothy Samuel Shah. "In Response to Persecution: Essays from the Under Caesar's Sword Project." *Review of Faith and International Affairs* 15 (2017) 1–11.

Pobee, John S. *AD 2000 and After: The Future of God's Mission in Africa*. Accra: Asempa, 1991.

Pohl, Christine D. *Living into Community: Cultivating Practices That Sustain Us*. Grand Rapids: Eerdmans, 2012.

Provost, Claire. "Nigeria Expected to Have Larger Population Than US by 2050." *The Guardian*, June 13, 2013. https://www.theguardian.com/global-development/2013/jun/13/nigeria-larger-population-us-2050.

Rhee, Helen. *Loving the Poor, Saving the Rich: Wealth, Poverty, and Early Christian Formation*. Grand Rapids: Baker Academic, 2012.

Rufai, Saheed Ahmad. "A Foreign Faith in a Christian Domain: Islam among the Igbos of Southeastern Nigeria." *Journal of Muslim Minority Affairs* 32 (Sept. 2012) 372–83.

Rundle, Steven, and Tom A. Steffen. *Great Commission Companies: Emerging Role of Business in Missions*. Rev ed. Downers Grove, IL: IVP, 2011.

Russell, A. Sue. *In the World but Not of the World: The Liminal Life of the Pre-Constantine Christian Communities*. Eugene, OR: Pickwick, 2019.

Sanneh, Lamin. *Translating the Message: The Missionary Impact on Culture*. Rev. ed. American Society of Missiology. New York: Orbis, 2009.

Sauer, Christof. "Theology of Persecution and Martyrdom: An Example in Globalizing Theology." *Evangelical Review of Theology* 37 (July 2013) 267–74.

Sauer, Christof, and Richard Howell, eds. *Suffering, Persecution and Martyrdom: Theological Reflections*. Religious Freedom Series 2. Johannesburg: AcadSA, 2010.

Schirrmacher, Thomas. "Persecution." In *Dictionary of Mission Theology: Evangelical Foundations*, edited by John Corrie, 286–89. Downers Grove, IL: InterVarsity, 2007.

Sesan. "Miyetti Allah Admits, Clarifies N100bn Demand From FG." *Punch*, May 17, 2019. https://punchng.com/miyetti-allah-admits-clarifies-n100bn-demand-from-fg/.

Shaw, Brent D. *Sacred Violence: African Christians and Sectarian Hatred in the Age of Augustine*. New York: Cambridge University Press, 2011.

Smither, Edward L. *Mission in the Early Church: Themes and Reflections*. Eugene, OR: Cascade, 2014.

Stark, Rodney. *The Triumph of Christianity: How the Jesus Movement Became the World's Largest Religion*. New York: HarperOne, 2011.

Ste. Croix, G. E. M. de. *Christian Persecution, Martyrdom, & Orthodoxy*. Edited by Michael Whitby and Joseph Streeter. New York: Oxford University Press, 2006.

Stefanos Foundation. *Religious Intolerance: A Threat to Nigeria's Unity*. Jos: Stefanos Foundation, 2010.

Stewart, John. *Nestorian Missionary Enterprise: The Story of a Church on Fire*. Edinburgh: T&T Clark, 1928.

Sundkler, Bengt, and Christopher Steed. *A History of the Church in Africa*. New York: Cambridge University Press, 2000.

Tacitus. *Complete Works of Tacitus*. Edited by Moses Hadas. Translated by Alfred John Church and William Jackson Brodribb. Modern Library. New York: Modern Library, 1942.

Teach Democracy. "A Brief History of Jim Crow." Teach Democracy, n.d. https://www.crf-usa.org/black-history-month/a-brief-history-of-jim-crow.

Thiessen, John Caldwell. *A Survey of World Missions*. Chicago: InterVarsity, 1956.

Tieszen, Charles L. *Re-Examining Religious Persecution: Constructing a Theological Framework for Understanding Persecution*. Religious Freedom Series 1. New Haven, CT: OMSC, 2006. https://iirf.global/wp-content/uploads/Books/Re-Examining_Religious_Persecution.pdf.

Tietz, Christiane. *Theologian of Resistance: The Life and Thought of Dietrich Bonhoeffer*. Translated by Victoria J. Barnett. Minneapolis: Fortress, 2016.

Trochim, William M. K. "Analysis." Conjointly, n.d. https://conjointly.com/kb/research-data-analysis/.

Tson, Josef. "Suffering and Martyrdom: God's Strategy in the World." In *Perspectives on the World Christian Movement*, edited by Ralph D. Winter and Steven Hawthorne, 181–84. Pasadena, CA: William Carey Library, 1999.

Turaki, Yusufu. *Historical Roots of Ethno-Religious Crises and Conflicts in Nigeria*. Jos: Challenge, n.d.

———. *Tainted Legacy: Islam, Colonialism and Slavery in Northern Nigeria*. Kaduna, Nigeria: Real Eagles, 2010.

Uchendu, Egodi. "Negotiating Relationships in a Mixed Religious Society: Islam among the Igbos of Southeast Nigeria." *Journal of Third World Studies* 28 (Fall 2011) 207–31.

Ukanah, Philip Oluwole. *In God's Name: The Story of Nigeria's Religious War and Its Brutal Killings*. Ibadan, Nigeria: Divine, 2011.

Umeagbalasi, Emeka. "Imminent Extinction of Christianity in Southern and Middle-Belt Nigeria." *Today's Challenge Magazine* 14 (June 2018) 28–30.

UN High Commissioner for Human Rights. *Violations and Abuses Committed by Boko Haram and the Impact on Human Rights in the Countries Affected*. Digital Library, Dec. 9, 2015. https://digitallibrary.un.org/record/819031?ln=en.

Urofsky, Melvin I. "Jim Crow Law: United States [1877–1954]." *Britannica*, July 20, 1998; last updated Nov. 5, 2023. https://www.britannica.com/event/Jim-Crow-law.

Vickers, Peter, and Maxine Offredy. "Developing a Healthcare Research Proposal: An Interactive Student Guide." Higher Ed BCS, n.d. https://higheredbcs.wiley.com/legacy/college/offredy/1405183373/index.htm.

Willard, Dallas. *The Great Omission: Reclaiming Jesus's Essential Teachings on Discipleship*. New York: HarperCollins, 2006. Kindle.

Workman, Herbert B. *Persecution in the Early Church*. London: Oxford University Press, 1980.

Wynn, Philip. *Augustine on War and Military Service*. Minneapolis: Fortress, 2013.

Yahaya, John. "Ethnic and Religious Conflicts in Kaduna and Plateau States: Implications for Development in Nigeria." PhD diss., University of Nigeria Nsukka, May 2011.

Yoder, John H. *Reinhold Niebuhr and Christian Pacifism*. Zeist, Neth.: De-BUSSY, 1953.

———. *The War of the Lamb: The Ethics of Nonviolence and Peacemaking*. Edited by Glen Stassen et al. Grand Rapids: Brazos, 2009.

www.ingramcontent.com/pod-product-compliance
Lightning Source LLC
Chambersburg PA
CBHW062023220426
43662CB00010B/1456